CHINESE ECONOMIC REFORMS AND FERTILITY BEHAVIOUR: A STUDY OF A NORTH CHINA VILLAGE

T0299956

Chinese Economic Reforms and Fertility Bahaviour

A STUDY OF A NORTH CHINA VILLAGE

Zhang Weiguo

Routledge
Taylor & Francis Group

LONDON AND NEW YORK

First published in 2002 by China Library

2 Park Square, Milton Park, Abingdon, Oxon OX14 4RN
711 Third Avenue, New York, NY 10017, USA

Routledge is an imprint of the Taylor & Francis Group, an informa business

Chinese Economic Reforms and Fertility Behaviour
A Study of a North China Village

First issued in paperback 2016

British Library Cataloguing in Publication Data
A CIP catalogue entry for this book is
available from the British Library

ISBN 978-1-873410-49-3 (hbk)
ISBN 978-1-138-99327-3 (pbk)

Typeset in Stone 9¼pt on 11 by Mark Heslington, Scarborough, North Yorkshire

To Liu Yan and Zhang Yifei

Contents

List of Tables and Figures

Figures

Acknowledgements

This book comes out of a PhD project on rural Chinese reforms and fertility at the Institute of Social Studies, The Hague, The Netherlands. I owe special thanks to my supervisors, Professor Marc Wuyts and Professor Frans Willekens, who provided me with valuable comments, guidance and encouragement. I wish to thank my local supervisor, Professor Feng Litian, who gave me many valuable comments and much needed support during my year-long fieldwork in China. I am grateful to Professor Ashwani Saith and Professor Geoffrey McNicoll for their detailed comments. The fellowship provided by the Institute of Social Studies for the study, and the facilities provided by the Capital University of Economics and Business (then the Beijing College of Economics) during my fieldwork are very much appreciated.

I wish to thank Professor Ben White and Professor John Cleland, who gave me valuable and critical comments on my initial research design. My thanks go as well to Dr Bridget O'Laughlin, who went through many of my chapters and gave me comments despite her busy schedule. I also owe my thanks to numerous staff members of the Institute of Social Studies for their comments and encouragement during various stages of the study. Among the many I could mention, I wish to thank Dr Gabriele Dankert, Dr Eric Ross, Dr Mahmood Meskoub, and Dr Aurora Galindo, Linda McPhee, and Joy Misa.

This study also benefited from comments I received on conference papers and journal articles based on my dissertation project. I particularly wish to thank Professor William Lavely, Professor William Skinner, Dr Thanh-Dam Truong, Dr Peng Xizhe, Dr Govind Kelkar, Professor Tim Dyson, Dr Ines Smith, Professor Elisabeth Croll, Dr Flemming Christiansen, Dr Zhang Junzuo, Dr Joan Kaufman, Dr Hadgu Bariagaber, and many anonymous readers for their valuable comments. I am grateful to Dr Griffith Feeney, who gave me valuable comments on my application of parity progression ratio in the analysis in Chapter 9 of the thesis.

I wish to thank the staff members of various libraries, especially the libraries of the Institute of Social Studies, the Sinological Institute at Leiden University, the Netherlands Interdisciplinary Demographic Institute, and the Institute of Population and Economics of the Capital University of Economics and Business for the generous help and cooperation.

I am grateful to Mona Mehta, Imani Tafari-Ami and Dr Skye Hughes for their correction of my English of my draft chapters, conference papers and journal articles, and Linda McPhee for her professional editing of my PhD thesis.

I am grateful to Dr Mohammed Mazouz and Dr Patrick Molutsi, the coordinator of the Global Training Programme in Population and Sustainable Development and director of the project at the University of Botswana, for their continuous encouragement.

Above all, my thanks go to the village cadres and people, whose cooperation with my year-long fieldwork in the village is very much appreciated. Special thanks go to my host family, who treated me as one of the family and helped me in many ways to understand the life of the village people in general and their family lives in particular. Many thanks go to county and township officials and people who helped my investigation in the county town and assisted my selecting and settling down in the research village. My thanks also go to my survey assistants for collection of the quantitative data and many institutions and individuals in China who provided facilities and help inputting the data. Without their assistance I cannot imagine how I would have completed my fieldwork.

My wife Liu Yan helped me greatly during my fieldwork and shared with me the joy and distress during my research programme. My parents and my brother and sister's family showed their support and concern throughout the years of my study, and did their best to offer help during my fieldwork. My newly born son, Zhang Yifei, added a lot of joy and happiness to the family while I was busy with modification of the thesis into the present book.

Briefer version of Chapter 5 appeared in 'Dynamics of Marriage Change in Chinese Rural Society in Transition: A Study of a Northern Chinese Village,' *Population Studies* 54: 57–69. Briefer versions of parts of chapters 3, 4 and 7 appeared in 'Economic Reforms and Fertility Behaviour: An anthropological and demographic enquiry,' *European Journal of Population,* 15(4): 317–348. Briefer versions of parts of Chapter 9 appeared in 'Earlier, Denser, but Fewer: Fertility Transition in a North China Village,' *Genus* LVI(1–2): 77–98. Chapter 8 appeared in 'Implementation of State Family Planning Programmes in a Northern Chinese Village,' *The China Quarterly,* 157: 202–230. Earlier version of parts of Chapters 4 and 6 appeared in 'Rural Women and Reform in a North Chinese Village.' In Flemming Christiansen and Junzuo Zhang, eds. *Village Inc. – Chinese Rural Society in the 1990s,* Curzon, Richmond, 1998, pp. 193–211.

Zhang Weiguo

Preface

This study is based on both empirical and theoretical considerations. Empirically, many scholars remain puzzled about the causal process underlying the Chinese fertility decline experienced in the last few decades. Theoretically, the puzzle of Chinese fertility decline in particular, and of human fertility transition in general, is related to the fact that many existing fertility studies ignore or fail to incorporate the social context of fertility behaviours.

This research adopts an institutional approach to fertility studies through an intensive study of a village in Northern China. Its object of inquiry is political economy. This study is to situate fertility within a historical and institutional perspective of development and change in rural China and within the context of the culture and political economy of Chinese society. Theretically, it is based on the consideration that the main fertility theories that locate fertility at different levels of macro- and micro-analysis do not incorporate the institutional context in their analyses. Classical demographic transition theory assumes invariant institutions that the functions of institutions and the principles governing demographic change are seen as uniform even for different societies. Microeconomic fertility theory assumes inevitable institutions that all non-neoclassical explanations of human behaviour are thus shunned. I argue that a clearer understanding of human fertility cannot be achieved when individuals are assumed to rationalize their behaviour in the same way, independent of context, or when human fertility is seen as a result of socially determined processes only at the aggregate level without consideration of the individuals who are making such processes. Social demographers try to link socio-economic factors and fertility and they adhere that macro socio-economic factors must work to affect fertility through intermediate fertility variables. However, the model of intermediate variables of fertility fails to recognize that the nature of the effect of macro socio-economic factors on fertility is filtered as well as reshaped by existing social institutions.

The study focuses on rural China during the period of economic

transformation since the 1978 reforms and it uses the period of collectivization as its starting point. My primary concern is with the way
deliberate state policies of institutional reform affect fertility
outcomes through processes which are both filtered by, as well as
reshape, existing social institutions regarding marriage, family and
local authority and power. It is these intermediate institutions which
shape as well as filter the nature of the effect of macro socio-economic
policies on intermediate variables and hence, on fertility. With a
combination of anthropological methodology and demographic techniques, this study, based on fieldwork from June 1992 to November
1993 in a Hebei village, hopefully shed lights on the linkages between
macro-economic reforms and micro fertility behaviour in rural China.

Although many scholars suspected that economic reforms would
simply strengthen the motivation of rural couples to have more children, especially sons, this has been found not to be the case in the
village. This study shows that the mechanisms and processes through
which state instigated economic reforms influence individual fertility
perception and fertility decision making are complex, and there are
economic mechanisms at work which constrain fertility. Since the
reforms, rural Chinese are more likely to marry at earlier ages and to
have children earlier with shorter birth intervals; nevertheless, they
also stop their reproduction earlier with fewer children. This study
shows that the timing of marriage and of childbearing have been
shifted to earlier ages, and yet the individual fertility level has
declined. Declining age at marriage and shorter birth intervals are not
mechanisms at family level for increasing fertility.

Processes and mechanisms of the reforms that are influencing individual fertility behaviour may vary in different villages. Variations
among villages may reflect different local economic, ecological, political and social circumstances to which individuals must respond.
Chinese macroeconomic policies and population programmes may
change overtime, this village study may thus have its findings with
characteristics representing a period of transition from a certrally-
planned economy to a market-oriented economy.

Notes on Measures
1 mu	= 1/15 hectares	=1/6 acre
1 jin	= 0.5 kilogram	= 1.1 pounds
1 yuan	= approximately U.S. $0.125 in 1993	

Introduction

China's rapid fertility decline in the last few decades is not following the pattern of conventional fertility transition in Western European countries observed by the fertility transition theorists. Its total fertility rate (TFR) fell from 5.9 in 1950 to 2.6 in 1981 (CPIRC 1983), to 2.3 in 1989 (Ji 1992) and to around the replacement level of 2.1 by 1992 (Zeng 1996).[1] This is the most rapid fertility decline on record for any large population. Socio-economic development is believed to be unable to account fully for such tremendous fertility decline, and some scholars argue that family planning programmes have played a determining role (Aird 1978, 1990, Arthur Wolf 1986, Banister 1987). Feeney & Wang (1993) assert that it is likely that at least half of the decline in Chinese fertility in the last few decades may be attibuted to government family planning programmes. Others (Tien 1984, Birdsall & Jamison 1983, World Bank 1993, Li & Wu 1985, Wu 1986, Posten & Gu 1987, Gu 1987 & 1996, Zhu 1989) argue that the Chinese accomplishments should not be regarded solely as success for administratively-induced family planning programmes, and that Chinese fertility decline would not have been possible without socio-economic development.

In addition to its magnitude and rapidity, other features concerning China's fertility decline have been noted. Firstly, China's fertility fell rapidly in urban areas between the mid-1950s and the mid-1960s even when the effects of the Great Leap Forward are discounted and well before the strong 'later-sparser-fewer' family planning policy was implemented in the early 1970s (Greenhalgh 1990a). Secondly, when a more ambitious one-child family planning policy was implemented in the 1980s, fertility did not decline further, but fluctuated (Wang 1996). Thirdly, there exist significant variations in fertility decline among China's provinces, autonomous regions and municipalities (hereafter refered to as provinces) and between urban and rural areas (e.g. Coale & Chen 1987, Tien 1985, Peng 1989, 1991, and 1993, Freedman et al. 1988, Poston & Jia 1990).

China's experience in fertility decline is only one example of the

failure of classical demographic transition theory; there are man
others. Using aggregate-level historical data from over 700 Europea
districts, demographers have found that in many parts of the cont
nent the pattern of demographic change failed to follow th
three-stage path enshrined in demographic transition theory (cited i
Greenhalgh 1990b). As stated by Greenhalgh (1990b), the closer w
get to understanding specific fertility declines, the further we mov
away from a general theory of fertility transition.

In contrast to conventional demographic transition theory, whic
posits relations between socio-economic development and demc
graphic change at the macro level, microeconomic theories of fertilit
focus on individual fertility behaviour at the micro level. What
common between conventional transition theory developed b
demographers and microeconomic theories of fertility developed b
economists is that both ignore or fail to incorporate social context i
individual fertility decision-makings in their analyses. Demographi
transition theory tends to abstract societies, because differences i
institutions and institutional change among different societies ai
treated as less important, different societies are seen to follow th
same general pattern of demographic transitions. Microeconomi
theories also tend to decontextualize individual decision-makinɡ
working with the static assumption that individuals will invariabl
maximize their objectives under whatever conditions. Micrc
economic theories of fertility also ignore power relations withi
families and within the society which determine the reproductiv
behaviour of individual couples. Neither demographic transitio
theory nor microeconomic theories of fertility allow adequate analys
of the complex and dynamic human reproductive processes an
mechanisms and linkages between macro socio-economic factors an
micro fertility behaviours.

Following these theoretical streams, there are extensive fertilit
studies employing correlation and regression analysis at both aggr
gate and individual levels.[2] These studies use fertility indicators c
intermediate variables as dependent variables, and use socio-economi
indicators (and sometimes family planning indicators) as inde
pendent variables, and see causality in terms of the effects c
socio-economic and family planning variables on intermediate var
ables and fertility outcomes. Such studies may give us useful hints an
reveal interesting patterns, providing they can avoid superficial c
misleading interpretations (see Dixon 1979, Caldwell 1985). Howeve
such analyses pay little attention to the concrete social contexts tha
structure such relationships, obscure observed regularities and thei
underlying mechanisms, and ignore the essenttially contextual an
systematic nature of these mechanisms (Wuyts 1997).

Many studies have been ubdertaken on human fertility over th
last few decades by scholars ranging from demographers, economist
to sociologists and psychologists. However, fertility determinants an
mechanisms and processes of social factors influencing individuɑ

fertility behaviour remain largely a mystery. The important role social institutions play in human fertility behaviour and fertility change has been noted by scholars in the last two decades (e.g., McNicoll 1975, 1980, 1985 & 1994, McNicoll & Cain 1990, Potter 1983, Greenhalgh 1988 & 1990b, Herbert Smith 1989, Hammel 1990, Hayes 1994, Stokes 1995, Ye 1991, Zhou 1995 & 1996). Studies of *family systems* by Lesthaeghe (1980), Hajnal (1982), Richard Smith (1981), Caldwell & Caldwell (1987) and Goody (1990), of *societal control* of human reproduction by Lesthaeghe (1980), of *labour market, social security, education and gender* (Cain 1983 & 1991, Caldwell 1980, Nugent 1985, Vlassoff & Vlassoff 1980), etc., have brought much insight to our understanding of the interrelation between socio-economic changes and population growth. Though the influences of institutional contexts on individual behaviour have received theoretical attention, there have been relatively few empirical studies in China and elsewhere. There is a lack of empirical research on how rural transformation and its institutional reforms are reshaping the fertility perceptions and motivations of rural Chinese people, on how individuals cope, in terms of fertility, with the changing context where they work and live, and on how fertility decisions are made at the micro level, with both families and local administrations trying to influence the reproductive processes of reproductive couples. There is also insufficient knowledge of how China's stringent state family planning programmes are actually implemented, and of how individuals responding to the rapidly changing context in turn affect the implementations of the family planning programme. Many questions concerning Chinese socio-economic development, family planning policy and fertility change remain controversial and unanswered. This study is not, however, an attempt to develop an alternative fertility theory. Based on the primacy of the importance of context in delimiting human behaviours, this study brings social institutions into the picture and hopefully sheds light on the mechanisms and processes through which macro socio-economic factors influence micro fertility behaviours through institutions that exist at various levels in society.

FOCUS AND OBJECTIVES OF THE PRESENT STUDY

This empirical study focuses on the rural Chinese context in a particular transition period of institutional reforms initiated at the end of the 1970s and lasting into the early 1990s. Its main focus is the interrelations between macroeconomic reforms and micro fertility behaviour, mediated and linked by intermediate institutions and intermediate variables of fertility. Specifically, the research asks how the economic reforms which started in 1978 and changed the context in which rural Chinese live and work, are affecting individual fertility behaviour in rural China.

Post-1978 reforms have shifted the state's emphasis from Mao's social equity to post-Mao economic efficiency. A series of reforms, ranging from introducing responsibility systems, dismantling the commune system, loosening control over labour mobility, permitting the coexistence of a private economy, etc., have been adopted to increase individual incentives in production and to promote economic development. The centrally-planned economy is gradually being transformed into a so-called socialist market economy.

These economic reforms have dramatically changed the social context in which the rural Chinese live and work. Many scholars have noted the changes in individual fertility motivations and in the roles of cadres in implementing family planning programmes. They suspect that the shift towards a household responsibility system and greater reliance on market mechanisms in rural China will increase fertility, because (1) peasants' demand for children as labour and security has been increased (e.g., Davin 1985; Saith 1987; Croll 1988; Cao 1985, 1989, 1990; Wu and Zhong 1992; Lin and Yao 1993; Chang 1996) and (2) the roles of local cadres in the implementation of state policies have been weakened (e.g. T. White 1987, Peng 1990, Wei 1988, 1989, Greenhalgh et al. 1994).

Many scholars argue that Chinese economic reforms will promote socio-economic development which will ultimately lead to low fertility in the long term; however, in the short term, they believe that fertility may increase due to increasing demand for children as labour and as old age security. For example, Cao argues:

> Along with the processes of reforms and opening to the outside world and the development of commodity economy, it is inevitable that peasants will tend to want many children, especially sons, after they reach prosperity at the initial period of the reforms. It is a historical inexorability at the initial stage of socialism which is transforming from a partially self-contained economy to the commodities-based one. Present China is at this stage. However, from the long term perspective, peasants will get richer and richer with the deepening of reforms and further development of the commodity economy; the traditional fertility ideas of 'more sons, more happiness' and 'the superiority of men over women' will be limited and changed from wanting many children to few children. This is also historical inexorability. (Cao 1990: 23–4, original text in Chinese)

Many studies have focused on the impacts of economic reforms on the implementation of family planning work in rural China. The aspects these studies have considered can be grouped into three categories: (1) population education and propaganda; (2) formulation and effectiveness of incentive and disincentive structure; and (3) administrative means. Most studies have focused on the influences of new social and economic changes on the last two aspects, while there has been little study of the influence of population education.

Most studies have argued that the economic reforms have weakened the role of cadres and undermined the mechanisms by which the population policy was to be enforced. The main arguments can be summarized as follows. Firstly, some have argued that the rise in peasant family incomes impaired implementation by enabling couples to pay fines for violating the policy rules without suffering great hardship (Greenhalgh 1993). Many peasant households, as they become better off, are increasingly willing and able to pay the financial penalty levied for extra births (Peng 1990, 1991, Cao 1985). Secondly, the abolition of the commune disabled the system of economic incentives and disincentives by which the population policy was to be enforced (Greenhalgh 1993). Thirdly, economic reform exacerbated implementation difficulties by reducing the power and prestige of local cadres. As the reform progressed, the administrative function of the Party and government is diminishing and the power of local cadres has been undermining (Peng 1990, Greenhalgh et al. 1994, Wei 1988, 1989). Fourthly, the market reforms increased the mobility of rural population, which increased the difficulties for local cadres in implementing population policies (Yang 1991, Wu & Zhong 1992, Peng 1990). Finally, the health network established during the Cultural Revolution has now been privatized (mostly in an *ad hoc* manner), and it is thought that as a result, the distribution of family planning services has deteriorated in many rural areas (Peng 1990: 9).

Literatures analysing the impacts of economic reforms on fertility based on intensive empirical study are thin. The main weakness in the existing literature is that it ignores the complexities of the roles of intermediate institutions concerning marriage, family and local authority in mediating the relations between reforms and fertility. Instead, (1) changes in marriage are seen as peasants' responses for enforced fertility motivation in the reforms period, rather than as changes of the intermediate institution brought about by economic reforms and shaped by individual reactions, which then have consequences on fertility; (2) cost and benefits of having children are analysed without considering changes in familial relations which determine the processes of fertility decision-makings; (3) local government organizations and local cadres are seen as representatives of the state and a coherent whole, rather than as agents, or actors within a social context in which there exist internal conflicts and cooperation which need to be disaggregated and analysed.

This study argues that a clearer understanding of human fertility cannot be achieved when individuals are assumed to rationalize their behaviour in the same way, independent of context or when human fertility is seen as a result of socially determined processes only at the aggregate level without consideration of the individuals who are making the processes. It will show that institutions influence individual behaviour by many ways, and that institutions and behaviour change over time, since both are dynamic and evolutionary by nature. The policy-induced institutional reforms in China are altering the formal institutional set-up, which in turn affects social institutions in society. Individual responses to changing contexts also reshape the character of social institutions.

This research, recognizing the importance of social context in influencing human fertility behaviour and the importance of social institutions in the mediation of state policies and individual fertility behaviour, and focusing on certain salient institutions which bear on fertility and have drastic changes in the reform era, puts forward the following overall proposition:

> Economic reforms, which have opened up various opportunities for social upward mobility, at the same time increased vulnera-bilities, risks and uncertainties, by shifting responsibility for individual well-being from collectives to households, and by stressing economic efficiency rather than social equity, have changed the whole context within which the rural Chinese work and live. The rural reforms, together with the responses of rural Chinese people to the changing context, are reshaping the character of intermediate institutions such as marriage, family and local authority. This in turn is having a deeper effect on individual fertility perception and on interactions in the fertility decision-making processes within individual families and between families and local cadres.

Within this overall proposition, this research sets out four sub-propositions, as follows:

(1) Increasing opportunities as well as risks and vulnerabilities are asymmetrical between genders and between generations; this leads to new form of cooperation, competition and conflicts within the domestic sphere. New forms of the divi-sion of labour and division of household property are determining new forms of gender and intergenerational rela-tions. The family relationship is changing, in that the traditional primary relation between father and son is gradu-ally being replaced by the relation between husband and wife. Thus the roles of family members in the decisions of fertility of reproductive couples have been changed, so that the young play an increasingly important role in reproduc-tive processes.

(2) Decollectivization, together with market-oriented reforms (in which collective resources and work opportunities have been reallocated and individuals have gained freedom to arrange their labour and to make use of increasing non-agricultural opportunities both inside and outside the village) have changed the position of local cadres in relation to the peas-antry. Decollectivization reinforces the roles of individual households in decision-making in both the productive and

the reproductive spheres. At the same time, local cadres have gained autonomy in relation to higher authorities. These changes have in turn reshaped the character of fertility control; in short, the state's family planning policy is increasingly mediated by both individual households and by local administrations.

(3) The roles of children as contributors to the household economy, as insurance against increasing risks and various contingencies to the family and as contributors to family efforts to achieve social upward mobility, have all changed in the reform period. Also, childbearing and childrearing have become increasingly costly, including particularly the costs of children's marriage, education and related direct expenses, but also the indirect opportunity costs. These roles and costs also differ for boys and girls. These changes and differences are reshaping and differentiating the individual fertility perception and motivation of different family members.

(4) Individual fertility behaviour is incorporated in and adjusted as part of the strategic response of rural people and their households to the changing context, which is the consequence of state-instigated reforms; it is also reshaped, in turn, by the multiple ways in which individuals respond. Rural couples tend to adjust the timing of marriage and of childbearing and the desired number and sex of children. Differentiation in fertility behaviour also exists among different social groups, because reforms affect different social groups differently and their responses to the changing context vary.

While this study will focus on relations between economic reforms and fertility behaviour in the reform era, it nevertheless takes the relation between socio-economic development and fertility under the collective institutions as its starting point. Also, because this study will focus on micro processes influenced by macro forces, it should be seen in relation to the macro context and kept within the macro perspective. Questions concerning macro-micro linkages and historical comparison of the roles of institutions and institutional change on relations between socio-economic development and demographic change will always be noted in the analysis.

RESEARCH METHODOLOGY AND FIELDWORK

The study combines anthropological methodology with demographic techniques in the study of a Northern Chinese village with 471 households and a population of 2,104 individuals.[3] Methodologically, there are two considerations. Firstly, I want to have more accurate and complete data in order to uncover the real situation. Secondly, I also want to have a better understanding of intermediate level institutions, to see how institutions are shaped by macro policies and individual responses, and how macro forces affect intermediate variables and thus fertility outcomes through intermediate institutions.

Findings based on inaccurate data will be misleading, yet it is difficult to collect good data on personal subjects such as fertility perceptions, because interviewees may intentionally or unintentionally mislead researchers or try to influence policy-making to their advantages (see Appendix I and II). Gathering accurate data requires intensive study, and can be accomplished only through long-term residence. Intensive village study, incorporating anthropological methods, is needed to understand the complex institutional structures, their institutional dynamics, and their roles in influencing individual behaviours. Unlike many large-scale demographic surveys such as the World Fertility Survey (WFS) and the Demographic and Health Survey (DHS) which provide important information but no explanation (Caldwell 1985, Boerma 1996), village-level studies can help researchers understand changes, processes and mechanisms. The dynamic processes and mechanisms of macro forces on micro behaviours cannot be simply studied by macro investigation at the aggregate level. The essence of these processes and mechanisms is how certain institutional changes bring forth adjustments and adaptations in the social institutional fabric of society, because changes in any one institution or institution-set produce changes in other institutions. Intensive study of a single locality allows one to examine changes in each area of life separately and to piece together a picture of the change process (Greenhalgh et al. 1994).

Such a study needs to identify the most salient fertility-relevant institutions in which significant changes have been induced by economic reforms and which are significantly influencing demographic behaviour. This study has few references to previous research, and proceeds mostly through empirical explorations, because no other intensive village study of economic reforms and fertility behaviour has been conducted in rural China.[4] It studies institutions in the society not only to know how individuals *perceive* how such institutions work, but to see how they actually do work; this in turn required intensive study, including interaction with people and participation in their work and daily life, during a long-term residence (Cain 1983). This micro study is the first step toward a complete, clear picture that may emerge through ongoing study and debate. Its reliance on long-term fieldwork also guards against unwarranted generalizations based on the analysis of observed associations between macro aggregates. Comparative study with a focus on particular institutions (proposed by Herbert Smith 1989), and questionnaire surveys supplemented by intensive study of a few communities (Caldwell 1985), though much needed, remain to be done.

Fieldwork was carried out from July 1992 to November 1993 in a Hebei village that I will briefly discuss here (see Appendix I for detailed discussion). The fieldwork consisted of a two-step investigation: first in the county town and second in the village. The village was chosen based on background information on the whole county and some of its villages. I started the village investigation in early October 1992. I lived with a village family for the whole period, arranged by the village cadres. During the fieldwork, I particularly concentrated on the most salient fertility-relevant institutions that have changed significantly in the reform era, and on the characteristics of the implementation of family planning programmes at the local level.

Because I was living in the village and had developed rapport with the villagers, I was able to have detailed discussions with them on many important issues. I participated in their work and daily life in order to have a sense of certain institutions such as marriage and the family, and local authority and power. I participated in marriage and burial ceremonies, worked in the fields, in household enterprises and at the collective kiln, observed family planning campaigns and visited migrants who worked in the cities. I wanted to understand what has changed in social, economic, and political structure in the village, what the most salient fertility-relevant institutions are, how these changed in the collective and post-reform periods, what institutions mean to local people and how institutions influence people's behaviour. Before the fieldwork, I made an exhaustive list of almost all institutions that might potentially play important roles in shaping individual fertility behaviours. Only during the months of intensive fieldwork, however, was I able to identify the institutions that are actually important in fertility behaviour; these I then studied in great detail, and the institutions which are unimportant for human reproduction were dropped from the study.

Based on the knowledge gained at the initial stage of the fieldwork, my survey questionnaires were modified to capture quantitatively significant changes in marriage, family and gender relations and fertility. Population census and surveys of married couples in which wives were aged between 15–59, of ever-married women aged between 15–59, of unmarried young people aged between 6–24 and of elderly people aged 60 and over were conducted at various stages of the fieldwork. Questions addressed marriage, family, schooling and economic activity of the young, welfare of the old, fertility motivation of married couples, birth histories and contraceptive use by ever-married women, etc. The population census was assisted by two men from the village who worked in the county town. The surveys were assisted by a woman from the village and a female M.A. student majoring in Anthropological Demography at the Central Institute of Nationalities in Beijing. According to the village census, the village had 471 households and 2,104 residents in early 1993. The survey of ever-married women aged between 15–59 on their birth history and contraception included almost all eligible women (450 women, 97.4 per cent). Of the married couples, 254 (59.8 per cent) were interviewed, of the young 244 (33.2 per cent) and of the old 95 persons (66.5 per cent).

To insure the quality of the quantitative data, the population census was conducted after a three-month stay in the village during which a rapport developed with villagers. The survey concerning births and contraception was conducted at the very late stage of the fieldwork, i.e., nine months into the fieldwork. By cross-checking the data through informants and through processing the data immediately during the fieldwork, data quality was ensured. However, certain problems remain, for example, data on questions concerning ideal and real number of children in the family, and the contraception methods of reproductive couples, have certain problems, although these problems were reduced as much as possible.

Starting with background information on socio-economic development and fertility change and variations among Chinese provinces at the macro level, this study then considers economic reforms and socio-economic transformations in the selected county and village, and then the intermediate institutions with regard to marriage, family and local authority. The final part of the thesis discusses fertility outcome and the related patterns of contraception.

Chapter 1 discusses the various theoretical approaches found in fertility studies, in order to develop an institutional approach to studying Chinese economic reforms and fertility behaviour and to provide an institutional framework for the study. Chapter 2 covers provincial variations in socio-economic development, family planning policy and fertility at the macro level, to provide the national and provincial context for this particular study.

Chapter 3 discusses reform processes, the evolution of population policies and general information on economic development and population growth in the county. Chapter 4 begins to present the empirical data on the village, focusing on the reform processes and socio-economic transformation in the village, as these are reflected in structural changes in labour, ownership, income, social differentiation, the position of cadres, and education, health and social welfare.

Chapter 5 discusses what has changed in the marriage institution and marriage patterns, including changes in the meaning of marriage to local people, marriage finance, brideprice and dowry and marriage decision-making in the reform period. Chapter 6 focuses on family institutions, mainly in terms of changes in family structure and family relations, for example family size and composition, household division, division of labour and inter-household and intra-household relations in the reform period.

Chapter 7 considers how changes in the institutional context reshape individual fertility perceptions, discussing how economic reforms define new opportunities and different problems for the rural Chinese, and describing the strategies adopted by reproductive couples and other family members for taking up these opportunities and solving newly-emerging problems. Chapter 8 discusses how the changing context is reshaping the characteristics of the implementation of state family planning policies at the village level, and how the family, as well as local administration, mediate state policies.

Chapter 9 investigates fertility and contraception patterns: the number of children, their sex ratio, the timing of childbearing and the methods of family planning used. The adoption of children, as a way for infertile couples to have children, and as a strategy fertile couples use to ensure their desired number and sex of children while avoiding family planning penalties, is also discussed. The conclusion of the study summarizes the research findings and recontextualizes them in a rethinking of the relations between economy, intermediate institutions and fertility in rural China.

Notes

[1] According to a national sampling survey conducted by the State Family Planning Commission in 1992, Chinese TFR in 1992 was 1.72, far below replacement level (see Jiang et al. 1994). With an adjustment for underreporting in the survey, Chinese fertility may have been close to replacement level during the early 1990s (see Peng 1993, Feeney & Yuan 1994, Zeng 1996).

[2] Such studies are too numerous to be listed here. The notable studies which analyse interrelationship between socio-economic development, family planning and fertility at the national level include, e.g., Mauldin & Berelson (1978), Freedman & Berelson (1976), Anker (1975), and Hernandez (1981); similar studies at sub-regional level within a country like China include Birdsall & Jamison (1983), Poston & Gu (1987), Poston & Jia (1990) and Jiang (1986). Studies using individual as unit in studies of Chinese fertility include Wang (1988) and Zhang (1994).

[3] Theories and methods from anthropology and demography have been discussed by some scholars (see Lorimer 1954, Howell 1986, Handwerker 1986, Caldwell et al. 1987, Greenhalgh 1990b & 1995 and Hammel & Friou, 1997).

[4] Anthropological work on Chinese villages since 1949 are few, and most of these focus on southern China, including Hong Kong and Taiwan (e.g. Cohen 1976, Parish & Whyte 1978, Chan et al. 1984, Huang 1989, Potter & Potter 1990), the rural north has been studied relatively little, although there are a few recent exceptions (e.g., Judd 1994). In the last few years the number of PhD dissertations on rural Chinese society by Chinese scholars has increased, e.g., Han Min (1993), Wang Hongsheng (1995).

CHAPTER 1

Economy, Institutions and Fertility: Theoretical Explorations

Fertility behaviour is essentially private in nature. Yet it is shaped both by social norms and an important determinant of societal dynamics. Both these aspects – the private and the social – interact in complex ways. However, existing theories and studies on human fertility, such as the microeconomic theories of fertility and classical demographic transition theory, tend to gravitate towards one pole or the other, i.e. either towards individual decision-making and choice or towards socially determined processes, without adequately addressing the social determinants of private choices and behaviour and the effects of private behaviour on societal transformations. Models that use intermediate variables to link socio-economic factors and fertility outcomes represent an attempt to come to terms with macro determinants and micro outcomes in fertility behaviour, but leave out the changes in institutional contexts brought about by changes in socio-economic policies; they also leave out the way these institutional transformations alter the mechanisms of transmission through which socio-economic factors influence fertility through the intermediate variables. An institutional approach, which links the macro economic reforms and micro fertility behaviour and embraces both elements of the social determinants of private choice and of individual behaviour on societal transformations, is thus adopted in the study.

This chapter begins with a search for an institutional approach in fertility studies. I do not intend to have a complete review of numerous fertility studies (for this, readers may refer to Van de Kaa 1996, and UN 1990) but instead will pinpoint the lack of institutional analyses in mainstream of fertility theories and studies, i.e., demographic transition theory at the macro level, economic theory of fertility at the micro level and the model of intermediate variables of fertility. After showing the weaknesses of present fertility studies, and discussing preliminary efforts to apply an institutional approach in fertility studies, I will then re-explore the theoretical discussion on institutions and human behaviour in institutional economics, a field which has experienced tremendous development in recent decades. Finally, I will discuss the use of the institutional framework to analyse relations between macro economy and micro fertility, which will be applied in the analysis of reforms and fertility in the rural Chinese context.

FERTILITY STUDIES: SEARCHING FOR AN INSTITUTIONAL APPROACH

Demographic transition theory

Demographic transition theory as developed by Thompson (1929), Davis (1945) and Notestein (1945) is one of the early attempts to understand human fertility dynamics. It originates from a description of historical trends of fertility and mortality in nineteenth-century Western European countries (UN 1990). Basically, the classical theory states that both the mortality and the fertility of a population will decline as a result of socio-economic development. The transition process typically passes through three stages, from high fertility and mortality to a near-zero rate of natural increase as a result of low fertility and mortality rates, with declining mortality and declining fertility lagging behind in between.

   Although it is called a theory, demographic transition theory only tries to describe regularities of demographic changes which in fact vary in different societies. It also has a number of weaknesses and ambiguities. One of the weaknesses is that it fails to provide the specific information needed for explanation and prediction in particular situations (Greenhalgh 1990b: 88, Willekens 1991: 6). When applied to the markedly different social and economic circumstances of the present developing countries, its explanatory and predictive power is further open to question. For example, China's rapid fertility decline in the last few decades is not following the pattern of conventional transition theory (Tien 1984, Peng 1991). Even developed nations like France did not follow the three-stage path enshrined in demographic theory, since French fertility may have declined before there were substantial declines in mortality (UN 1990). Further, as the study of fertility decline in northern Italy (Kertzer & Hogan 1989) shows, macro-level social and economic changes affected members of different classes living in the same community differently, and in Casealecchio there occurred not one but four distinct and discontinuous fertility transitions, a finding that challenges the assumption that all regions and countries undergo the same demographic transitions. As McNicoll suggests, the theory needs to discard its unilinear-evolutionary presuppositions, stop seeing societal change as unilinear movement from 'traditional' to 'modern' society, and recognize that there are, in fact, multiple paths for societal and demographic change (McNicoll 1994, Ng & Gu 1995).

At the same time, transition theory treats differences in institutions and institutional change among different societies as less important, since the functions of institutions, and the major principles governing human population change, are seen as the same (Notestein 1983: 350, 351). The classical theory tends to abstract different societies regardless of institutional variations. It also omits any explanation of the mysterious adaptation of individuals to socioeconomic context, or of the way in which these individual adaptations reshape the character of the socio-economic context within which people live and work. It provides no framework to analyse social and demographic change in various societies.

Microeconomic theories of fertility

Unlike classical demographic transition theory's macro generalizations on fertility change, the microeconomic theory of fertility attempts to explain fertility by focusing on individual fertility behaviour under the constraints of price, time, income and taste. The groundwork for microeconomic theory was laid by Leibenstein, and the version developed by Becker became the core of the 'new household economics'. Within this theory children, who are assumed to have utility values to their parents, are treated as 'consumption goods', and parents make a rational choice to have children of their own[1] as they do with other consumption goods.

The new household economics approach developed by Gary Becker can be formally expressed in terms of a single-period household utility function, where children and other commodities provide utilities, and a series of household production functions describe final untraded consumption commodities, subject to a budget constraint defined in terms of the wife's time and non-earned income (Becker 1965). Thus, according to economic law, the demand for children and reproduction would increase as the price of children decreased or as household income, the taste for children, or the prices of other household goods increased (Becker 1976); the demand for children would decrease as the value of human time increased (Becker 1965).[2] As increase in income does not lead to increase in demand for number of children in empirical records, it is argued that parents make a trade-off between quantity and quality.

Easterlin & Crimmins extended Becker's new household economics theory (which had aimed merely at determining demand for children) by adding the supply side of fertility and the cost of fertility regulation (Easterlin & Crimmins 1985). Unlike Becker's assumption of permanently stable preferences (Hodgson 1988: 117, Hayes 1994: 9), preferences are treated as endogenous variables. Cultural values, norms and beliefs can enter into the specification of tastes thereby affecting the demand for children, and into the specification of subjective regulation costs. However, Easterlin & Crimmins (1985) did not pursue the influence of social institutions systematically.

Microeconomic theories of fertility have many rigid assumptions. They assume a single joint household utility function, and an once-and-for-all decision at the beginning of marriage setting the number of children parents would like to have in their lifetimes. In addition to the assumption of static fertility decision-making, they also assume, quite problematically, that households are homogeneous and cohesive units with perfect altruism, and that individuals have the same utility function and thus the same interests. Such assumptions ignore the importance of sequential decision-making and its link to life course or domestic cycle. The further assumption that fertility decision-making is concerned only with the number of children ignores preferences parents have concerning the sex and the timing of births. Theories in this paradigm ignore the formation, development and dissolution of households, as well as the asymmetrical relations between family members, and thus pay little attention to what actually happens inside the household. Household models that eschew the problem of conflict within the family and treat the household as a given rather than an explicandum, miss something quite central to an understanding of the family as an institution (Sen 1990: 72). Further, without going beyond market, price changes, household income, and time value, and looking into forces and causes behind them, it would be impossible to see changes in fertility perceptions and preferences and their relation to interactions among family members and between family members and state and community-imposed social control of human fertility.

Furthermore, microeconomic theories of fertility are neo-classical in nature, assuming that individuals are rational beings, and proposing that the individual, as a rational economic agent, will attempt to maximize explicit objectives within the boundaries of clearly defined options. This assumption is strongly individualistic, decontextualized and more concerned with the outcomes of choice than with the decision process by which an outcome is reached (Simon 1978: 2, Lea et al. 1987: 104 cited in De Bruijn 1992: 11). They also make strong assumptions with regard to the awareness of choice, objectivity, intentionality, and the locus of control, leaving no room for the processes by which individual decision-makers shape their preference structure, reduce available information to a limited number of salient considerations, give meaning to behaviours, and cope with uncertainty, dependency and social pressure (De Bruijn 1992: 11).

The neo-classical assumption of rationality faces many criticisms for failing to consider the complexities of the real world, with its imperfect knowledge, uncertainty and limited computational capacity. In response, the model of maximization of utility has been modified to a model of satisfying, and rationality has been modified to become the 'bounded' rationality developed by Simon (1978), in which individuals are recognized as facing complicated decision-problems that they cannot be expected to solve instantly and optimally and which they thus must act to 'satisfy' because they lack the wits to 'maximize' (Langlois 1986: 225). The most common use of rationality, in its original neo-classical definition and its modified versions, refers to the centrality of the 'means and ends' pair in displayed human behaviour (De Bruijn 1991: 3). What is lacking is that both means and ends are affected by social institutions, as are the concepts and framework of human perceptions, and any information perceived through this framework. Individuals interact with each other to solve the conflicts between them, and they need coordination and cooperation (Hardin 1990). As Parsons emphasizes, human behaviour takes place within an institutional framework. In institutional economic terms, human behaviour is structured by human-devised constraints, namely the institutions in the society (North 1990). However, this approach to institutions as human-devised constraints and as devices for reducing transaction costs in economics does not depart far from the concept of the individual as maximizer or satisfier: individuals are still economic actors. It does not recognize that individual perceptions, purposes, means, etc., are themselves socially defined. Lindenberg (1990) suggests integrating economics and sociology in explanations of human behaviour; human beings should not be treated as either *homo oeconomicus* (maximizer) or *homo sociologicus* (role-playing) but as homo socio-oeconomicus. This is not to deny that individuals have their self-interests; however, it is stressed that the contents, or objectives, of self-interest are themselves socially constructed.

The model of intermediate variables of fertility

The description of and generalizations on empirical fertility patterns provided by demographic transition theory provide no explanation of underlying processes of fertility change. Microeconomic theories of fertility assume the inevitability of the institutions and organizational settings which shape fertility decisions. Demographic transition theory and the microeconomic theory of fertility never meet. Demographic transition theory does not bother to touch micro fertility processes, and microeconomic fertility theory ignores the incorporation of the societal context in analysing micro fertility behaviours.

Davis & Blake (1956) specifically put forward the notion of intermediate variables as a framework to study the influence of socio-economic factors on fertility. They compiled a list of critical variables in the reproductive process, from intercourse and conception, to gestation and parturition, through which social economic variables must work to affect fertility. The model of intermediate variables was later developed and popularized by Bongaarts (1978, 1982). With empirical analysis he shows that the majority of variation in fertility is accounted for by four primary intermediate variables: marriage, postpartum infecundability, contraception, and induced abortion (Bongaarts 1978: 125, 1982: 179–80).

This model of intermediate variables of fertility brings macro socio-economic forces and micro fertility behaviour together through intermediate variables. It can reveal certain relationships between socio-economic variables and fertility linked by intermediate variables and provide a helpful guide for the analysis of the complex, inter-linked socio-economic and fertility processes (cf. RIVM 1994). Bongaarts' model is, however, basically static. It has not incorporated individual life stages with different problem situations. What is also lacking in the model is that it does not seek an explanation of the mechanisms and processes through which socio-economic variables operate to influence fertility through various intermediate variables. The model implies that the process of transmission could be purely quantitative in nature. It does not note the importance of qualitative changes in institutional context brought about by changes in socio-economic policies and the way these institutional transformations alter the mechanisms of transmission (Wuyts 1997). It fails to see how the *intermediate institutions* shape (filter) the nature of the impact of macro socio-economic effects on the intermediate variables and, hence, on fertility. What matters is to explain how micro outcomes are restructured not only as the macro context changes, but also as the filters (through which its effects are transmitted) change. Bongaarts' version of the intermediate variables model is not meant to analyse the institutional factors affecting fertility, as was intended originally by Davis & Blake in the mid-1950s.

Institutional approaches to fertility

The importance of social institutions in influencing human fertility and fertility change has been noted by various scholars in the 1980s and 1990s. For example, McNicoll (1975, 1980, 1994) and others (Cain 1981, Lesthaeghe 1980, Potter 1983) have called attention to the institutional determinants of fertility change. McNicoll argues that two components missing from fertility studies are (1) an adequate model of individual decision-making which take into account institutional factors and (2) an understanding of institutional change itself (McNicoll 1980). He maintains that although fertility behaviour takes place in a particular institutional and cultural envi-ronment, it responds not to this environment as a whole but to a series of domains, within each of which behaviour is adaptive. He later (1985) develops the decision environments as 'objective' institu-tional environments within which individuals are placed, and as cognitive environments which are the immediate context of indi-vidual decision-making. Also, McNicoll & Cain (1990) show how institutions mediate rural development and demographic processes; the institutions included family system, community organization, local government administration and the international system. In a 1994 revisit to the institutional analysis of fertility, McNicoll (1994) offered a thorough discussion on institutions and institutional change, and the relationship between institutional endowments in a society and its fertility transition, in the light of an additional decade of demographic experience and developments in institutional theory.

The work on fertility decline by Parish & Whyte (1978), which concerns the impact of social change in rural Guangdong from 1949 until the 1970s, is frequently cited to show how convincing explanations of fertility levels and trends can be produced by careful analysis of institutional settings (cf. McNicoll 1980, Greenhalgh 1990b, Potter 1983). This intensive study of the rural changes which occurred·when China experienced socialist transformation starting in the 1950s, and when it set up the commune system in 1958 (which continued through the 1960s and the 1970s) shows persuasively that the nature and extent of the rural change did not correspond in any clear and simple way to government priorities and pressures, but instead reflects peasant responses to the new social structure in the transformations of the 1950s. It argues that fertility decline (though interpreted as primarily a response by parents and communities to the changed rural social structure and consequent shift in economic incentives), must also have been facilitated by expansion of the health care system and encouraged by government anti-natalist and delayed-marriage campaigns. With reference to such campaigns, however, Parish & Whyte concede that for marriage at least, official efforts were relatively ineffective. 'We don't claim that the government's proclaimed marriage ideals . . . have little impact. We do argue that their implementation depends to a very great extent on the concrete features of village life, features which support some changes and obstruct others' (Parish & Whyte 1978: 199).

Greenhalgh (1988) uses an institutional approach to elucidate the features of the Chinese experience that help explain the remarkable rapidity of the recent fertility declines in areas of Sinic culture including China. She divides societal institutions into two realms: the security/ mobility system and the institutional environment. The security/ mobility system refers to the class structure, the unit of socioeconomic behaviour (usually the family or household) and the security and mobility goals and strategies of that unit; the institutional environment includes the regulative principles and the formal and informal organizations that structure the world in which people live. The two institutional realms affect fertility in a great many ways. In the simplified schema she developed, the security/ mobility system determines the security and mobility benefits of children to parents and other older-generation family members. The institutional environment defines the cost of children and the terms in which cost-benefit calculations about children are made. Culture, she added, influences how closely behaviour, including fertility, follows from cost-benefit considerations.

In a later article, Greenhalgh (1990a) analyses fertility trend in China by looking into links between state-society relations and the politics of fertility decision-making, and between social institutions and the economics of childbearing. She argues that the explicit fertility policies of the 1970s and the 1980s were necessary but not sufficient conditions for the fertility decline that occurred in China. The sufficient conditions include a range of implicit fertility policies – economic and political policies that restructured family and community institutions and state-society relations in ways that fundamentally altered both the economics of childbearing and the politics of fertility decision-making. She notes that beginning in the mid-1950s a host of changes in family and community life lowered the value of children to parents while vastly enhancing the control of state cadres over the lives of ordinary peasants. This institutional context was crucial to the success of the later-longer-fewer policy in raising contraceptive use and lowering fertility in the 1970s.

Studies of fertility taking account of social institutions shed much insight, however, we still face many problems and difficulties in institutional analysis of fertility change. We still do not know much about the functions and mediation patterns of social institutions, and we do not know much about sources of institutional changes. McNicoll's (1980) initial institutional approaches in studying fertility change employs Herbert Simon's bounded rationality and, further, he limits his discussion of roles of institutions with respect to transaction cost. Potter (1983) reviews the study which aims to explain the role of social institutions on fertility behaviour, but many aspects are sparsely connected. Further, he does not include the 'complexities of decision-making and behavioural response' which are important issues regarding the sources and functions of institutions.

INSTITUTIONS, INSTITUTIONAL CHANGE AND HUMAN BEHAVIOUR

There have been further developments in institutional economics in the 1980s and the early 1990s. As a demographer trying to apply an institutional approach to analyse macro-economic reforms and micro-fertility behaviour, there is a need to step in the economic field and bring useful elements in the analysis.

Institutions: Concept

What constitutes an 'institution' is a subject of continuing debate among social scientists. Some scholars simply use 'institutions' without specifying the intended meaning. Eisenstadt (1968: 410) gives a formal definition of institutions as 'regulative principles which organize most of the activities of individuals in a society into definite organizational patterns from the point of view of some of the perennial, basic problems of any society or ordered social life'. North (1990: 3) defines institutions as the humanly devised constraints that shape human interaction. Institutional constraints include both what individuals are prohibited from doing and, sometimes, the conditions under which some individuals are permitted to undertake certain activities. Institutions are not behaviours themselves, they are the rules used by individuals; they provide the framework within which human interaction takes place (North 1990: 4).

The terms 'institution' and 'organization' are commonly used interchangeably and this also contributes to ambiguity and confusion. However, they can be distinguished if organizations are defined as groups of individuals bound by some common objective, created with purposive intent in consequence of an opportunity set resulting from an existing set of constraints (institutional ones as well as the traditional ones of economic theory), and able, while acting in the course of attempts to accomplish their objectives, to be major agents of institutional change (North 1990: 5).[3] More concisely, institutions, together with the standard constraints of economic theory, determine the opportunities in a society. Organizations are created to take advantage of these opportunities.

An institution must be accompanied with enforcement mechanisms and sanctions which limit the behavioural deficiencies of individual actors. In informal institutions, conventions are self-enforcing. Norms of behaviour are enforced by a second party (retaliation) or by a third party (societal sanctions or coercive authority) (North 1990: 385). In formal institutions, punishable offences, penalties, and the responsibility for taking punitive action are fairly well defined. Some actors or set of actors have the task of monitoring institutional behaviour, and the same or other actors have the task of punishing those who are viewed as having violated the rules (Levi 1990).

Institutions have the following four defining characteristics: (1) institutions are principles or rules to regulate human behaviours, which exist at different levels and in different spheres; (2) institutions form human habits and routinized behaviours and they have relative durability over time; (3) institutions are created and changed by intended design, inherited from the past, and/or reshaped by individual behaviours and actions, which may lead to unintended consequences; and (4) institutions have monitoring mechanisms which are either self-policed by individuals themselves or by external authorities.

Roles of institutions in shaping human behaviours

While it is recognized that institutional analysis can make an important contribution to understanding human behaviours, no consensus has been reached about how institutions exert their influences. North (1990) notices reduction of transaction cost and uncertainty nature of institutions. He also acknowledges the role of institutions in delimiting choices so as to avoid or, when necessary, resolve societal conflicts (see also Langlois 1986, Levi 1990). Langlois (1986) and Cook & Levi (1990) note that institutions serve as behaviour guides that reduce the knowledge and cognitive skills necessary for successful action.

Many theories of institutional economics are modifications of neo-classical economic theory (see North 1994). They argue that institutions matter, and that they matter since transactions in the economy are costly. Institutions emerge and persist when they are cumulatively seen to be in everyone's interest. Individuals are simply constrained by opportunities, transaction costs, and imperfect information defined by institutions in the society. In this perspective, the human world consists only of self-interested individuals; this is similar to the notion of 'bounded rationality' developed by Herbert Simon (1982), who rejects the global maximization hypothesis. However, the behaviouralist model of 'bounded rationality' is still calculating rationality, and human behaviour is still governed by rational deliberation (Hodgson 1988: 100). As remarked by Hodgson (1988: 100), 'the behaviouralist alternative does not stray a great deal from its orthodox model'.

O'Driscoll & Rizzo, two Austrian School economists, point out that institutions can convey information and transmit knowledge. Firstly if people can rely on others to fulfil certain roles then their expectations are more likely to be coordinated; Secondly, institutions convey knowledge in the sense that the routine courses of action they embody are efficient adaptations to the environment (O'Driscoll & Rizzo 1985: 39). However, subjectivism, the presupposition that the contents of the human mind, and hence decision-making, are not determined by external events, is unacceptable. As Hodgson maintains, although information and knowledge have important subjective and individual features, the concepts and theories that are used in their acquisition are not, and cannot be purely subjective, as if they resulted from an isolated individual (Hodgson 1988: 7).

The cognitive processes of individuals are essentially social as well. As Hodgson argues, the mechanisms of human perception and knowledge acquisition are unavoidably social and unavoidably reflect culture and social practice. The nature of information and knowledge and the social processes involved in their acquisition are closely related to social institutions. He argues that the socio-economic and institutional environment has a significant effect on the kind of information we receive, our cognition of it, our preferences, and thereby much of our behaviour (Hodgson 1988: 71).[4] This is not to deny that individuals have their self-interests, but those self-interests are themselves socially defined (cf. Parsons 1940: 197, cited in Hodgson 1988: 124, Platteau 1991).

Path dependence and evolutionary nature of institutions

The emergence and development of social institutions may be led by intentional design or by unintentional individual actions. Institutions can be intentionally created, however, as McNicoll (1994: 201) noted, efforts at institutional design must reckon with the fact that any society is a mass of habits and interests ready to distort or wholly subvert the best intentions of social planners. Institutions can also be inherited from the past. Rules become institutions as they are institutionalized, or vanish as they cease functioning or are destroyed. Social institutions are of an evolutionary nature; they involve human habits, interactions, bargains and negotiations of individuals with different interests. Changes of institutions, in aspects like timing, speed and extent of change, vary. As North puts it, while formal rules can change overnight, the informal norms usually change only gradually (North 1994: 366).

Changes in power relations reshape the changes of institutions. Assuming (1) that individuals create institutions, which then constrain the subsequent choices of the same individuals or future generations, (2) that those making decisions often have divergent interests from those whom their decisions affect, and (3) that there is an unequal distribution of power among those who constitute the institution, Levi argues that one source of institutional change is the redistribution of the coercive and bargaining power within the institutions (Levi 1990). She points out that institutions resolve societal conflicts and serve the interests – of the many or the few – and all facilitate and regulate the resources of power.

She also argues that if an institution depends only on coercion for the successful implementation of its policies, the costs of enforcement will be insupportably high. Thus, institutional leaders will search for alternative means to create compliance. She argues that besides coercion, side payment and norms, a fourth dimension, *contingent consent,* is also a principle means to induce individuals to comply. Contingent consent possesses both normative and utilitarian elements. However, the 'weak' are not powerless; the most important of the 'weapons of the weak' (Scott's term) is the ability to withdraw compliance. Levi notes that most institutional change is incremental rather than totally reconstructive or destructive; some change results from the intentional actions of institutional managers, and some institutional transformations evolve from the unintended consequences of routine decisions. She also points out that often the important catalysts to incremental institutional change are decisions of institutional managers and staff that have the unintended consequences of undermining their power.

Present institutions and their directions of change partly depend on past institutions and past institutional change; in other words, institutions are path dependent. As Mackintosh (1995: 35) put it, 'the past institutional development . . . shapes the present perception of what is "done" and what is possible. . . . [T]he path you have been following constrains the future possible paths', or, to put it more positively, established norms can make certain future paths possible to you but not to others'.

Sources of institutional change are many; they derive from changes in relative prices, technology innovation, demographic growth, wars, revolutions, natural disasters, etc. (North 1990). The state or institutional entrepreneur can create, design or modify certain institutions to achieve certain purposes by trying to influence individual behaviours by providing behaviour orientation, shaping individual perceptions, and imposing monitor mechanisms. Individuals are not passive followers. Their responses will shape the characteristics of those institutions. As Wuyts shows, institutional changes propelled as a result of public action, whether by the state or other forms of collectivity, centre on changing perceptions of public need emerging from changing economic and social conditions (Wuyts 1992: 29–37).

Institutions are not designed for 'one-shot' games. Individuals do not make once-and-for-all decisions. Both institutions and decision-making should be seen as processes. Institutions change and the making of decisions proceeds, coordinating with and counteracting institutional changes. Institutions and human actions interact with each other, and they run parallel courses in human history.

ECONOMY, INSTITUTIONS AND FERTILITY

For analysing relations between macro economic reforms and micro fertility behaviour within the rural Chinese context, I have the following three premises: (1) institutions matter, (2) they do not all matter to the same extent as far as fertility behaviour is concerned, and (3) it is useful to focus on the mechanisms and processes through which changes in social institutions are propelled by deliberate policies of institutional reforms to affect fertility outcomes.

Institutions exist as both contexts and processes at different levels and in different spheres, and a study is usually restricted to a certain time and place, thus some institutions become salient and overt while others fall into the background. For example, the existing land market can have important implications on risk environments for peasants and their strategies to adapt to the risk environment as studied by Cain in Bangladesh; however, this is not the case in China, where land is collectively owned. Nor are institutions at the international level, like international politics, international law and international trade and market, for example, the focus of the present study, though in many contexts they are likely to be relevant in understanding fertility.[5] At the societal level, institutions like those governing agricultural practices (an example used by McNicoll & Cain) can be omitted from the analysis, since including such trivial though interesting issues may obscure the main lines linking rural development and demographic process.

The impact changing government policies have for individual behaviours is dependent on intermediate level institutions which 'filter' and mediate government policies (Messkoub 1992). Such perspective is useful in analysing transitional societies such as present-day China, where some institutions may have experienced important changes, others may persist unexamined, and in some cases the new context may reinforce the old ways rather than doing away with them (Potter & Potter 1990: 196–97).

Social institutions influence fertility to different extents and in a great many ways. Some institutions are directly related to fertility behaviour while some others are indirect influences. For example, the marriage institution is more directly related to individual fertility behaviour than the funeral institution in rural China. As I will discuss in the following chapters, marriage is not only the prerequisite for giving birth to children among the rural population, the family formation processes and the expenses involved in marriages determine both familial relations (and thus fertility decision-making), and fertility perceptions and motivations. Funeral practices can also influence parents' fertility perception and motivation because children have a role in funeral rituals.

Although institutional roles in influencing the cost-benefit of children and people's perception of this have been of less concern in microeconomic theories of fertility, some contributions to this area have been made. Potter (1983) reviewed extensively how institutions would influence economic costs and benefits of children. Labour arrangement and social welfare, as studied by Mead Cain in Bangladesh and India, have a significant impact on children's value as labour and as a source of security and insurance. Institutions structure the cost of children's food, education and health and the cost of the needed time. Ben White (1976) in his study of Indonesia, found that the cost of children includes not only the cost of food, education and health, but also the considerable costs related to social and ritual obligations incurred from the time of the mother's pregnancy until the child reaches adulthood.

Equally important but of less concern in fertility studies is that institutions structure options. Having children may be too costly, returns from children may be less than cost, children may be an imperfect source against risks; however, if there are either no alternatives or only inferior alternatives, children will be nevertheless be highly valued (Cain 1985: 220). Having children can offer solutions to adult problems in that, as noted by Greenhalgh (1988: 667), 'childbearing aspirations are not primarily ends in themselves, but means to other, larger ends'. Children can provide security and risk insurance not only to their parents but also to other family members; they contribute their labour to the household economy and they may be important sources for household social mobility (Greenhalgh 1988).

It would be difficult to develop well-constructed typologies of institutional settings which influence fertility (see McNicoll 1980, 1994), especially because institutions are changing over time. In the case of Chinese rural society under the reforms, some institutions have changed rapidly and have had great impact on the changing fertility behaviour, and others have changed little and had little impact; the latter, though they may have some relevance, are insignificant enough to be relegated to the background. Also, some economic reforms have no real ties with fertility behaviour and thus can be omitted from consideration.

Rural reforms, which introduced responsibility systems and market mechanisms and stressed economic efficiency rather than social equity, have meant that individual welfare relies more on individual families than on the collective. The reforms of formal institutional setups have structured new options with new problems. Rural Chinese now have more opportunities and widening options, and they have the freedom to arrange their labour; at the same time, however, they face increasing uncertainties, risks and vulnerabilities, and they must rely on themselves for covering these risks and contingencies. The officially instigated institutional reforms may thus have greatly influenced the intermediate institutions of marriage and family systems which influence both fertility motivation and fertility decision-making. The meanings of marriage and familial relations may have changed. This goes beyond the notion that institutions influence individual fertility behaviour by only determining cost-benefits of having children for reproductive couples.

Economic reforms also change the context for policy implementation. Social demographers have shown that a population programme is one of the determinants of fertility.[6] However, many studies, as argued by Simmons et al. (1983), are unable to provide substantial insights into the dynamics of programme functioning or into the organizational and political determinants of programme success or failure. Simmons et al. call for an institutional analysis of population programmes that incorporates political-administrative system, public policy and population programmes in the analysis. I do not, however, intend to analyse systematically the making of population policies and programme success or failure in the Chinese context; I am more concerned with how economic reforms reshape the character of family planning implementation at the local level. This study focuses on how population blueprints made at the national or provincial level are translated into action at the local level, how local cadres interact among themselves and how they interact with individual households, and how these interactions in turn influence individual fertility behaviour. As noted in studies of centre and sub-region relations in China, it would be wrong to assume that local government has the same interests as the centre (cf. Zhao 1996). State policies would be mediated and filtered by its local government administrations.

Thus, the main line of the present study is to analyse how economic reforms, together with individual responses, shape the character of intermediate institutions which in turn influence inter-mediate variables and fertility outcomes. The primary intermediate institutions dealt with here concern marriage, family and local authority and power, in their complex and manifold ways. For instance, marriage is the starting point of childbearing in Chinese society, where pre-marital and extra-marital births are socially unac-cepted. Family is the centre and immediate context in which fertility decisions are negotiated. Authority and power at the local level are vital in Chinese society, where social control of fertility is tremendous. I will show in the following chapters that since reforms have begun, these intermediate institutions have experienced significant changes in the studied village (a finding likely to be indicative of the situation in other villages of rural China as well), and that they play important roles in the complex and dynamic relations between reforms and fertility in rural China.

Notes

[1] Becker (1965: 193) assumes that '[e]ach family must produce its own children since children cannot be bought or sold in the market place'.

[2] Becker (1965) also assumes that only the wife's time is relevant to the 'production' of children; husbands are assumed not to contribute to childbearing, and thus, as the value of wife's time increases, the demand for children will decrease.

[3] North uses the example of rules and players in a game to distinguish institutions and organizations. 'The purpose of the rules is to define the way the game is played. But the objective of the team within that set of rules is to win the game – by a combination of skills, strategy, and coordination, by fair means and sometimes by foul means. Modelling the strategies and the skills of the team as it develops is a separate process from modelling the creation, evolution, and consequences of the rules' (1990: 5).

[4] This is, however, different from arguing that institutions structure options, where institutions are seen as merely constraints. Hodgson used the status of women to illustrate the difference: 'The argument presented here is not simply that women may face a more limited opportunity set, but that their goals and choices are actually molded by culture and routine so that many may actually choose to stay in the same positions and occupations, even when choices and incentives are available' (see Hodgson 1988: 136).

[5] Greenhalgh emphasizes the importance of international economy, global communication, and international politics in understanding the conjuncture of local and global processes (Greenhalgh 1990b: 95). McNicoll noted the importance of the international system in linking rural development and population change (McNicoll & Cain 1990).

[6] There are studies analysing impact of population programmes coupled with socioe-conomic factors on fertility, using increasingly sophisticated measures of programme input or strength and a range of social and economic indicators as independent variables, and using fertility or contraceptive prevalence rates as dependent variables. Such studies have been conducted both at cross-national level and at a cross-regional level in China (e.g. Mauldin & Berelson 1978, Posten & Gu 1987).

■ CHAPTER 2

Chinese Reforms and Fertility: Macro Context

The Chinese Communist Party (CCP) has continuously paid attention to institutional reforms as an instrument to propel purposeful
change since it came to power in mainland China in 1949. At the
initial stage of socialist construction in the early 1950s, the Party reor-
ganized virtually the whole of China's agricultural system in rural
areas following the Soviet model (Putterman 1993). The equity-
oriented commune system, set up in 1958, survived for 20 years in
rural China until it began to be dismantled at the end of 1978 by
reformers led by Deng Xiaoping, who aimed to develop an efficient
Chinese economy. The new economic reforms have drastically altered
the set-up of formal institutions, and have brought about changes in
almost every aspects of social life. This study uses the Chinese
commune system and fertility patterns of that period as a starting
point, and also considers Chinese development and fertility at the
national level. This chapter starts with the evolution of economic and
population policies, socio-economic development and fertility at the
macro level since 1949. This background information on policy
evolution, socio-economic development and fertility change provides
a context for understanding Chinese rural reforms and fertility.

TRANSITION FROM PLANNED ECONOMY TO MARKET ECONOMY: INSTITUTIONAL REFORMS AND RURAL DEVELOPMENT

Chinese society has experienced several dramatic transformations
since 1949. Its national macroeconomy, and its rural development
have experienced dramatic changes. Schematically, Chinese rural
economic development since 1949 may be divided into three main
phases: the 1949–57 land reforms and transformation of socialist
economy under central plan; the 1958–78 communization and collective economy with its stress on social equality; and from 1978 to

present the transformation of the planned economy to a market economy with an emphasis on economic efficiency (Ahmad & Hussain 1991; Xu 1982). The periodization, key economic and population aspects and key economic and demographic characterization during each of these periods are listed in Table 2.1.

The pre-reform era was the main period of radical policies. During the Great Leap Forward (1958–60) and the early years of Cultural Revolution (1966–68) the commune system was formed, a higher level of accounting was propelled, and private elements of economy like private plots, household sidelines and rural market fairs, all considered 'capitalist remnants', were restrained or prohibited (Liu & Wu 1986). After the death of Mao Zedong in 1976, the radical policies were criticized. Economic construction began to replace 'class struggle' as the focus of the state's work. In rural China at the end of 1978 state introduced various household responsibility systems; later it carried out the market transformation (Liu & Wu 1986).

Pre-reform period: Transformation and construction of socialist economy

After land reform was completed in 1953, China carried out a socialist transformation of its peasant economy. Between 1954 and 1957, socialist cooperatives were established, first as elementary cooperatives and then in an advanced form (Xu et al. 1982). By pooling the land, large agricultural tools and capital, peasants were led onto a road toward common prosperity, producing an egalitarian society in which individuals would work for the common good rather than to advance the interests of their own family. Starting at early 1958, small coops merged into large ones. In August of the same year, people's communes were promoted in rural China since they were 'bigger . . . and of a more developed socialist nature' (Liu & Wu 1986). The communes merged with the basic organization of political power in the countryside, according to the principles of integrating government administration with commune management and combining industry, agriculture, trade, education, and military affairs. Under the commune system, land is owned by the collective. The communes took over the peasants' private plots, poultry and domestic animals as well as household sideline occupations, thereby eliminating the remnants of the so-called private ownership of the means of production. Communes exercised control and management over almost all aspects of rural production (Liu & Wu 1986: 233–35, 242–43).

The great famine which occurred in the following years (1959–61) affected large areas of rural China, with an estimated loss of life of 30 million (Ashton *et al.* 1984: 619). The radical policies were modified, and economic readjustment continued until 1963. The work points system was adopted, public canteens were closed down, and private plots, household sidelines and rural market fairs, which had been eliminated or severely constrained during the establishment of the commune system, were resumed. However, the three-level system of

Table 2.1 Periodization, policy context, and economic and demographic changes since 1949

A: Policy context

Period/Periodization	Key economic policy	Key population policy
1949–57		
Land Reforms (1949–52)	Confiscating the means of production of the landlord class, distributing them to the poor peasants.	Multiple births promoted
Socialist transformation of agriculture (1953–57)	Private property abolished; Mutual-aid teams, and elementary and advanced cooperatives set up.	Birth control advocated
1958–78		
Great Leap Forward (1958–60)	Rural collectivization, infrastructural works and rural industrialization; Commune system set up.	Family planning curtailed
Readjustment of Economy (1961–65)	Mild restrictions on private activities and rural markets; egalitarian distribution minimized.	Short-lived birth control (1962–66)
Cultural Revolution (1966–76)	Dazhai model promoted; class struggle emphasized.	Population policy came to a standstill (1966–70)
The era of Hua Guofeng (1976–78)	'Continuing the revolution'; Taking class struggle as the key link'.	'Later, sparser and fewer' birth policy (1971–78)
1978–		
Responsibility systems (1979–83)	Contracting out land and production quotas to the household.	'One-child' policy (1979–)
Development of market economy' (1984–)	Mandatory sale of grain to state abolished; Free mobility; Private economy & hire of labour permitted.	

(Continued)

Table 2.1 (Continued)

B: Economic and demographic changes

Period/Periodization	Economic performance	Demographic dynamics
1949–57		
Land Reforms (1949–52)	Economic recovery and economic improvement: From 1952 to 1957, growth of national income 9% annually;[d] GOVA* increased by 25%;	Fertility remained high & rapid mortality decline: CBR* remained around 32 and 37 per thousand between 1953–57;[f] TFR remained around 6.[j] Life expectancy had risen from 32 years in 1949 to 57 in 1957;[a]
Socialist transformation of agriculture (1953–57)	The consumption level was 34.2% higher; Farmers household income increased by nearly 30%;[e]	
1958–78		
Great Leap Forward (1958–60)	Great famine (1959–61): From 1957 to 1960, GOVI* increased by 134.4%; GOVA* & grain output dropped by 22.7% & 26.4%;[e] More than 20 million lives died of starvation between 1959–61.[a]	CDR* reached high, CBR* & NGR* low peak in 1960.
Readjustment of Economy (1961–65)	Revitalization of economy: The average annual increase in national income 14.5%; agriculture increased by 11%.[d]	Fertility compensation: CBR* and TFR* reached peaks of 43.37 per thousand[f] and 7.5[j] in 1963.
Cultural Revolution (1966–76)	Setback of economy: sharp decline of GOVI* & GOVA* 10% in 1967, and 4.2% in 1968; Grain output in 1968 4% less than that in 1967; National income 7.2% drop in 1967, 6.5% decrease in 1968.[e]	Sharp fertility decline: CBR* declined sharply from 33.43 per thousand to 18.25 in 1978;[f] TFR* from 5.81 in 1970 to 2.72 in 1978.[j]
The era of Hua Guofeng (1976–78)	Economic ups and downs, slow growth.	

Period/Periodization	Economic performance	Demographic dynamics
1978–		
Responsibility systems (1979–83)	Rapid economic growth: Between 1978 to 1994, the annual increase rate of GNP* and GDP* reached 9.78% and 9.80% respectively; Per capita GNP* increased by 8.28% yearly; GOVA*, grain output increased annually at 6.2% and 2.4%.[f]	Fertility remained low: Life expectancy further increased to 68.5 in 1990.[h] TFR* reached around the replacement level in the early 1990s.[i]

Notes

* CBR = Crude Birth Rate; CDR = Crude Death Rate; NGR = Natural Growth Rate = CBR–CDR; GOVI = Gross Output Value of Industry; GOVA = Gross Output Value of Agriculture; GNP = Gross National Products; GDP = Gross Domestic Products; TFR = Total Fertility Rate.

Sources

a: Ashton et al. (1984);
b: CASS (1987: 628);
c: Zweig (1989: 54);
d: Johnson (1988: 226);
e: Liu & Wu (1986: 193–9, 266, 354–5)
f: SSB (1992: 64), (1995: 20–1, 32, 278–9);
g: Zhang (1980), cited in Watson (1983: 707);
h: SSB (1995: 70);
i: Zeng (1996);
j: Peng (1991: 110).

ownership of the means of production, namely, production team, production brigade and people's commune, with the production team as the basic accounting unit, was reaffirmed. Under the commune system, income differentials were dramatically reduced within rural production teams (G. White 1992: 237–38; Johnson 1988: s230); their basic form lasted for more than 20 years before being dismantled.

The leftists believed that private plots, household sidelines, and free markets were inadequate for building the communist society of the future.[1] Thus, during the peak years of Cultural Revolution (1966–69), the unit of accounting again was shifted from production team to production brigade in some villages. Payments were based on not only skill and effort, but also on people's enthusiasm and political attitude. Task-based payments were seen as undesirable because they would foster inequality and the selfish pursuit of individual gain. Private plots were restricted in size or even abolished (Zweig 1989: 56–58). In the early 1970s China's villages were given approval to make changes according to their concrete condition (Zweig 1989).

Reforms period: Transition of planned economy to market economy

Following the death of Mao Zedong in 1976 and the political rehabilitation of Deng Xiaoping in the late 1970s, the CCP decided in the third plenary session of the eleventh Central Committee of the Party that the central focus of the Party's work should be shifted to socialist modernization (Liu & Wu 1989). In the late 1970s, while upholding public ownership of land and other basic means of production and the principle of distribution 'to each according to his (or her) work', China conducted a series of rural economic reforms and developed new agricultural economic policies.

The immediate objective of rural economic policy in 1979 was to ensure a stable increase in agricultural production by increasing labour productivity through improvements in peasant incentives (ZGNYNJ 1980: 56–62). With the introduction of responsibility systems around 1980 linking peasants' working performance with their payment to increase their incentives, the Chinese government also encouraged the development of household sidelines and promoted the diversification and specialization of the economy; private plots were allowed to be enlarged; and the procurement prices for grain and other agricultural products were also increased.

The Chinese government initially allowed various experiments with different responsibility system forms only if not contracted to individual peasants households.[2] It was not until September 1980 that contract output to individual households (*baochandaohu*) was permitted in poor and remote areas. However, forms of the responsibility system, including contracting everything to households (*baogandaohu*, or *dabaogan*), spread quickly to other areas, and *baogandaohu* is now the main and the most radically decentralized form of production responsibility system.[3] Under the *baochandaohu* system, the households contract with the team to farm a particular area of land and to hand over a proportion of the production in return for an agreed work point payment. The system virtually abandons all aspects of collective management. Initially the contract of land to households was normally valid for only one to three years; in 1994 this was extended to 15 years or more.[4]

As the *dabaogan* system spread all over China, reformers realized that the commune management system was not appropriate for furthering agrarian development (cf. G. White 1992: 238–39, Watson 1983). Reformers argued that the commune acted as a unified unit of government administration and economic management without guaranteeing the autonomy of the production team. They believed that the direct intervention of the state and the commune in the production team would result in many coercive commands and in blind leadership, and that this would weaken the role of the production team in economic management, confuse the relation of interests among production teams and brigades, and block the further economic development of the production team. The separation of government administration from economic management was thus an aspect of the transition to reliance on economic levels and economic rules (Wang & Wei 1986, Ash 1988: 539). In 1982, the state constitution re-established the township governments. By the end of 1984, communes had virtually disappeared from rural China (ZGNYNJ 1985: 121). The three levels of production team, production brigade and commune have since been replaced by the village residents group (*cunminxiaozu*), administrative village (*xingzhencun*) and township (*xiang*). All economic units, such as small factories and stores, previously owned by the commune, have become independent cooperative enterprises.

Since the reforms, private plots have been expanded, previous restrictions on domestic sidelines have been removed, and village fairs and markets have been re-established. The number of farm products subject to compulsory state purchase was reduced gradually. More and more goods are allowed to be sold in markets. The rural supply and marketing system, which controlled the rural commerce until 1982, has also been reformed to fit the new conditions. In 1985, the state monopolies over purchasing and marketing of major farm products were abolished and a contract system was introduced (ZGNYNJ 1985: 1–3). Grain and other farm produce over and above quotas fixed in the contract to the collective can also be sold in free markets.

Elements of private economy are allowed to coexist with socialist economy. Peasant households are allowed to employ casual labourers (*linggong*), helpers (*banggong*) and apprentices. Peasants can look for paid jobs in urban areas (Zhao Dexing 1989: 609–10). The green light for the private economy and the opening of the labour market have made it possible for tens of thousands of Chinese peasants either to run enterprises or to look for paid job outside the village. Rural-urban migration has increased rapidly; it reached 100 million in 1992 (Zhou 1996: 231).

Rural development since 1949

Rural economic development since 1949 has experienced ups and downs closely related to Chinese macroeconomic policies, political variations and institutional change and adjustments. The economy was in tatters in 1949 following 12 consecutive years of war. Compared with the peak year before 1937, the output value of agriculture in 1949 had dropped by more than 20 per cent, with grain output down 22 per cent; the period from 1949 to 1958 saw a tremendous recovery of economy, with over 7 per cent of annual growth rate of agriculture output value and over 6 per cent annual increase of grain output (Liu & Wu 1986: 17).

From 1958 to 1978, the gross value of agricultural output increased by 2.3 per cent annually, with the grain output averaging 2.1 per cent. Agricultural producers performed reasonably well compared with other Third World countries (G. White 1992: 237). However, during this period the population was growing rapidly, expanding from 659.94 million in 1958 to 962.59 million in 1978 (SSB 1992). In consequence, there was very little improvement in agricultural output per capita during this period; in fact the growth in grain output translated into only a slight increase in per capita terms, rising from an average of 303 kg in 1958 to only 317 kg in 1978 (Table 2.2).

China's agriculture is now set to embark on a radically different path of development from that which characterized the 20 years between 1958 and 1978; agricultural production has been developing rapidly since the 1978 reforms. Between 1978 and 1994, the gross

Table 2.2 Selected national economic indicators, 1949–94

	GOVA (billion yuan)	Grain output (10,000 tn)	Grain output per capita (kg)	NICP (yuan)
1949	31.07	11 318	208.9	NA
AAGR (%) (1949–58)	(7.4)	(6.5)	(4.2)	NA
1958	58.92	20,000	303.1	60.0[a]
AAGR(%) (1958–78)	(2.3)	(2.1)	(0.2)	(2.5)
1978	92.11	30,477	316.6	98.3
AAGR (%) (1978–94)	(6.2)	(2.4)	(1.0)	(13.5)
1994	241.15	44,510	371.4	743.4

Notes
GOVA = Gross Output Value of Agriculture at 1952 constant prices; AAGR = Average Annual Growth Rate; NIPC = Net Income per Capita in *yuan* for agricultural population at 1950 constant prices; a: Net income per capita in 1957, Johnson 1988: 234. NA = Not Available.

Sources
SSB 1992: 206; 1993: 59, 81, 345, 364; 1995: 32, 20–21, 278–79.

value of agricultural output increased by 6.2 per cent a year, more than double the rate of the previous period.

The percentage increase in grain output since 1949 shows that China's grain production has been good, except during Great Leap Forward and Cultural Revolution when grain production was set back by unfavourable state policies and political chaos. Though many criticize the internal problems of collective institutions or external macro policies, the apparent success of rural reforms focusing on market-led growth is most likely based on the success of pre-reform rural development (Saith 1994). Increasing population and decreasing arable land meant that Chinese per capita grain output could not increase significantly even after certain constraints from the pre-reform period were removed and land productivity rose substantially (output of grain crops per *mu* rose from 169 kg in 1978 to 239 kg in 1988, see G. White 1992: 244). The reform period also saw an increase in the annual growth rate of grain output per capita of only 1 per cent, which, though small, is much higher than during the collective period, when yearly grain production hardly increased at all (Figure 2.1).

The incomes of farming people have increased since 1978. In current *yuan* the per capita income of peasants was 134 in 1978, 425 in 1986 and 1220 in 1993 (see Johnson 1988). With the raising of peasants' living standards, the growing inequality in rural incomes has also become apparent; official measures of income inequality indicate an increase in income inequality in the countryside since 1978 (*Beijing Review*, 22 July 1985: 22).

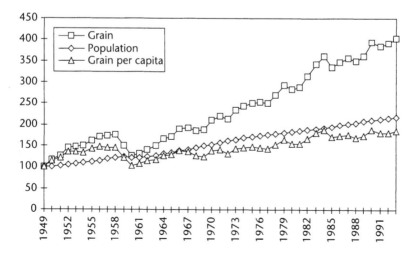

Figure 2.1 Indexes for grain output, population, and per capita grain (1949 = 100)
Source: SSB 1993: 59, 81, 345, 364.

EVOLUTION OF POPULATION POLICIES

The forming and changing of population policies in China since 1949 has been and continues to be a dynamic process related to the socioeconomic and political changes of the country. Starting from initially encouraging more births, to exhortation to have 'births in a planned way' (Mao 1957, cited in Liu et al. 1983), to strict control over rapid population growth, China has experienced dramatic changes in population policies. The evolution of population policies can be roughly divided into three phases: the forming of population policies in the late 1950s and the early 1960s; the policy of 'later, sparser, and fewer' births in the 1970s; and the so-called 'one-child' policy in the 1980s and the early 1990s. As noted by Hull & Yang (1991: 181), Chinese family planning in these different periods are not stages in the development of family planning programmes; rather, they are different styles of family planning based on the different stages of the development of government structures in China. This distinction is important as it helps to explain the fragility of family planning policy in the face of administrative and socio-economic changes.

The forming of Chinese population policies

In the initial stage of the newly established China, Mao Zedong's view that a large population was a great asset predominated. Families with multiple births were financially assisted and the mothers were rewarded. Birth control was rejected as immoral. Abortion and sterilization were strictly constrained. It was only in 1954, as women pressured for expanded access to contraceptive methods, and the government needed to complete the first five-year plan by reducing the rapid population growth, that the pro-natalist policy was formally shifted (T. White 1994). In 1955, a directive on birth control was issued, and control over childbearing was advocated. In 1956, China started its first family planning programme (Peng 1991: 19–20).

However, in 1957, radical population theory gained predominance. It was argued that more people would provide richer human resources, making it possible to develop the socialist economy at greater speed. People supporting birth control were identified as Malthusian and criticized.[5] With the launching of the Great Leap Forward, official family planning activity was curtailed.

In 1962, as the nation recovered from the chaos of the Great Leap Forward and from great famine, the State Council once more called on the various localities earnestly to promote birth control measures in order to bring the runaway growth rate of the population under control and gradually to bring childbearing into the orbit of state planning. In 1964, the State set up a special agency to take charge of matters pertaining to family planning – the Family Planning Office of the State Council – with corresponding offices in each province, municipality and autonomous region. This laid the organizational basis for earnest implementation of family planning and control of population growth throughout China. But this second family planning programme was also short-lived. When the 'Cultural Revolution' began in 1966, the work of the state family planning agencies came to a standstill. Their personnel were disbanded and there was virtually no official family planning activity (Hou 1981).

'Later, sparser and fewer': Population policy in the 1970s

The family planning campaign was reactivated in 1969 with the realization that high population growth was extremely detrimental to the health of the population and the economy. In 1971 a population target was incorporated in the Five Year Plan and large-scale implementation of a family planning programme resumed. The first two family planning campaigns in China were largely urban-oriented and left the dominant rural area almost untouched. This time the campaign spread to rural villages nationwide as well.

The campaign reached nationwide in late 1972. In 1973, the State Council set up a steering group for family planning which was to be responsible for carrying out the family planning programme country-wide and instituting a more comprehensive policy to limit fertility. The policy's theme was 'later, sparser and fewer', and this theme was to remain the dominant one in family planning policy until 1979. The word 'sparser' advocated a four-year interval between births, both to promote maternal and child health and to reduce population growth. 'Fewer' advocated having two children, and 'later' encouraged marriage at a later age.

In 1974, contraceptives were made available free of charge. The well-established health networks and hundreds of thousands of bare-foot doctors in rural areas helped the dissemination of contraceptives. By mid-decade the government was trying to require urban couples to stop at two children and rural couples to stop at three. In 1976, birth control received a short setback after the death of Mao Zedong, but in the autumn of 1976, after the fall of the 'Gang of Four', efforts were made to get the family planning campaign rolling again. In 1977 a new intensification of the campaign took place, and it was announced that rural as well as urban couples must cease childbearing after two children (Banister 1984).

'One-child-per-couple': Population policy in the 1980s and the early 1990s

Concurrent with the shift of the Party's work on economic development, China's family planning programme was intensified in the 1980s. In June 1979 the work report of the State Council to the People's Congress recommended the provision of incentives and rewards to couples giving birth to only one child. This recommendation was adopted the next year at the third session of the Fifth National People's Congress in 1980, which put forward a general call for 'one-child-per-couple'. In September of the same year, the Party's Central Committee issued an open letter to all members of the Communist Party and the Communist Youth League asking them to take the lead in fulfilling this call (*People's Daily*, 26 September 1980). Since that time the basic content of birth control policy has been to encourage having one child, to control the second birth and to prohibit the third birth. In March 1981, it was decided to set up a State Family Planning Commission, which was to be in charge of national family planning work (Zhao 1989: 829). In this period, intensive mass education and propaganda campaigns were conducted.

In April 1984, the rigorous population policy was modified and implemented along more pragmatic lines (Wang Wei 1985); local family planning offices were given more autonomy in devising regulations and setting targets according to their concrete conditions. The policy condemned coercion, urged voluntarism and persuasion, and advised a flexibility of approach which would allow more couples to have a second child (T. White 1990). In May 1986 the Party Central Committee called on local governments to learn from past experience, overcome mistakes and perfect population policy (Peng 1991: 25), and since then greater flexibility has been introduced into population policy. The modified measures emphasise the promotion of later marriage and late childbearing in order to generate fewer but healthier births. In 1988 the family planning policy was again modified, one change being that couples in rural areas with one daughter were allowed to have a second child (Davin 1990). By the end of 1988, in 18 provinces, single-child peasant families with a daughter were permitted to have a second child after an interval (Peng 1991: 26). Since then, there has been no major change in governmental population policy, though there have been official reports that family planning efforts were strengthened in the beginning of the 1990s.[6]

CHINESE POPULATION AND ITS FERTILITY: NATIONAL TREND
AND REGIONAL VARIATIONS

China's population was 542 million in 1949 (SSB 1985: 185). It reached 1.2 billion at the mid-1990s (1.199 billion at the end of 1994, SSB 1995: 59). China's population growth remained high in the first two decades after liberation, due to rapid decline of mortality and continuing high level of fertility (see Figure 2.2). By 1957, China's crude death rate had already been halved from pre-1949 levels. In 1970 China reported a national crude death rate as low as 7.6 per thousand population. However, the birth rate did not decline simultaneously. As late as in 1968, China's birth rate remained high, almost the same as in 1949 (Figure 2.2). The rate of population growth fell beginning in the early 1970s, owning to marked fertility decline during that decade, and since the mid-1970s China's population has grown at a relatively low annual rate of around 1.2 per cent. However,

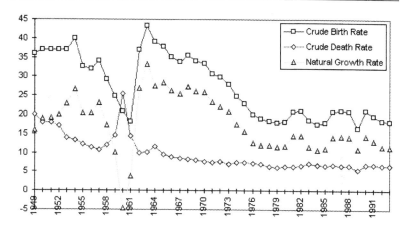

Figure 2.2 National crude birth rate, crude death rate, and natural growth rate (per thousand) since 1949
Source: CASS 1994: 497.

given its large population base, the annual net increase in population is around 14 million.

Since 1949 there have been significant changes in both urban and rural fertility trends. The crude birth rate and crude death rate (in Figure 2.2) provide a general view of the trend in population growth since 1949. However, crude birth rate is influenced by the population's age-sex structure, and its change might reflect changes in the population structure without specifying the change of fertility level of reproductive population. For example, fertility peaks in China in the 1980s are to a great extent influenced by a baby boom in the 1960s. However, for my purpose, total fertility rates over the years are used to illustrate the general trend of fertility change. Figure 2.3 shows the total fertility rates over the past 40 years from 1949 to 1992 for China as a whole and for the urban and rural population separately.[7]

National fertility remained high in the early years of the People's Republic. The total fertility rate actually increased slightly in the 1950s and reached a peak in 1957. Fertility experienced a sudden and remarkable decline after the setback during the Great Leap Forward. In 1959 a disastrous drought caught the country unprepared, and famine devastate the most populous areas for over two years (see Hull & Yang 1991). In 1961, fertility dropped to its lowest point prior to the 1970s. In 1962 and 1963, fertility had a short-term rebound to unprecedented levels as the national economy recovered and normal life resumed. In the other years of the 1960s, national fertility level remained as high as in the 1950s, though there were some variations associated with the early years of Cultural Revolution.

During the 1970s China experienced a sharp fertility decline. The total fertility rate (TFR) reduced from 5.7 in 1970 to 2.3 in 1980, a

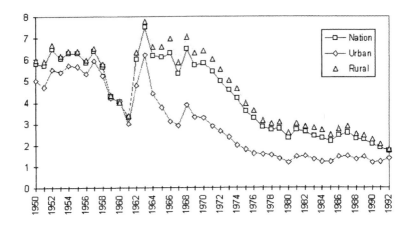

Figure 2.3 Total fertility rates in China, 1950–92
Sources: Peng 1991: 110, Peng 1990: 17, Jiang et al. 1994: 222–24.

decline of over 50 per cent in only one decade. Since the 1980s, fertility has remained at low levels, with slight fluctuations. In both the early and the late 1980s fertility showed a slight increase; the low for the decade was reached in 1984–85, and its peak in 1987, then declined rapidly at the end of the decade. The level of fertility in 1990 was lower than ever, with a TFR of 2.0. A national fertility survey conducted by China's State Family Planning Commission in 1992 shows that China's fertility fell below replacement level during the early 1990s.

In the process of fertility change, urban and rural China experienced a similar trend over the past few decades, but the trend differed in timing and pace. While there were close similarities in fertility change in urban and rural China in the 1950s, the fertility gap between urban and rural areas appears to have become significant after the sudden decline followed by a brief compensatory increase in fertility in the early 1960s. Urban fertility started to decline rapidly in the mid-1960s, a trend that continued through the last half of the decade, although rural fertility remained as high as in the 1950s. In the 1970s, family planning services reached vast areas of rural China, and rural fertility declined more deeply than urban fertility, and the gap between the two started to shrink. In the 1980s, the urban total fertility rate fluctuated below 1.5. Rural fertility has continued to decline since 1987, after a zigzag in the early 1980s. The fertility gap between urban and rural areas became even smaller in the early 1990s.

In addition to variations between China's urban and rural areas, fertility change over the last few decades also varies by region.[8] These variations can be shown using box plots, which show directly the fertility variations among China's provinces, autonomous regions and municipalities.[9] Figure 2.4 shows total fertility rates at five-year inter-

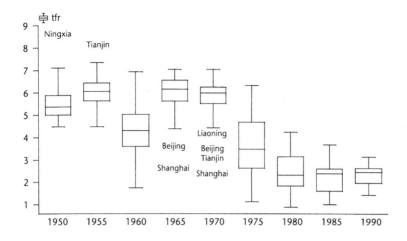

Figure 2.4 Box plots of provincial total fertility rates in selected years, 1950–90

vals for 28 provinces, municipalities, and autonomous regions (excluding Taiwan and Tibet) since 1950 (see also Table 2.3 for a summary of the data used in the figure).

The spread and the level of fertility of the different provinces have changed tremendously since 1949. The spread remained low and the level high from 1950 to 1970 (except in 1960, when the spread was much higher and the level much lower than any other year during the period). With their extremely low fertility, Shanghai and Beijing became outliers in 1965, joined by Tianjin and Liaoning in 1970. The spread suddenly leapt to 2.1 in 1975, around 2.3 times more than that in the 1950s (and the widest spread since 1949), while the fertility level declined sharply. After 1980, the spread started to decrease, though it remained high, and only in 1990 did the spread fall to 0.7, the lowest since 1950. This shows clearly the pattern of overall fertility level and its variations among provinces of China.

The mid-spread in 1950 was as small as 0.9, but the median was as high as 5.4, indicating that high fertility was a common feature for all provinces across the country in the initial stage of the Communist China. Fertility tended to be high in more developed provinces like Beijing and Tianjin, and low in less developed provinces like Qinghai and Xinjiang. The pattern was, however, not clear, because the TFRs in most more-developed and less-developed provinces were interwoven. Of the outliers, Ningxia had an extremely high TFR (8.7). China's TFR increased to 6.1 in 1955, while the mid-spread remained low (0.8), meaning that regional difference was still small. Fertility rose in almost every province, probably primarily as a result of peaceful social conditions, better health care and the modernization process (Coale 1984).

Table 2.3 Summary of total fertility rates of 28 Chinese provinces in selected years, 1950–90

Year	1950	1955	1960	1965	1970	1975	1980	1985	1990
5-point summary									
Maximum	8.7	7.9	6.9	7.0	7.0	6.3	4.2	3.7	3.1
Upper Quartile	5.9	6.4	5.0	6.5	6.3	4.7	3.1	2.6	2.6
Median	5.4	6.1	4.3	6.2	6.0	3.5	2.3	2.4	2.5
Lower Quartile	5.0	5.6	3.6	5.6	5.5	2.6	1.8	1.6	2.0
Minimum	4.5	4.5	1.7	2.6	2.3	1.1	0.9	1.0	1.4
Range									
Midspread (IQR)	0.9	0.8	1.4	0.9	0.7	2.5	1.3	1.0	0.7
Range	4.2	3.4	5.2	4.5	4.8	5.2	3.4	2.7	1.7
Outlier									
Upper Outlier	NX								
Lower Outlier		T		BJ, SH	LN, BJ TJ, SH				

Notes
Midspread = Inter Quartile Range (IQR); NX = Ningxia; TJ = Tianjin; BJ = Beijing; SH = Shanghai; LN = Liaoning.

Sources
Coale & Chen 1987, SSB 1989, Feng 1995.

Fertility levels in 1960 were a direct consequence of the Great Leap Forward. The TFR level decreased to 4.3, much lower than before. The mid-spread increased to 1.4, meaning that provincial differences in fertility were quite considerable. The effect of the economic depression on fertility in different provinces was different. Roughly speaking, the central part of China, e.g. Anhui, Hubei, Henan, Sichuan, and Qinghai and Ningxia, suffered the most serious fertility loss, while the vast far north regions were only moderately affected (Peng 1987). Fertility in 1965 showed high compensation; TFR was over 6 and the mid-spread decreased to 0.9 (slightly higher than in the 1950s) indicating that TFR remained high in most provinces, but tended to be lower in more developed provinces like three municipalities, and higher in less developed provinces like Guizhou, Yunnan and Xinjiang. This is partly because in the early 1960s the Chinese government started to carry out a birth control programme focusing on the urban population, though no compulsory measures were adopted (Peng, 1987). Shanghai and Beijing appeared as outliers under this situation.

The Cultural Revolution, which started in 1966, totally stopped all family planning work, but fertility levels declined (slightly) nonetheless. In 1970, the TFR level was 6.0, and the spread only 0.7. Fertility in most provinces remained high, although Shanghai and Beijing were joined by Tianjin and Liaoning as outliers. TFRs in the eastern provinces of Zhejiang and Jiangsu also declined. This clearly shows that fertility began to decline in some developed provinces even before systematic implementation of any family planning programme, while fertility in other provinces remained unchanged.

In the early 1970s more vigorous and efficient family planning measures were introduced as the 'Later, Sparser and Fewer' policy. TFRs in 1975 showed the impact of the family planning programme on fertility decline. But implementation of family planning programme was uneven, varying by region. Family planning programmes for minority nationalities did not work regularly until 1984 (Zhang Tianlu 1989) and as a result, a number of more developed provinces had a dramatic decline in fertility, while declines in other provinces were much smaller. In this period the provincial differences in fertility widened dramatically, with the mid-spread at the post-1949 high of 2.5 in 1975.

In 1980, as family planning work proceed steadily, TFRs continued to decline except in the municipalities and in some eastern provinces where TFRs fluctuated around replacement level. The northwest and southwest provinces had also quite considerable declines in fertility. Provincial differences in fertility tended to be smaller than in 1975. The TFR was also low, at 2.3. In 1985, fertility levels remained almost the same as in 1980, and the mid-spread remained 1.1. Most provinces where fertility fell below replacement level either remained at the same level, or fluctuated slightly. In provinces where the fertility level remained high (over 3.0 in 1980) TFRs continued to decline. In 1990, the fertility level had a tiny increase. The spread, however, became even smaller – the lowest since 1950. This means that the fertility level among the 28 Chinese provinces has become close at a low level.

The box plots in Figure 2.4 show a mixed picture, namely that what is significant about Chinese fertility transition is not just change in fertility level, but also the marked variations among China's provinces. Fertility in some provinces started to decline even before population policy became affirmative, though it was not unrelated to availability of family planning facilities. The box plots show that China's fertility transition is a process of diffusion (cf. Tien 1984); sustained fertility decline started in a few large municipalities and some eastern provinces and then the transition gradually spread to the interior.

Notes
[1]   The leftists included Lin Biao, Chen Buoda, and the 'Gang of Four', see Zweig (1989).
[2]   See 'Decisions on some questions for promoting agricultural development' approved at the fourth plenary session of the eleventh central party committee. It should be noted that the responsibility system was not a new invention. During the elementary cooperative period and in the three difficult years after the Great Leap Forward, forms of responsibility system were used to promote peasants' production incentives. See Zhou (1996).

3   By the end of 1980, about 30 per cent of all production teams had imple-
    mented household contracts (ZGNYNJ 1981: 80), and in early 1982 this
    system covered 90 per cent of production brigade of the nation (Zhao 1989:
    596). Though the state still did not want the *baogandaohu* system to
    develop widely, by 1983, 94.2 per cent of China's rural brigades had
    adopted *baogandaohu* (ZGNYNJ 1984: 69).

4   See 'Zhonggong zhongyang guanyu 1984 nian nongcun gongzuo de
    tongzhi' (Circular of the Central Committee of the CCP on Rural Work in
    1984), (ZGNYNJ 1984: 1–4).

5   Ma Yinchu, who wrote the article 'New Population Theory', which
    appeared in People's Daily on 5 July 1957 and promoted birth control, was
    criticized.

6   Although Chinese family planning policy has been commonly referred to
    as a 'one-child' policy, this is however not a unified national policy across
    China. For example, minority nationalities and Han nationality face rather
    different family planning regulations. Also, China's provinces have made
    their own, not necessarily same, family planning regulations.

7   Chinese demographic data in general, and fertility data in particular,
    became available after the 1980s. In the 1980s and the early 1990s, two
    population census and three fertility surveys were conducted at the
    national level. The total fertility rates, estimated by the censuses and
    surveys, were reasonably consistent (see Feeney & Yuan 1994). TFRs from
    1949–82 are derived from data collected in China's 1982 One-Per-Thousand
    Fertility Survey (Peng 1991: 108–10). TFRs from 1983–85 are available from
    the Planning and Statistical Department of the State Family Planning
    Commission (Peng 1990: 17). TFRs from 1986–92 are derived from Fertility
    Sampling Survey conducted by State Family Planning Commission in 1992
    (Jiang et al. 1994). For survey methods and evaluation of data quality, see
    Coale & Chen (1987), Jiang et al. (1994). Though there exist small gaps for
    TFRs in overlapping years from different surveys, I hope the TFRs shown in
    the figure can however depict the general trend of TFR changes at the
    national level since 1949.

8   It should be noted that Hebei has followed the general transition pattern of
    China with regard to fertility changes and family planning practice (Wang
    Feng 1988, Larsen 1990).

9   In the box plot, the middle 50 per cent of the distribution is represented by
    a box, the median is shown as a line dividing the box. Whiskers are drawn
    connecting the box to the adjacent values, the data points which come
    nearest to the inner fence (the data which is 1.5 times the mid-spread
    higher than upper quartile or lower than lower quartile) while still being
    inside or on them. Values further out than the inner fence are outliers. Box
    plots allow a fine visual inspection of a distribution and convey informa-
    tion of level, spread, shape and outliers of a variable. Readers may refer
    Marsh (1988) for detailed discussion.

CHAPTER 3

The County: Reforms, Family Planning, Economy and Population

The county is located on the alluvial plain to the east of Taihang mountains and at the south of the North China plain. It is south of Hebei province, 194 km south of Shijiazhuan, the provincial capital (HDW 1991). The county consists of 23 towns and townships, with 421 administrative villages (HDBW 1989). According to the government's 1990 population census, the county had a population of 521,612 in the mid-1990, and its rural population represented 503,867 of that number, or 96.6 per cent of the county's population (CSB 1991). It is primarily an agricultural county with wheat, corn and cotton as its main agricultural products. Of the land planted for agricultural crops in 1990, 42 per cent was planted with wheat, 26 per cent with maize, and 14 per cent with cotton, with the remaining 18 per cent planted with beans, peanuts, rape, vegetables, etc. (CSB 1991). The county has 750,000 *mu* of arable land, making per capita land only 1.5 *mu* (CSB 1991). The county was nevertheless categorized as one of the provincial grain base counties. Owing to deficiencies in industrial resources, the industry of the county is weak. According to the county officials, industry contributed only one-quarter of the financial income of the county in the early 1990s, and in 9 of the 23 townships there were no township- or village-run industrial enterprises in 1993.[1]

REFORM PROCESSES

Household responsibility system

In 1980, in response to the state call for economic reforms, the county introduced various responsibility systems linking payment with performance. The process of introducing various forms of responsibility system varied among villages of the county. In spring 1981, 60 per cent of villages had implemented some forms of responsibility system.[2] According to county officials, by the end of 1982, 75 per cent of the 2,330 production teams of the county used the responsibility system of *baochandaohu*; and 16.7 per cent used the system of *baogandaohu*. *Baogandaohu* later became widespread and stabilized. In 1983, 98 per cent of the villages carried out *baogandaohu* (see note 1). In that year the county's agriculture output reached its post-1950 historical peak, with bumper harvests in almost every village in the county. In 1984 the county had another bumper harvest year, in which agricultural output surpassed that of the previous year, even with less favourable weather (see Figure 3.1 later in the chapter).

Baogandaohu differed among villages of the county. Various contracts were initially made according to either the household size or combination of household size and quantity of household labour. The quota, however, was based on the size of the parcel of land contracted. Starting in the early 1990s, the county made new guidelines called the 'double-field system' (*liangtianzhi*) and the 'triple-field system' (*santianzhi*). In *liangtianzhi*, collective land is classified as either a 'grain ration field' (*kouliantian*) or a 'responsibility field' (*zerentian*). 'Grain ration fields' served to secure the basic food consumption of each individual in the collective (not by getting a food ration as in the pre-reform collective period, but by getting a 'grain ration field' which was to be worked to gain food for consumption). 'Responsibility fields' were contracted to the collective with certain quotas as peasants' responsibilities. Each person (both labourer and dependent in the household) with valid agricultural household registration (excluding unregistered unplanned births) in the village collective could get a piece of 'grain ration field' without any quota on it. The labourers in the household could also get a 'responsibility field' for which they must fulfil certain quotas contracted with the collective. In the 'triple-field system', the collective land is divided into 'grain ration fields', 'responsibility fields', and 'collectively-managed fields'. The 'collective-managed field' was supposed to be managed by the collective. Under various responsibility systems, households get more freedom and flexibility. They may contract the 'responsibility field', and they can release their contracted land to others. Most villages in the county started the 'double field system' soon after the call from the county governments. The 'triple-field' system has been tried in only a few villages, where it was initiated by the county government.

Non-agricultural enterprises

During the introduction of various responsibility systems in the early 1980s, non-agricultural enterprises, especially those township and village enterprises developed during the commune era, were greatly enhanced. Various responsibility systems were tried out for township and village enterprises, including director and manager responsibility systems in which certain quotas, awards and punishments were specified in the contract. Contracting the main responsibilities of enterprises to one person or a group was, however, discouraged. Instead, contracting with the workers as a collective, with directors and managers in charge of management, was promoted.

Individual enterprises developed rapidly during the period. As early as 1981, 1,645 individual enterprises were registered in the county, almost 18 times the number in 1978.[3] In 1983, the county government was still carefully guiding the development of an individual economy of a private nature, and trying to promote its development 'adequately'. In 1984 the county called on cadres of every levels greatly to enhance the development of collective as well as the individual household enterprises. In this single year, the registered number of individual households of industry and commerce (*gong-shanghu*) doubled (see note 3). In 1984, the county government decided to waive the relevant management fee. However, some individual enterprises ceased to function in 1985 because of high taxes and many restraints imposed by the relevant government departments. To promote the development of non-agricultural enterprises and diversification of the rural economy, the county government decided that some newly created township, village and other cooperative enterprises could be exempted from product tax, added-value tax and income tax for their first one or two years.

According to officials from the Bureau of Industry and Commerce, the years of 1986–88 brought the first high wave of the development of town, township, and individual enterprises in the county. After a setback in 1989–90, the county started officially to encourage the development of private economy in 1991. In 1992 and 1993 when I did my fieldwork in the county, the county government was trying to initiate another high wave of non-agricultural enterprise development. The county called for cadres at every level to mobilize all possible resources to enhance the development of non-agricultural enterprises of all forms, including state enterprises, collective enterprises, individual, or private enterprises and any forms of cooperatives. Starting in the early 1990s when the county was listed as one of the counties open to the outside world, it also started to absorb some foreign investment (see note 3).

Market reforms

In the collective era, the commodities which were permitted to be sold in the free market by individual households were limited. Only a few live pigs and sheep, vegetable seeds, woods and other small commodities could be sold by individual households. Almost all consumer goods were controlled by the Provision and Sale Department. Rural labour was also strictly controlled. Recruitment of labour for industry, construction, mining, transportation, etc. was arranged through various level of government departments. Non-agricultural sidelines was mostly organised by the collectives.

Since the 1978 reforms, free markets have gradually opened. Fruits, fresh vegetables and similar agricultural products were permitted to be sold in the markets as early as 1980. Grain and oil could be sold in free markets after the sale quota to the collective and state was met. The circulation of important means of production in the market was made possible in the late 1980s. Resources in short supply, like fertilizer, machine oil and pesticides, were partly controlled by the state and partly circulated in the market. Cotton, the main agricultural product of the county, remained controlled by the state.

Along with the reforms, free market fairs and trade streets have been set up in various locations. The county government provides information to guide the peasants to change their crop structure and diversify their economy. In the early 1990s, one township market was set up in the county as 'special economic zone', in which some commodities which in the past had been strictly controlled by the state – e.g. colour televisions, refrigerators, fertilizer, pesticide, machine oil, cigarettes, etc. – could be freely sold without restrictions (see note 3).

Free flow of labour has also become possible. In the early 1980s, the county tried to control the outflow of rural labour seeking employment in towns and cities, to relieve some of the burden of urban unemployment. However, as of 1985 peasants were allowed to relocate to urban areas to seek employment and set up individual or private enterprises, with food provision taken care of by themselves.[4] Skilled and manual labour can form specialized contract teams, like those that construct buildings, roads, gaslines and other urban infrastructure. In 1987, the county government requested that every township government set up a labour service agent to develop the labour market and to promote the outflow of labour. The county also set up its own representatives in some cities like Beijing and Taiyuan (see note 3).

EVOLUTION OF FAMILY PLANNING PROGRAMMES

The family planning leader's group was set up in Hebei in 1954. Family planning work in the 1950s and the 1960s was mainly urban-oriented and relied primarily on education (HDBW 1987). It was interrupted by the Great Leap Forward and the Cultural Revolution. Starting in the early 1970s, the state, the province and the county focused again on family planning work. In 1973, the 'later, sparser, fewer' policy was formally introduced in provincial family planning (HDBW 1987: 180). According to county family planning officials, the county also made its own family planning regulations according to the provincial principles of family planning work. Late marriage, which was defined as 25 years for men and 23 for women, was promoted in rural areas. Flexibility was also allowed, so that the marriage of a man of 23 with a woman of 25, or both at 24 counted as late marriage. The preferred birth interval was fixed as four years or over. The government encouraged that each couple have two children at the beginning. In the late 1970s this was shifted to a preference for one child, and at most two.

Family planning in the 1970s mainly consisted of education and propaganda through various means, including study groups. It also focused on setting up relevant institutions for carrying out the family planning programmes (HDBW 1987). Attention was paid to gaining experiences in family planning work. The county government required that by the end of 1973 every commune and production brigade had one doctor in charge of family planning work. It also required at this initial stage of the family planning programme that every commune made a trial in one or two production brigades, gain experience, and then spread the campaign to other villages.[5]

By mid-1979, the county had made trial family planning regulations, in which one-child-per-couple was promoted and an award and penalty system was introduced. In 1981, the county added supplementary regulations, in which one-child-per-couple was stressed, and conditions for couples having a second child were fixed while the birth interval was fixed as over four years (see note 5). For couples who had only one child, the brigade or the production team would award cash equivalent to between 7–10 per cent of the value of the average annual income of a labourer. For couples with extra births, a penalty of 10 per cent of the value of the average labourer's annual income would be imposed, with no differential to reflect the number of extra births. The county specified that rural peasants were given 15 days of marriage leave to the couple and 45 days of maternity leave to women for a late marriage and a late childbirth, and these couples were given priority in the distribution of housing plots, as well as in children's education and health care (see note 5).

According to county level family planning officials, family planning was intensive in 1983. Surgical forms of family planning (*jihua shengyu shoushu*, including IUD insertion, abortion and male and female sterilization, locally called *sishu*, or the four operations) in 1983 were overwhelmingly more common than previous years. However, the intensified family planning programme faced many complaints. At the end of 1984, the county modified its family planning regulations, in theory to open 'a small hole and block a big one', i.e. to relax the conditions in which couples would be allowed to have the second child, while under no circumstances permitting the third birth.

The county issued a stricter regulation at the beginning of 1986. It decided that couples had to get a birth permission certificate before they gave birth to a child (see note 5). The certificate was valid for only one year, but could renewed. Those who gave birth to a child without certificates were treated as having had an unplanned birth and would be economically punished. In the new regulation, marriage before the minimum legal marriage age and childbirth before age 24 would also be economically fined. However, the county did not specify the financial penalty for early marriage, early childbirth or births without permission certificates. In the spring of 1986, the county issued a regulation specifically on adoption of children, because some couples insisted that one or more of their natural children was adopted, in order to give birth to more children or escape punishment.[6] It was decided that those having children of their own were not allowed to adopt children. Couples where both partners were aged 36 or over who remained childless after five years of marriage could gain official permission to adopt children. Unmarried person also could adopt children if they wished to (see note 5).

A comprehensive provincial family planning regulation, issued in March 1989 after approval by the Provincial People's Congress, included some modifications reflecting the new situation since reform (see note 5). Grassroots family planning organizations and infrastructure were enhanced in the early 1990s; townships set up family planning commissions with the assistant governor appointed as the director. Each township should have special family planning officials in charge of propaganda, statistics, technical services and finance. Family planning commissions should also exist at the village level, with one or two special family planning cadres. Around 30 women of reproductive age form one family planning group, with a group leader in charge of the group's family planning work. In each village, a family planning activity room should be arranged for family planning propaganda, arranging study groups, etc.

According to officials from the county family planning commission, family planning work in the county went well in the early 1980s; then in 1982 the family planning scheme of the county was introduced to other counties in the prefecture. In the mid-1980s, the county's family planning work was assessed as backward in the whole prefecture, and it was not until the early 1990s that the family planning programme again achieved great success. In 1993 the county was listed as the third in the first family planning campaign and the fifth in the second family planning campaign among the 16 counties in the prefecture. The county's experience with family planning work was described in *Hebei Daily, Hebei Population Daily* and *Handan Daily* (see note 5). This family planning work has gradually been regularized, formalized and institutionalized.

When the various production responsibility systems were introduced in the early 1980s, a 'double contract' system linking production and reproduction was adopted. According to county family planning officials, this was to meet the new challenge in the family planning work during the reform period, since old-style family planning work through administration was seen as inappropriate in the new situation. Peasants not only deliver grain quotas to the collective in exchange for the right to farm a given area of land, but also need to limit their reproduction. The 'double contract' system in the county followed from the experiences of other counties set up as models by the province, and was widely applied elsewhere in rural China.

In the late 1980s, the family planning 'one vote veto system' (*yipiao foujue*) for cadres was introduced (see note 5). Cadres' performance in economic and family planning work were evaluated together, with their family planning work as the top priority for evaluation. They would be awarded if both economic and family planning work was performed well, but would be punished if their performance in family planning was bad, no matter how well their economic work was. One 'vote' of bad performance in family planning work can 'veto' their achievements in other aspects of their work. Through this system, the county pushed cadres to take family planning work seriously.

ECONOMIC CHANGE AND POPULATION DYNAMICS

This county is traditionally agricultural; industry started to develop only after 1949 and agricultural output value (AOV) was higher than industrial output value (IOV) from 1949 to 1990. Figure 3.1 shows that AOV grew little during the first 20 years after liberation. The increase in AOV in the 1970s could have been due to the massive improvement of soil during the collective period. The dramatic increase in AOV in 1983 and 1984 was due to the favourable weather, and to the peasants' production incentive having been released by the various responsibility systems. AOV started declining in the second

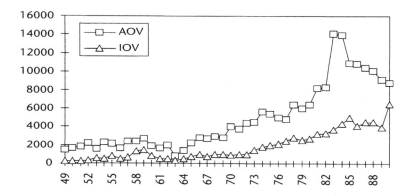

Figure 3.1 Reported agricultural and industrial output value in the county, 1949–90
Note: AOV = Agricultural Output Value in 10,000 yuan in 1950 constant prices; IOV = Industrial Output Value in 10,000 yuan in 1950 constant prices.
Sources: CSB 1974, 1975 ... 1990.

half of the 1980s, though it is still much higher than in the previous decades. The Great Leap Forward in the late 1950s had a more significant impact in industry than in agriculture, and in the early 1960s industrial output value (IOV) dropped dramatically. The pace for industrial development started to quicken in the 1970s, due to the development of the collective enterprises. Industry experienced a high growth rate in the mid-1980s, before it stabilized in the late 1980s. The year 1990 saw an unprecedentedly high growth in IOV. Peasant income has also increased sharply since reforms. It is officially reported that the per capita yearly peasant income increased from 141 *yuan* in 1982, to 328 *yuan* in 1985, and to 559 *yuan* in 1990 (CSB 1982, 1985, 1990).

Figure 3.2 shows that fertility and mortality have experienced rapid changes in the county since 1949. Notably, its transition pattern is similar to the national one (see Chapter 2), though fertility increased more dramatically from 1953 to 1957. Fertility started to increase in the 1950s, peaked in 1957, then declined dramatically during the famine period. After compensation in 1963, fertility remained high, then once again declined dramatically, from 1973 to 1977. It levelled off, then peaked again in 1981, went down for a few years, and came up and reached another peak in 1990. Mortality remained high in the 1950s though there was a declining trend. In 1960 when famine was most fierce, mortality was extremely high. Starting in the first half of 1960s, it remained low throughout the 1970s and 1980s. It should be noted that the official reported data suffer from serious problems. It is often manipulated, even though falsifying any reported statistics is expressly forbidden. One should be thus careful in interpretation of this data.[7]

The estimated annual growth rate that can be extrapolated from

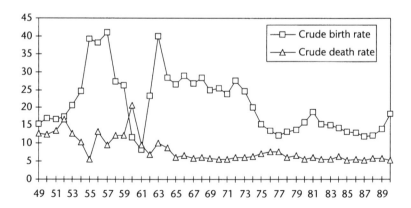

Figure 3.2 Reported crude birth rate and crude death rate (per thousand) in the county, 1949–90
Source: CSB 1991.

official population censuses shows that population growth in the county accelerated over time. Between 1982 and 1990 the annual growth rate was one-third higher than between 1964 and 1982 (see Table 3.1). This was different from the national trend, but was in line with the provincial trend (though the increasing annual growth rate of the province was less significant). It should be noted that the population was overwhelmingly agriculture-based (96.6 per cent in 1990, and even higher in previous years, see Table 3.1), and that the fertility level of the agricultural population is usually higher than that of the urban population (see Banister 1987: 142). The low population growth rate between 1953 and 1964 was mainly due to the high mortality in the period, and the exceptionally low fertility and high mortality rates due to three years of famine. The much higher population growth rate between 1982 and 1990 would be partly because members of the population born during the birth boom in the 1960s entered their reproductive ages. It is also possible that family planning programmes in the period were less effective than expected. Furthermore, the dramatic decline in age at marriage in the county, starting from early 1980 (see later in the chapter), also contributed to an increase in the number of women of childbearing age.[8] The high population growth in the most recent decade can also be seen in the county's population pyramid (see Figures 3.3 and 3.4). In 1982, the base of the pyramid shrunk a bit at the age group 5–9 years, but started to expand at the age group 0–4; in 1990 the base of the pyramid expanded widely.[9]

The tremendous demographic changes that have followed the 1978 reforms can be observed in marriage and fertility patterns at the county level. In the 1980s, both men and women married at younger ages, with the decline in men's age at marriage more significant than that of women. According to the official population census, the singulate mean age at marriage (SMAM) for women declined one year (from 21.7 in 1982 to 20.8 in 1990) and the SMAM for men declined over

Table 3.1 Population and population growth in the county

Year	1953	1964	1982	1990
Population	267,008	313,232	431,272	521,612
Agricultural population	264,602	307,737	419,956	503,867
(%)	(99.1)	(98.3)	(97.4)	(96.6)
Non-agricultural population	2,406	5,495	11,316	17,745
(%)	(0.9)	(1.7)	(2.6)	(3.4)
Annual growth rate (%)		53–64	64–82	82–90
Nation-wide		1.6	2.1	1.4
Hebei province		1.4	1.7	1.8
The county		1.5	1.8	2.4

Sources: HDBW 1989; CSBPCO 1982, 1990; CASS 1994.

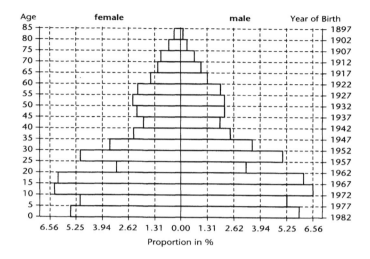

Figure 3.3 Population pyramid of the county in 1982
Source: Government population census of the county 1982.

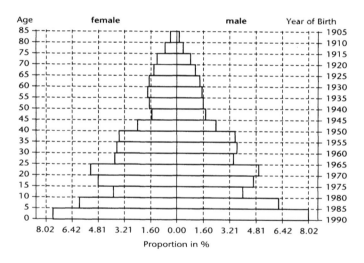

Figure 3.4 Population pyramid of the county in 1990
Source: Government population census of the county 1990.

three years (from 24.5 in 1982 to 21.1 in 1990) (CSBPCO 1982, 1990). The percentage of single men in the 20–24 age group declined from nearly 50 per cent in 1982 to 30 per cent in 1990, and for women the decline was from around 29 per cent in 1982 to around 23 per cent in 1990 (see Figure 3.5).

The higher share of births of higher parities (third and fourth

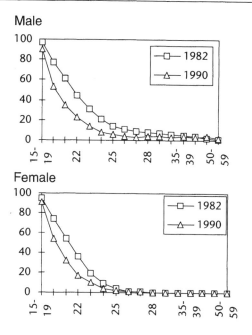

Figure 3.5 Unmarried male and female population by age groups in the county in 1982 and 1990 (per cent)
Source: CSBPCO 1982, 1990.

parity) and lower share of births of lower parities (first parity) in 1990 than in 1982 may indicate a higher fertility level in 1990 than in 1982 (Figure 3.6); it could be the result of stronger family planning programmes in 1982 than in 1990 (as described in the previous section). The increase in numbers of newly married couples in 1982 may also have contributed to the larger share of the births of the first parity. The TFRs increased from 3.5 in 1982 to 3.7 in 1990 (CSBPCO 1982, 1990). Figure 3.7 shows the fertility patterns in 1982 and in 1990: there is little difference in fertility for women aged 30–34 and over in the two years; the years of peak fertility of women aged 25–29 in 1982 flattened in 1990, and fertility for the lower age groups in 1990 was higher than in 1982. It is clear that the higher TFR in 1990 than in 1982 was not due to overall increase of age specific fertility rate (ASFR), but mainly due to a greater share of women having births at younger ages in 1990 than in 1982.

It is difficult to show post-reform fertility trends through the TFR and ASFR of the county in two years. The parity progression ratio (PPR),[10] calculated using live births of women aged 15–64 in 1982 and 1990, could better show fertility changes over time. Figure 3.8 shows that the PPRs for women aged 15–64 in 1982 and 1990 exhibited a similar progression from marriage to first birth, from first to second birth and from second to third birth. However, a smaller proportion

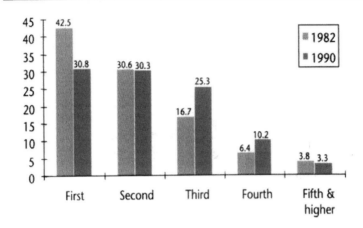

Figure 3.6 Proportion of births by birth order in the county in 1982 and 1990
Sources: CSBPCO 1982, 1990.

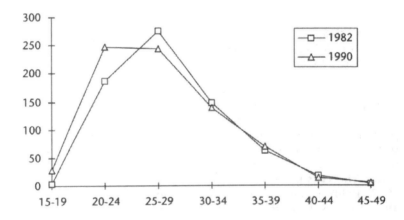

Figure 3.7 Age specific fertility rate in the county in 1982 and 1990 (per thousand)
Sources: CSBPCO 1982, 1990.

of women in 1990 continued to have births of higher parities (from third to fourth birth and so on) than women of the same age in 1982. This shows that women's fertility levels in the county did decline over years.

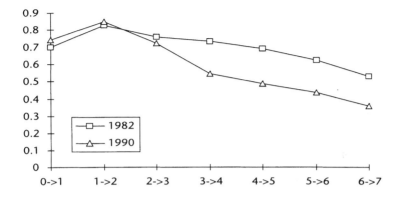

Figure 3.8 Parity progression ratio for women aged 15–64 in the county in 1982 and 1990
Sources: CSBPCO 1982, 1990.

Table 3.2 Basic social, economic, and population information for 23 townships in the county

Township No.	Population 1990	PCAOV 1990	Illiteracy % 1990	Agri. Pop % 1990
1	39,286	197	19.5	72.8
2	17,889	355	34.4	98.5
3	25,263	326	30.3	98.7
4	20,410	305	33.1	98.4
5	19,257	370	33.8	98.8
6	34,076	313	31.5	98.6
7	22,554	346	32.5	98.5
8	26,751	430	32.6	98.8
9	40,267	373	35.7	99.1
10	17,759	367	30.9	97.8
11	14,228	416	21.3	98.7
12	37,046	271	31.5	98.3
13	13,750	400	37.2	98.4
14	31,940	287	29.0	97.6
15	10,665	334	30.6	98.1
16	18,483	353	31.5	98.2
17	27,140	304	35.6	98.9
18	23,221	385	32.3	98.7
19	13,716	362	27.9	98.0
20	14,471	265	26.6	98.8
21	20,614	296	35.4	99.1
22	9,420	356	31.9	99.0
23	23,406	311	29.2	98.6
Total	521,612	327	30.9	96.6

(Continued)

Table 3.2 (Continued)

| Township | Per capita income (*yuan*) | | CBR | | CDR | |
No.	1975	1980	1985	1990	1990	1990
1	50	115	478	742	25.0	3.8
2	51	89	289	485	34.0	5.8
3	50	83	347	554	26.4	4.3
4	48	60	387	560	29.8	5.9
5	48	85	258	546	28.4	5.3
6	56	117	324	571	25.4	5.5
7	47	90	365	640	25.6	4.4
8	37	66	227	635	25.8	6.3
9	36	63	414	596	31.0	4.9
10	50	99	395	570	33.1	7.0
11	52	105	382	604	36.6	6.1
12	39	52	249.5	471	31.0	5.0
13	37	65	303	528	38.3	6.2
14	49	82	339.5	580	28.0	5.5
15	41	64	275	543	15.5	6.4
16	35	56	372	485	31.3	7.3
17	40	52	230	541	34.1	6.0
18	35	53	206	495	33.3	5.7
19	50	97	299	397	32.0	4.6
20	34	48	212	522	28.6	4.4
21	44	78	314	478	31.2	4.4
22	47	79	315	480	31.8	6.7
23	43	123	471	618	27.7	4.5
Total	44	78.8	327.5	558	29.4	5.3

Note
PCAOV = Per Capita Agricultural Output Value; Agri. pop = Agricultural population in persons; CBR = Crude Birth Rate per thousand; CDR = Crude Death Rate per thousand.

Sources
CSB 1975, 1980, 1985, 1990; CSBPCO 1990.

DISPARITIES AMONG TOWNSHIPS AND VILLAGES

Socio-economic development is uneven among townships and villages in the county. In the northern part of the county, where townships and villages are close to the county town, their economic development is more rapid than elsewhere in the county. They have a more diversified economy and people tend to migrate out for non-agricultural activities. In less developed townships and villages, people mainly engaged in agriculture. Though there is little difference in the percentage of agricultural population in each township (except township one, where the county town is located, see Table 3.2 for a list of basic indicators showing the variations among the county's townships), per capita income varies a great deal, due mainly to the different economic structures.

Implementation of family planning programmes also vary. County-level family planning officials said that in some townships family planning work was doing well while in other townships it was not satisfactory.[11] They said that in one of the townships no abortions or sterilizations occurred as a result of the 1991 family planning campaign. Evaluation of the fourth family planning campaign in 1993 shows that 6 of the 23 townships fulfilled their family planning work, two only completed half of the requirements, and the other townships were listed in between.

The performance of township and village cadres in implementation of state policies since the reforms may depend to a great extent on the development of collective economy in their townships and villages. In townships and villages where collective economy is strong, it may be easier for the cadres to carry out state policies. According to economic development and cadres' performance, the county government grouped their constituent village governments into three categories: I: good; II median; III backward. In 1992, among the 421 villages in the county, 124 were categorized as 'good', 258 as 'median', and 46 as 'backward'. The village governments of these 46 villages were regarded as 'paralysed' or 'half-paralysed', meaning that the assigned tasks could not be well completed.[12]

Notes

[1] Personal communication with county government officials.

[2] In the township where the study village was located, it was 70 per cent (personal communication with county officials).

[3] Personal communication with county officials from the Bureau of Industry and Commerce.

[4] Household enterprises employing fewer than seven labourers were grouped as individual households of industry and commerce, and individual enterprises employing more than seven labourers were classified as private enterprises.

[5] Personal communication with county-level family planning officials.

[6] The national adoption law was promulgated much later, in 1991. See ZGFLNJ (1992: 169–71).

[7] The county's yearly report data in 1990 was inconsistent with the data for the county registered in the prefecture. The county obviously manipulates the data on the of number of births by counting births as immigrants. For problems with official statistics, refer Appendix II.

[8] China's crude fertility rate increased between 1984 and 1988 (see Figure 2.2 in Chapter 2). Based on a decomposition of increases in the crude birth rate into components attributable to changes in age structure, marriage pattern and marital fertility, Zeng Yi, Tu Ping, Guo Liu et al. (1991: 435) demonstrate that the increase in China's crude birth rate during the period was 'caused mainly by the rising proportion of women of peak reproductive age and the declining age at marriage', and the contribution of the absolute change in marital fertility was 'much less important'. It is difficult to use the decomposition method, however, to show the relative importance of

age structure, marriage pattern and marital fertility in fertility change and population growth in the 1980s in the county, since crude fertility rate data was problematic. See Appendix II.

[9] The patterns of the pyramids in 1982 and 1990 are similar to the national patterns, though the base of the county's pyramid in 1982 started to expand a bit, and the base of the pyramid of the county in 1990 expanded much more widely than the national one (cf. CPIRC 1993).

[10] PPR is the probability of having another child given that one has already had a certain number of children. Thus, a_0 represent the proportion of women who become mothers, and a_1 represents the proportion of women who have the first child and continue on to have a second child, and so on.

[11] Personal communication with county family planning officials.

[12] Personal communication with county officials.

CHAPTER 4

The Village: Institutional Reforms and Social Change

Rural reforms, which stress economic efficiency rather than social equity, have opened up various opportunities, and at the same time brought increased uncertainties, vulnerabilities and risks. Changes in formal institutional set-ups not only altered the set of opportunities, risks and uncertainties but also reshaped the ways rural people utilize increasing opportunities and deal with escalating uncertainties and risks; they also resulted in many other social changes. Newly defined opportunities and risks, together with newly reshaped means adopted by individuals for achieving security and social upward mobility, are producing a new context within which rural Chinese work and live; these trends are also triggering their own sets of responses. Dramatic reconstruction of formal institutions instigated by the state and alterations to other social institutions accordingly have produced both changes as well as continuities.

This chapter deals with the changes and continuities of the village society since the reforms, and in particular how state-initiated institutional reforms were conducted in the county and the village, and what salient changes have been produced at the village level. It firstly presents the background information on the village and its reform processes, followed by a discussion of the various changes in the village, in its economic structure, social differentiation, grassroots village party/government administration and social welfare programmes. This will show that reform processes in the village have brought changes in the economic structure, have enlarged social differentiation, have changed relations between cadres *vis-à-vis* the peasantry and have affected the roles of the collective in social welfare.

GENERAL PROFILE OF THE VILLAGE

The village is approximately 35 km away from Handan city, and 10 km from the county town. It is close to the main road to other nearby cities and towns. The village is located in a densely-populated area, with per capita arable land of only 0.8 *mu*.[1] The reported annual per capita income was around 700 *yuan* in 1990 (CSB 1991), this is the average for the 12 villages in the same township, and not far from the provincial average of 683 *yuan* (CPIRC 1993). The township, in turn, was relatively wealthy compared to the 23 townships of the county. Modern appliances such as televisions and tape-recorders are common. Quite a few families own colour televisions, washing machines and motorbikes. However, there are still families living in old houses without much furniture and without modern facilities.

No reliable data is available on the population size of the village at the beginning of the liberation year, though a few senior villagers estimated that there was a population of approximately 580 during land reform in the early 1950s. Official population censuses show a population of 1,531 in 1982 and a population of 1,886 in 1990, with an annual population growth of 2.6 per cent. This is faster than the 2.4 per cent annual growth rate of the county as a whole in these years. My own population census shows that in early 1993 the village's population with agricultural household registration was 1991 persons, and there were 113 people who held urban household registration status.[2] Among the 113 people who held urban registration, 91 were aged 15 and over with men accounting for 80 per cent.

The age-sex structures in the village in 1982 and 1990 differ from those of the county population (see Figures 4.1 and 4.2), in that the base of the pyramid of the village in 1990 shrank somewhat, while the base of the pyramid for the whole county expanded significantly.[3] Two features in the age-sex structure of the village population can be observed. Firstly, there is a significant shrinkage of the age group, both for male and female, born 1957–62 (Figure 4.1), during the great famine that followed the Great Leap Forward. Secondly, the age-sex pyramid of the village population is asymmetric, particularly in certain age groups. As Figure 4.1 show, there are many more women than men in age groups born in 1947–52, while (see Figure 4.2) there are more boys than girls in the age group born in 1980–85, and then a further reversal (see Figure 4.3) with more girls than boys in the age group born in 1988–93. The features of the pyramids could be related to historical factors such as war, famine, institutional transformations and state family planning programmes in recent decades, which cannot be easily explained here.

The village comprises one branch of the Party commission affiliated to the township Party commission, the village government and six residential groups. These correspond to the earlier Party commission of the production brigade, production brigade and production team respectively. According to the village household registrations,

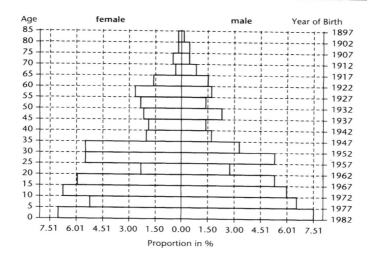

Figure 4.1   Population pyramid in the village in 1982
Source: Government population census of the village 1982.

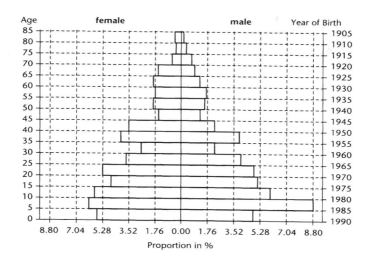

Figure 4.2   Population pyramid in the village in 1990
Source: Government population census of the village 1990.

each residential group consists of 70 or so households (approximately 300 individuals). The production brigade is now referred to as the village. However, villagers still refer to the residential groups as production teams.

The village households belong to different family clans; there are about 10 surnames. According to my population census, *Huang* is the major surname, accounting for over half of all households. The second most common surname is *Guo*, accounting for just under 30 per cent of village households. Families of the same surname might be divided into subgroups, identical to family clans. Villagers divided the *Huang* families into three *Huang* family clans (*san Huang*); the division between the two *Guo* family clans (*er Guo*) is said to be based on their memorized genealogical records for nine generations. Family clan is an important fundamental organization in village society. Main village cadres, including the Party secretary and the head of the village government during the period of my fieldwork, come from the *Huang* families. The two *Guo* family clans want to strengthen their relations by involving all clan members in organizing marriage and burial ceremonies, which used to be done separately. They have tried this, but discontinued the attempt because the households and members were simply too numerous to be easily organized.

The village has one collective-owned brick kiln built in 1979. There are also two small privately-owned plastics factories, three private stores, four private health clinics, one public credit cooperative, one primary school, and one junior secondary school. The village has electricity provided by the county government, and drinking water supply to family yards is provided by the village government.

The village is not atypical in any sense except that it is well known that the village people are good at making bricks and running brick enterprises. Some of the villagers contract the collective brick kiln; quite a few groups contract brick kilns outside the village, some in nearby villages, some outside the township. One group contracts with a village outside the province around Taiyuan in Shanxi province, which is around 400 kilometres away.

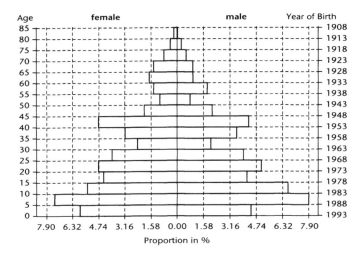

Figure 4.3 Population pyramid in the village in 1993
Source: Research population census of the village 1993.

REFORM PROCESSES

Household responsibility system

During the commune system, the production team was the basic account unit. Each household was allocated small piece of the collective-owned land of 0.1 *mu* or 0.2 *mu* as a private plot (*zilioudi*). Production, labour and collective resources were arranged by production leaders under a national plan. According to village cadres, immediately after the Third Plenary Session of the Eleventh Central Party Committee held in 1978, each production team was subdivided into two smaller production groups. Each group arranged their own labour independently from the other group in the same production team, and each had its independent accounts. This was the initial means of specifying responsibilities and initializing labour enthusiasm.

In 1980, village cadres carried out the responsibility system of *baochandaohu*. At the initial stage, the cadres only contracted cotton and maize production to households, keeping wheat under the collective unified production. The contract was made according to household size and number of labourers in the household.[4] Contracted households were to complete certain work requirements and quotas, they would keep the surplus and receive a certain number of work points. During this period, ploughing the land, planting, threshing and distributing grain and the distribution of cash were all arranged by the production teams, while daily management of the land and harvesting were the responsibility of individual households. In 1980, the basic means of production, like agricultural machines and tools, cattle, and tractors, were still owned by the collective. These basic means of production were sold to individuals through public bidding in 1982, when the two-year *baochandaohu* period ended.

In 1982 the village, like many other villages, started the *baogandaohu* system. This time the contract was made only according to household size. The initial contract term was fixed to last for five years. Contracted land was not adjusted to reflect changes in household size in this period. In mid-1987, the village cadres renewed the contract. The state's standard for the contract was 15 years. However, village cadres did not specify the time period for the contract. Since the late 1980s, peasant households have been allowed to transfer their contracted land, on the condition that they still fulfil their contract quota, no matter how arrangements have been reached among the households concerned. However, the transfer of land to others was not significant in the village. Only around five households have transferred all or part of their land to their relatives or friends.

In 1993, the county issued a guideline for carrying out the 'double-field' and 'triple-field' system. However, the village cadres did not make the corresponding adjustments. They had no initiative to change the present arrangement. Adjustment of land for the whole village is a complex task, and village cadres said that they wished to avoid the conflicts that they knew from experience would be inevitable in the redistribution of land resources. Furthermore, the 'double-field' and 'triple-field' system initiated by the county was still in its experimental, small-scale stage.

The collective enterprises

As early as 1974, the production brigade organized a sideline team for repair and maintenance of the railway in Handan city. Members were recruited from each production team and awarded a certain number of work points. Their food and travelling expenses were paid by the production brigade. Profits were contributed to the collective welfare fund, accumulation fund, and also earmarked for distribution. According to the village cadres, the number of labourers recruited was around 20 persons at the beginning and reached over 70 at the end of the 1970s. In 1978, the production brigade organized construction team of around 50 persons. These two small sideline teams lasted until the initiation of economic reforms.

After introduction of the responsibility system, the two collectively organized teams had less and less contact with the collective, and became the responsibility of the main manager of the teams. However, until 1988 the sideline teams still provided part of their earnings to the village. After the state permitted the coexistence of a private economy with the state-planned economy, these collective sideline teams became independent private enterprises; the managers of the teams, who come from the village, became the owners of the new enterprises. The enterprises started to recruit labourers by themselves. In the early 1990s, the railway team had only few labourers from the village, since earnings were low. However, many labourers were attracted to the construction team, which by 1993 had developed into a large enterprise, with ten construction brigades, one housing company and around 1300 workers, mainly recruited from the village and nearby villages.

The collective brick kiln built in 1979 is still owned by the collective; since 1982, it has been contracted out through public bidding for two-year terms. Recruitment and arrangement of labour, daily management of the enterprise and sale of the bricks were all the responsibility of the contractors. Village governments played a mediating role if there were conflicts between labour and contractors, or between the enterprise and higher government departments concerning tax collection, environmental protection, land management, etc. The village government made a strict rule that all contractors must prepay the quota contracted with the collective. In the late 1980s and the early 1990s, the brick kiln profited when peasants who had become richer started to buy bricks and build houses. The fee for the contract also increased. In 1990, the yearly fee for the two-year contract was 15,000 *yuan*. In 1992, when the village government made a new contract, the base of the yearly fee was 20,000 *yuan* but became 23,000 *yuan* after public bidding.

STRUCTURAL CHANGES

After reforms when the household resumed its function as the basic production unit, agricultural production was gradually led by market signals, in contrast to the collective system, when agricultural production was arranged by the collective under the national plan. In 1992, the village cotton crop suffered from a serious plague of insects. Peasants did not harvest much cotton that year, and the next year most households decided not to plant any cotton. Despite the overtures made by the state such as providing free loans, machine oil, pesticides, etc., to encourage peasants to plant cotton, no one responded. Such a situation would have been impossible when decisions regarding agricultural production were made by commune leaders.

Peasants in the village still plant their traditional crops like wheat, maize, and cotton. They have not planted vegetables, watermelons and fruits for sale in nearby towns and cities, as peasants in some other villages do. Only one young man with his parents has tried planting mushrooms in their simple greenhouse for sale in the local market.

In the collective period, both men and women worked together in agricultural and sideline productions. Opportunities for working outside in urban areas were extremely limited. According to some senior villagers, the system was like 'drawing a circle on the ground to serve as a prison' (*huadi weilao*); labour activity was much restricted and labour was mostly bound to the land. Though there were some labourers working in the sideline teams, or working as temporary or contract workers in urban areas, most labourers, whether male or female, were engaged in agriculture during the collective period, when grain production was much stressed. According to village and county cadres, the commune usually allocated 85 per cent of its labour to agriculture, with the remaining 15 per cent engaged in sidelines. Temporary or contract workers in state-owned enterprises in urban areas were few. In the collective period, the flow of labour to non-agricultural occupations was strictly regulated, and sometimes prohibited. The rural policy and the household registration system (*hukou zhidu*) effectively restricted free movement of labour and related economic activities in the collective period.

Most women retired from collective production work in their 40s to take care of household chores. Women having children had some difficulties working for the collective, because women were not allowed to bring children along and care for them during their work time. Women in some households with many labourers, or with members working in urban areas, could usually stay at home. Women staying at home had flexibility to arrange their time; they could keep some chickens and one or two pigs at home. They could also sell eggs and pigs to the collective, for which the household could receive cash (of 200 *yuan* or so per year) in hand. The value of work points was low. One normal labourer working the whole day in the collective used to be worth between 0.3–0.5 *yuan*. During the agricultural busy seasons, village cadres had to call on these women to participate in collective work when extra labour was most needed.

Opportunities available in the reform period were by no means equal. Most who took advantage of the new opportunities to engage in various occupations were men. Besides migrating outside for paid jobs, running various enterprises, or providing various services, they also have explored other opportunities inside their own village, like contracting or working in the brick kiln, or running small shops and providing various services like grain-processing, wood-cutting, etc. As Figure 4.4 shows, in 1993 around 80 per cent of men aged 20–49 engaged in non-farm activities as primary activities; less than 10 per cent of women over 20 reported their primary activity as non-farm. In the youngest age group, young unmarried women aged 15–19, one-fourth reported that their primary work was in non-farm occupations, which is a bit more than for boys of the same age. This is because girls tended to work in the village collective kiln and small family enterprises, and the boys in this group were too young to take the advantage of migration for non-farm jobs; the labour market within or near the village did not favour young boys over young girls.

Agricultural land is now mainly taken care of by women, with the help of their children and the older members of the household (Table 4.1). For some households, agriculture is mainly the responsibility of women in their 40s, and men and younger women are busy with non-

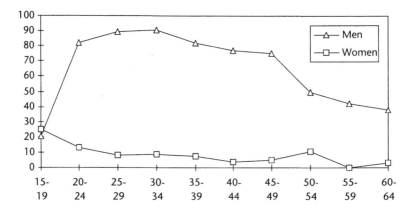

Figure 4.4 Non-farm job reported as primary activity by age and sex (per cent)
Source: Research population census of the village 1993.

agricultural activities. It is mainly women who take care of the daily management of crops, with male help during ploughing, planting and harvesting (the agricultural busy seasons). Women now undertake various jobs, from ploughing, seeding and watering, to harvesting, threshing, drying and storing the grain, many of which had been done by men in the past. At present, only a few men in their 20s and 30s are engaged in farming as their primary activity. These men stay in the village for agricultural work without engaging in more profitable non-agricultural occupations in the urban areas because they have too many children to take care of, or are supporting old or infirm household members. Essentially, every woman were engaged in farming, except those who were still in school and those who took care of household chores. Of those who reported their primary activity as farming, women worked much longer than men. As Table 4.2 shows, women worked seven months of the year in the fields, while their male counterparts worked less than 5.5 months. Those women who reported their secondary activity as housework worked more than four months in farming in a year. Men who did not primarily engage in agriculture usually helped for two months in a year.

Some women, most of them unmarried and young, worked in the brick kiln as their primary activity. This amounted to around five months in a year, during agriculture slack seasons. Some may work intermittently, an average total of around two months of work in a year. There are also a few women teachers in the village school, and a

Table 4.1 Age and sex structure of those aged 15 and over who reported their primary activity as farming

Age group	Men		Women	
	Cases	Per cent	Cases	Per cent
15–19	4	4.2	10	6.7
20–39	29	30.2	88	58.7
40+	63	65.5	52	34.7

Source: Research population census of the village 1993.

Table 4.2 Mean months of primary activities and secondary activities of those aged 15 and over by occupation and by sex

Occupation	Primary activity		Secondary activity	
	Male	Female	Male	Female
Farming	5.4	7.0	1.9	4.2
Working in brick kiln	8.9	5.2	4.5	2.2

Source: Research population census of the village 1993.

few found temporary jobs in a nearby factory, or work primarily in their household-run shops. One or two women primarily work as baby-sitters or hairdressers, or cooks for construction teams or in household-run restaurants.

Most men worked in construction in the urban areas. Of the 157 persons working primarily in construction, nearly 80 per cent worked as migrant labourers, with the rest working in the village or nearby villages. Previously, houses were constructed with the help of relatives, friends, or neighbours, without payment. However, this is no longer the case under the market-oriented reforms. Housing construction is now contracted out to a small construction team which the household pays. Most migrant labourers working in construction stay outside the village for about 8.5 months of the year. Over half (56 per cent) of the migrants working in construction in urban areas worked as long as ten months per year outside the village. Most returned home three times each year: twice during agricultural busy seasons, and once for the spring festival.

A large group of men (79) contracted or worked in the collective-owned brick kilns in or outside the village. Most of them (72 per cent) contracted or worked in the brick kiln enterprise in their own village. The rest contracted brick kiln enterprises outside the village.

Migration patterns for men and women aged 20–59 (Tables 4.3 and 4.4) who lived and worked outside the village show that nearly half of the village's male labourers have migrated out, mainly for economic activities. In contrast, very few women have migrated out the village for economic activities. A higher proportion of young men are working outside: three-fifths of men in their 20s, but just over one-fourth of men in their 50s have sought outside jobs. The occupations of migrant men are varied. Most work in construction teams. Some contract or work in brick kilns. Some work as itinerant furniture-makers, moving from village to village or in urban towns. A few engage in the catering trade in nearby towns, or as far away as Beijing. A few people are engaged in long distance transportation, or run small

Table 4.3 Months migrating out of the village by age group and by sex (per cent)

Age Group	No migration		Out < 6 months		Out ≥ 6 months		Total cases	
	Male	Female	Male	Female	Male	Female	Male	Female
20–29	40.3	94.9	11.9	1.7	47.7	3.4	176	175
30–39	55.7	95.6	10.4	0.9	33.9	3.5	115	113
40–49	69.3	97.7	9.9	2.3	20.8	0.0	101	132
50–59	72.5	100.0	7.5	0.0	20.0	0.0	40	48
Total	54.2	96.4	10.7	1.5	35.2	2.1	432	468

Source: Research population census of the village 1993.

Table 4.4 Months of primary activities of men aged 20–59 working outside the village in 1992

Occupation	Cases	Mode	Median	Mean	IQR	SD
Construction	124	10	10	8.8	2	2.1
Brick kiln	30	10	10	8.8	4	2.5
State/collective enterprises	28	11	10	9.0	4	3.3
Carpenter	14	10	9	8.7	3	1.7
Catering trade	7	11	11	11.1	1	0.7
Transportation	2	—	10.5	10.5	—	0.7
Commerce	2	—	8.50	8.5	—	3.5

Notes: IQR = Inter Quartile Range; SD = Standard Deviation; — = Few cases.
Source: Research population census of the village 1993.

businesses. Some people have temporary jobs in the factories in the nearby townships or towns. As Table 4.4 shows, the mean and median months of migrants working outside the village were both over eight months. A significant number stay outside the village most of the time; some return to visit their natal families only during the spring festival.

It is difficult for women to migrate out alone. Women follow either their husbands or their parents, seeking paid jobs. One woman in my census went together with her husband to Changzhi, where she worked in the restaurant for the construction team. Another woman went to Beijing with her husband to make and sell steamed bread. One unmarried girl from a poor family worked as a baby-sitter in the county town. In this respect the village resembled many other villages in the county, but this is not a national pattern; village women in southern and eastern provinces sometimes migrate to work as house-maids or migrate as a group to work in factories in various cities.

INCOME AND INEQUALITY

Along with the opening up of opportunities and diversification of the rural economy and the sources of income, peasants' standard of living has been greatly improved. Villages reported that during the collective period one work point was worth only a few cents and the wheat distributed from the collective would be consumed in only a few months. At present, peasant households have enough wheat stored to feed them for the entire year, and they sometimes sell their surplus wheat and corn in the free market.

Formal collective institutions and policies were egalitarian in nature (see Griffin & Griffin 1985, Griffin & Saith 1981, Lardy 1978, Nolan & White 1979). The limited work opportunities were more or less evenly shared. Grain distribution was made by considering labourers according their work points earned and the number of dependants in their household. However, inequality existed between households of different dependent and labour ratios, and between households in different production teams. The more young and/or infirm members of a household, the less labour it could offer and (because the per capita work points earned was low) the lower its consumption level. The households also varied in income and family property among different production teams due to variations in the ownership of per capita arable land, their economic performance, the management of agricultural work and the sidelines of the production teams. Inequality among different production teams could be reduced by the arrangement of grain distribution and labour opportunities organized by production brigades. For example, according to village cadres, the production brigade intentionally distributed a larger share of work opportunities and collective income to the poorer production teams, to equalize household income among different production teams.

With reforms, non-agricultural opportunities have increased peasant incomes, contributing a much higher share of household income. A manual labourer working on a construction team for ten months could earn 3,000 *yuan* or more; much more than the value of gain produced from the contracted land of the whole household.

Productivity in agriculture was also much higher after 1978. Villagers often calculate the cost and benefit of planting wheat in the reform period. The cost for planting one *mu* of wheat, for example, including seeds, fertilizer, pesticides, watering plants, ploughing, etc. was 123 *yuan* in 1993. If the yield per *mu* is 350 kg, this would then be worth 259 *yuan* (the wheat price was 0.74 *yuan* per kg in 1993). After paying the agricultural tax, collective levy and various other levies imposed by government departments, the net benefit of planting wheat in this example would be around 100 *yuan* per *mu*. Thus, a household of five numbers, with total land of 4 *mu*, could only produce a net profit of 400 *yuan* a year if wheat was planted. Peasants complained about the high cost of agricultural production and heavy levy imposed. They planted wheat mainly for own consumption.

Village labourers would engage in non-agricultural activities whenever they got the chance. However, the majority of households did not give up their contracted land, since this secured food provision. Only a few rich households leased their land or part of their land to relatives or friends, on the condition that they could easily take the land back if they wished. Giving up land and relying on the grain market for their daily food consumption was costly and too risky for peasants in the village.

Peasants who became rich rushed to build houses. Houses are the major household property. People traditionally prefer to spend most of their money to build more, taller and more modern houses. The newest houses in 1993 had modern facilities (like bathrooms) which many urban residents admired. In 1993, more than half of the houses in the village had been built after 1985, and around three-fifths of these households had built their houses after 1990. Households with young members spent their money on television sets, cassette recorders, washing machines and/or motorbikes. According to my household census, among four categories (housing, durable consumer goods, agricultural machinery and household livestock) that can roughly represent household wealth, housing accounted for 85 per cent of total household wealth.

Villagers see the emerging differentiation. Though the poorest households are better off than before, the richer households have become much richer. In 1993, two-fifths of all households still lived in houses built before the 1980s; a few poor households lived in houses built in the 1950s and the 1960s (Table 4.5). Villagers claimed that the gap between households in their village was not wider than in some neighbouring villages. Still, it is likely that Chinese society is a most egalitarian one compared to other societies in the world.

Another characteristic of household wealth distribution is that total wealth distribution is less skewed than each of its elements (see also McKinley 1993). The kurtosis of total wealth was also lower than for any of its components (Table 4.6). Agricultural machinery and livestock, which formerly belonged to the collective, were not elements that would differentiate households in the same production team. After the reforms, collective-owned machinery and livestock were sold to individual households. Households could also buy small tractors, and threshing, planting and cutting machines which became the important elements of their household property. However, many households own no agricultural machinery. Several households shared agricultural machinery among themselves. Agricultural machinery and livestock could be substituted with each other in agricultural production; that is, households that chose to buy agricultural machinery usually did not buy cattle, and vice versa. Those who

Table 4.5 Proportion of households living in houses built in different periods

Period	Households		Houses	
	No.	Per cent	No.	Per cent
1950–54	3	0.7	7	1.1
1960–64	5	1.1	14	2.1
1965–69	11	2.5	22	3.3
1970–74	40	9.2	61	9.2
1975–79	33	7.6	65	9.8
1975–79	83	19.0	136	20.5
1985–89	163	37.3	230	34.6
1990+	99	22.7	129	19.4

Source: Research population census of the village 1993.

Table 4.6 Mean value and variations of household wealth (in yuan) and of its contributing elements

Household asset	Total (%)	Mode	Median	Mean
Housing	85.5	11000	9000	8795
Agricultural machinery	5.5	0	0	568
Durable consumer goods	7.6	0	400	783
Livestock	1.4	0	0	147
Total wealth	100.0	8000	10400	10292
	IQR	SD	Skewness	Kurtosis
Housing	7000	9556	2.7	18.9
Agricultural machinery	0	1977	5.2	36.2
Durable consumer goods	1200	1180	2.7	13.5
Livestock	100	335	3.1	13.5
Total wealth	8500	7768	2.1	12.8

Notes: IQR = Inter Quartile Range; SD = Standard Deviation.

Source: Research population census of the village 1993.

bought durable consumers goods had little agricultural machinery and few cattle.

Much of the differentiation of household wealth was not due to differentiation in land ownership, in contrast to many other rural societies in other countries (see McKinley & Griffin 1993). Because land was contracted on a per capita basis, it could be adjusted according to the change of household size. The outliers of household with high per capita land are due to special contracts those households made on some less attractive, low quality land. One household which is not exceptional in any sense to others in the village contracted 10 *mu* of such land. Those have contracted large areas of land are not necessarily the richest families. However, if contracted land is not adjusted for long periods, as has tended to be the case in the village, differentiation from land ownership will become more significant. Private ownership of land, eliminated along with other sources of economic inequality in 1949, has not been re-instituted in the post-1978 rural reforms, and this may have buffered the otherwise strong potential for further social differentiation in rural China.

Much of the present differentiation has been due to variation of household non-agricultural activities. The opportunity for upward mobility is becoming much wider and the time period for change is becoming shorter. Some households which economically ranked as average before have suddenly become rich. Villagers believe that becoming rich does not necessarily depend on the number of labourers in the household, but on their capabilities. Yet capability is an elusive concept. People who have talents and have command of certain skills, who have social networks and are therefore in a better situation to access information, job opportunities, or loans, are believed to have capabilities. For example, since the reforms, cadres, doctors, dismissed PLA soldiers, intellectual youths, etc. have been better off than before. However, teachers, who used to be economically well-off and socially admired, have lagged behind economically. Some have quit their jobs and shifted to other commercial activities or sought jobs in private enterprises.

However, household size does exhibit some positive relationship with household wealth; richer households are also larger households. It could be either that the richer households were able to keep their household members longer, delaying household division, or that bigger household have an advantage that enables them to get rich quicker. The biggest household in the village in 1993 had 10 members: one couple in their 50s and their two married sons with their wives and children. The household, together with other households, contracted the collective kiln as a group in 1993 and 1994. Both of the married sons (as well as other family members) worked with the household head and kept their household undivided. For other large households, it could be much easier for them to divide their household labour and have a much diversified economy.

The positive correlation between household wealth and household size was also apparent in villages in northern China in the Republic era, according to several surveys in the 1930s, when land, the main household property, was privately owned (Gamble 1954, Buck 1937). Some scholars argue that in the collective era, household size may no longer correlated with wealth in rural China, and that the correlation is 'above all the product of life-cycle timing' (Selden 1993: 144, Davis & Harrell 1993: 7). In the village, many mentioned the dependant-labour ratio (renlao bilu) in the household rather than land, capital, or special skills as the main contribution to variations in household wealth in the collective period (see also Croll 1994). It could be the case that the positive correlation between household wealth and household size would have been much stronger if land had been privatized and had become an important element of household wealth, as in some other developing countries (see Krishnaji 1992).

VILLAGE CADRES

The institutional reforms, with the changing economic structure and increasing social differentiation, have reshaped the relations between cadres and individual households (Nee & Su 1990). The changing roles of cadres are influencing the collective social welfare, and are important in shaping individual fertility perceptions and fertility motivations. Further, these reshaped relations influence the implementation of state family planning programmes at the village level.

During the collective period, village cadres were embedded in the three-tier commune system. After the dismantling of the commune system, cadres at what was once the production team level no longer functioned as they had before. In the 1980s, at the initial stage of the reforms, leaders of residential groups assisted village cadres in the collection of agricultural tax and in family planning work. In the 1990s, the village cadres took in charge of various village affairs, and leaders of residential groups in fact ceased functioning. Village cadres said that it was too costly to pay for so many cadres in the village, and cadres of residential groups said it was not worthwhile to do so many difficult jobs with little payment.

Brigade and team cadres formerly exercised control over collective resources and work opportunities. Divisions of labour were made at the collective level. Villagers needed to ask for leave to visit friends or relatives. Those who found temporary jobs outside the village needed cadre approval. Labourers with physical disabilities used to be assigned certain jobs through which they could earn work points. Households with insufficient labourers could borrow grain. The old who had no other family labourers to care for them were cared for by the collective under the five guarantee programmes.

The role of cadres in influencing peasants' income and opportunities for upward mobility has declined since reform, because collective property such as agricultural machinery, storerooms, cattle, etc. were sold in the early 1980s and, although land is still collectively owned, individual households own usufruct rights. Currently, peasants rely to a great extent on their own abilities and their social networks rather than (as before) on the collective for their security and social mobility. Although the state contracts to provide a certain amount of fertilizer, pesticides and machine oil to individual households, many problems make peasant access to these resources difficult. The carrying out of the contract is not rigidly enforced. Peasants seldom receive sufficient agricultural inputs from the state, and they now rely mainly on the market for purchasing fertilizers, oil, pesticides, seeds, etc. There are also problems in using collective resources. Village cadres had not properly organized the use of the collective well for irrigation. The use and management of the village's collective water well was not contracted to individuals, something that has occurred in neighbouring villages. Instead, anyone with a pump can install it and charge high fees for their services.

The collective used to keep work points accounts. Cadres decided not only how much grain and cash should be distributed and how much should go to collective accumulation funds and welfare funds, but could also easily levy fines of any kind and collect them by deducting work points. Since the reforms, cadres have to go door-to-door to collect agricultural tax, various government levies, and fines. Sometimes cadres try to collect more grain than needed for agricultural tax, retaining the surplus as an advance on the collection of various levies and fines. This unofficial control mechanism is not always possible, since the villagers may refuse to pay any grain at all, complaining that they contributed more grain than required by the state for agricultural tax without seeing any money back.

Village cadres and their family members used to be refereed to as 'superior' commune members (*gaoji sheyuan*), reflecting their privileged positions. After the reforms, the cadres and their families were no longer the only group in a privileged position. Villagers were no longer bounded by and dependent on the collective. The 'superior villagers' include not only the cadres and their families but also those entrepreneurs or migrant labourers who earn more than the village cadres.

It is not always easy for cadres to gain compliance with state policies from rich and strong families. Cadres have a much greater need to adhere to the principle of fairness in their work; otherwise villagers may withdraw their cooperation. Now that social differentiation has become much larger, and cadres are not the only group with higher social status, village cadres do not always carry out a unified policy toward all social groups. The rich, or the privileged, may possibly deviate from official policy without much cost. Since the rich and the powerful can exempt themselves, the poor, and the less powerful villagers can also resist, by not cooperating using any means available.

Cadres are less well remunerated than previously; they usually engage in other economic activities as well. During the collective period, cadres earned the same (if not more) work points as other labourers. After the 1978 reforms, village cadres received fixed yearly salaries, and by the early 1990s this amounted to only 800 *yuan*,[5] much less than people earn by engaging in other activities. For example, a young male labourer in his 20s could earn a yearly income of 3,000 *yuan*, and skilled labourers in construction could earn 5,000 *yuan*. In 1993, village cadres were mostly in their 50s or 60s, and the youngest was in his late 40s. To supplement their income, they have busied themselves in their own area of expertise, or in their shops, or in businesses outside the village. The collection of agricultural tax and various levies, attending meetings and being involved in family planning campaigns, all require time and energy, and if cadres feel that their cadre work is too much of a burden, they can easily resign their posts. The political costs of resignation are much lower than in the past, especially in comparison to the Cultural Revolution period.

Since reform, villagers unsatisfied with cadres' work who want to take revenge by injuring cadres or their family members, or damaging their property, especially their crops, have found this easy to do. For example, the 1987–88 Party secretary was injured by a man who had conflicts with him, and the vegetables in his private plot were damaged. Cadres' properties have, since 1978, been damaged so frequently that the county insurance company has created an insurance policy especially to cover this. Each township can budget a sum to finance insurance coverage for the main cadres (the Party secretary and the village governor). However, the village cadres said they had not yet joined in the insurance program due to the financial difficulties of the township.

Prior to the introduction of reforms, cadres served for long periods. The Party secretary served from 1964 to 1987. The production leader served from the mid-1960s until resigning in 1979. Since reforms began, the Party secretary has changed frequently. After the first Party secretary was replaced in 1987, there were new Party secretaries in summer 1988, spring 1990, early 1992, and early 1994. The village governor also changed three times during the period. The Party secretary and the village governor appointed in 1994 are new faces, who held no position before. However, while the Party secretary and village governor frequently change, all have been from strong family clans and most are from and remain in the village leader's group (the 1992–94 Party secretary dropped out).

The township and the county Party committee and government have set up certain incentives to retain capable cadres. Besides setting up insurance of cadres' property, the county also plans to implement a pension system for the main village cadres. The township and the county have also tried to promote the collective economy by setting up more favourable policies than other economies of different nature. However, the collective and also state owned enterprises do not function well, and there are serious difficulties in local finance.

Although the role of village cadres has weakened,[6] they still control a share of the village's collective resources. They benefit from contracting out the village brick kilns, from administering a special fund for basic agricultural construction assigned from above (like irrigation), and from controlling private contributions made by certain entrepreneurs. In agriculture, cadres also organize the unified ploughing of the responsibility fields, the purchasing of seeds, and the distributing of a certain amount of machine oil, fertilizer and pesticides. Cadres are much involved in the provision of drinking water, and in the management of electricity, road-building, education and welfare programme. Cadres provide the certificates villagers need to marry, to run certain businesses outside the village, etc. This facilitates their ability to exercise influence over their villagers.

CHANGES IN SOCIAL WELFARE: EDUCATION, HEALTH AND SOCIAL RELIEF

Along with the institutional reforms, the weakening roles of the collective and of the village cadres have important implications for the maintenance of collective welfare in education, health, and social relief. The subsequent changes in education and health services for both the young and for adults, and in social security for the old, will not only strongly influence fertility motivations but are also influencing social relations which are important in fertility decision-making.

Education

The village has one primary school and one junior high school, which were set up in 1949 and in 1965 respectively. The junior high school makes efforts to provide sufficient positions for primary school graduates to continue their education, since the number of school-age students has been increasing in recent years. Previously, the junior high school graduates could continue their education in the commune's senior high school. However, the township senior high school closed in the 1980s, and there are only limited opportunities for junior high school graduates to continue their education in the three senior high schools available in the county.

There is a 'Training the Red' (*yuhong*) pre-school education class attached to the primary school, which was set up in 1985; it serves 100 or so young children aged around seven years.[7] In 1993, there were two classes for first year and second year primary students and one class each for the other primary students, each class with around 50 students. Junior high school education lasts for three years, with 75 first, 65 second, and 62 third year students in 1993. There were more girls (113) than boys (89) at junior high school.[8] This gives the impression that more boys than girls are dropping out of school. However, my sampling survey of 239 young boys and girls aged between 6 and 24 years, which included 43 school dropouts, suggests a different picture (see below).

There are 15 teachers in the junior high school. The quality of teachers has been tremendously improved following the resumption of recruitment of students for college and university education since 1977. Five of the 15 are college or university graduates, two are professional school graduates, seven are senior high school graduates and the only junior high school graduate has had much experience in teaching.

Available data from the 1982 and the 1990 official censuses outline the education levels of the village population and changes over time. Several patterns can be observed from Table 4.7 and 4.8. Firstly, in general, men have higher education levels than women in every age group; the proportion of those who are senior high graduates is much higher for men than for women while the proportion of illiteracy is lower for men than for women. Secondly, the young population has more education than its elders. Thirdly, the gap in the education level between men and women is narrowing. Finally, the proportion of senior high school graduates is declining. It is evident that the education level of the village population in general has been on the rise, in both the previous period and since economic reform.

Many parents did not send daughters to school in the collective period, or sent them for far fewer years of schooling than boys. The numbers of female senior high school graduates were small. At present, both boys and girls are sent to school. My sampling survey shows that almost every child was sent to school, except for cases

Table 4.7 Education structure for male population aged 6-59 in 1982 and 1990 (per cent)

Age group	Senior High 1982–90		Junior High 1982–90		Primary 1982–90		Illiterate 1982–90	
6–9					57.6	71.1		
10–14		1.1	14.1	13.3	80.4	85.8	4.3	0.9
15–19	13.4	5.2	59.8	54.2	23.2	36.5	3.7	4.2
20–24	26.2	2.2	42.9	46.7	23.8	45.7	7.1	5.4
25–29	14.6	5.2	36.6	55.8	31.7	29.9	17.1	9.1
30–34	4.0	11.4	36.0	29.5	40.0	45.5	20.0	13.6
35–39		7.6	34.6	41.8	42.3	31.6	23.1	19.0
40–44	4.5	2.4	31.8	35.7	40.9	42.9	22.7	19.0
45–49		11.1	11.1	38.9	30.6	33.3	58.3	16.7
50–54		4.3	4.8	34.8	19.0	17.4	76.2	43.5
55–59				3.3		23.3		3.3

Sources: CSBPCO (1982, 1990)

Table 4.8 Education structure for female population aged 6-59 in 1982 and 1990 (per cent)

Age group	Senior High 1982–90		Junior High 1982–90		Primary 1982–90		Illiterate 1982–90	
6–9					51.9	78.0		
10–14			23.3	19.8	67.0	79.3	9.7	0.9
15–19	8.8	1.1	26.4	54.0	37.4	28.7	27.5	16.1
20–24	15.2	2.0	6.1	31.6	18.2	39.8	57.6	26.5
25–29	9.6	2.9	6.0	18.6	22.9	47.1	60.2	31.4
30–34		1.9	2.4	17.3	22.9	34.6	74.7	46.2
35–39		1.3	10.7	12.7	32.1	41.8	57.1	44.3
40–44		1.5	3.7	15.2	14.8	33.3	71.5	50.0
45–49	2.9	3.4	2.9	13.8	2.9	20.7	91.4	62.1
50–54				8.8		8.8	97.2	82.4
55–59				6.1	2.4	9.1	97.6	84.8

Sources: CSBPCO (1982, 1990).

where children had physical or mental disabilities. Among 239 young people surveyed, only six have never had any education, and four of these are still very young (aged six or seven years) and would attend school later; the other two (aged 11 and 13) are mute and could not be accommodated by the village school, though their parents showed strong motivation for their education.

Children of seven years are admitted to the pre-school training class. There was no much difference in age of school entrance between boys and girls. From the sampling survey of the young, 94.7 per cent of boys and 94.8 per cent of girls entered school before age nine. A small number of children begin attending school at higher ages, mostly because their parents needed help from these children, usually girls, to take care of their younger siblings; parents believe that boys cannot be of much help at home. There was also not much difference between the rich and the poor in age of school entrance. Tuition and registration fees for children in families with economic difficulties can be waived. Most importantly, parents believe that young boys and girls cannot provide enough help to justify keeping them at home.

As mentioned, there was an impression that boys were more likely to drop out of school than girls. However, the sampling survey of the young shows that slightly more young girls than boys dropped out of school in 1993.[9] Among those surveyed aged between 6 and 24, of those who had ever been exposed to formal education, 16.2 per cent of male students and 17.9 per cent of female students dropped out of school. However, girls dropped out at younger ages, mostly during their primary school education. About 40 per cent of male dropouts dropped out before they were 15 years old, while 87.4 per cent of female dropouts did so. One-fourth of male dropouts dropped out of primary school, while nearly three-fourths of female dropouts discontinued their education while still in primary school. Strong discrimination against girls still exists in the rural society. Parents prefer to have their sons educated as much as possible, while they believe that it is enough for girls just to 'learn to read and write and do some simple calculations'. Some villagers believe that it was absurd that a girl of the village was sent to senior high school in the county town to continue her education. Some parents explained that girls who drop out of school earlier than boys could take care of their younger siblings and do household chores, while boys could only 'enjoy playing around' and provide little help. Nearly half of the boys dropped out of school when they are old enough to find paid jobs outside the village. Only one in ten male dropouts helped with agricultural work. However, nearly half of female dropouts engaged in agricultural fieldwork.

Health

In the collective period there had been one collective health clinic, and three barefoot doctors were trained during the late 1960s. Patients paid a small fee for the service, while doctors earned work points. Barefoot doctors, as the term indicates, often participated in agriculture or in sidelines. In the early 1970s, the village instituted the cooperative health care system, in which each commune member contributed a small amount of premium. However, village cadres said that it only lasted for two years. People simply did not have money for the health fund.[10]

In the early 1980s, the health clinic, including simple facilities and medicine, was sold to one barefoot doctor. Another two barefoot doctors also run their own health clinics. One demobilized soldier who had learned medicine in the army and who was working in the county town provided some medical services at home in his spare time. One young man, who just graduated from a special medical school in the county after 2.5 years' training, paid for by his family, started to run an independent health clinic in 1991. Being a doctor is an attractive career to villagers, since doctors can earn more money, and are well respected by the villagers.

Huang Yisheng, in his late 50s, had much experience in provision of medical care, and most villagers went to him when they were ill. He also immunized the newborn babies through an arrangement paid for by the township health care agency.[11] He sent his only son and his son's fiancee to be trained in a provincial medical school in the provincial capital of Shijiazhuang, all paid by the family. They graduated in 1993 during my fieldwork. The son helped his father in providing medical care for their fellow villagers. The son and his fiancee married after I completed my fieldwork. They were to inherit the father's medical practice, providing service inside the village.

In the collective era, poor patients who could not pay for health care could still see the village barefoot doctors; they received the service and paid later, and some households owed debts to the collective for years. Villagers said that they could also see doctors in the county town or other places, where again they received services first and paid later. After reforms, this became impossible because hospitals, like other enterprises, had various responsibility systems to carry out and these required that benefits be linked to payments to doctors. Patients now must deposit sufficient money before they receive health services. Some people, especially the poor, complain about the current cost of health services. Although a patient can still pay the village doctors after service has been provided, because the clinic is privately owned the poor who would find it difficult to pay such debts usually will not visit a doctor before their illness become serious.

For most villagers, basic health care has not been a serious burden in the reform period. In fact, villagers went more often than before to see doctors in the village clinic, in the township clinic, or, if necessary, in the county hospital. Women also had more prenatal health care; higher percentages of younger women than their older generations had prenatal care for their births (Table 4.9). Also, women of older generations used to give birth to children at home, with the assistance of older female family members or their neighbours. Now increasingly women are being assisted by midwives from the village or the township (Table 4.10), although some also give birth in the county hospitals. The availability of basic health care in the collective period in the 1960s helped to reduce infant mortality dramatically in the 1960s (except in the early 1960s when there was an extremely high infant mortality as a result of the great famine), and it remained low in the 1970s and 1980s. It has had a further slight decline in the early 1990s (Figure 4.5). People's health is in general improved, showing that the reforms have directly benefited the rural populace, though there exist variations among peasant households.

Welfare

During the collective period, the 'five guarantee' (*wubao*) system cared for all men aged over 60 and all women over 55 who had no labour capabilities and no children or close relatives to care for them. The collective provided their food, clothing, housing, and health care, and when they passed away, the collective provided burial. The production brigade might assign some people, usually women, to provide assistance and care to the 'five guarantee' households (*wubaohu*, most often single person households). The property of *wubao* households, mainly the house and housing plot, belonged to the collective. The level of life of *wubao* households was believed to have been higher than in households with more dependants per labourer.

Table 4.9 Prenatal care of married women, by age group

Age group	With prenatal care		No prenatal care		Total cases
	Cases	Per cent	Cases	Per cent	
20–24	15	65.2	8	34.8	23
25–29	22	51.2	21	48.8	43
30–34	16	50.0	16	50.0	32
35–39	9	32.1	19	67.9	28
40–44	13	26.5	36	73.5	49
45–49	6	17.1	29	82.9	35
50–54	3	25.0	9	75.0	12
55–59	3	25.0	9	75.0	12

Source: Research sample survey: ever-married couples 1993.

Table 4.10 Married women who deliver all, some or none of their children assisted by midwives

Age group	Assisted births		Assisted + unassisted births		Unassisted births		Total cases
	Cases	Per cent	Cases	Per cent	Cases	Per cent	
20–24	15	75.0	0	0.0	5	25.0	20
25–29	25	58.1	3	7.0	15	34.9	43
30–34	16	45.7	4	11.4	15	42.9	35
35–39	4	13.8	4	13.8	21	72.4	29
40–44	3	6.0	11	22.0	36	72.0	50
45–49	5	14.3	7	20.0	23	65.7	35
50–54	1	8.3	0	0.0	11	91.7	12
55–59	1	8.3	1	8.3	10	83.3	12

Note: Assisted + unassisted births = assisted births for some children and no for the others.
Source: Research sample survey: ever-married couples 1993.

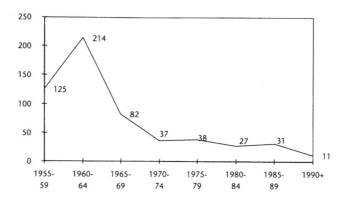

Figure 4.5 Change of infant mortality (per thousand) over time in the village
Source: Research sample survey: ever-married women 1993.

Wubaohu were few in the collective period. There were three *wubaohu* around 1978, two widowed women and one widowed man. They all had close relatives. However, both women had married into the village and had only relatives from their husbands' families, who were reluctant to provide the needed care. The widowed man joined the *wubao* households because his relatives were too poor to care for him. One single old women who did not marry due to her physical disabilities was cared for by her brothers' family members. The brothers did not want to be gossiped about for not fulfilling their responsibilities to care for their sister.

However, the *wubao* programme had problems after reforms. In 1993, no one was provided with the 'five guarantees'. Villagers explained that since people had become much richer, it was much easier for couples who had no children of their own to adopt children, though the expense of adoption was also much higher. The elderly who were without children could also get help from their close relatives, which was not possible before due to poverty during the commune system. However, I found one widowed woman in her 80s with only a daughter; she received 9 *yuan* per quarter directly from the civil affair department of the township government, much less than 15 *yuan* per quarter distributed to each *wubao* household by the village during the commune system.

It was impossible to get a clear picture of the village's financial situation. Village cadres collected levies of many different kinds and received many complaints, but villagers had no idea how their collective fund was managed. There was the suggestion that the 'five guarantee' programme did not function well because the collective had insufficient resources under its control. However, this was not the case in the village. Firstly, providing care for *wubao* households required little money. Secondly, though cadres claimed that they had paid debts in previous years and that as a result there was not much money left, the cadres had money for other projects such as the new village government site, they also used collective money to pay family planning fines (see Chapter 8), and they were preparing to build a new road at the end of 1993. Village cadres simply had no incentive to run the *wubao* system. Further, main village cadres were frequently replaced, and they were most likely to busy themselves by concentrating on short-term jobs, rather than on long-term ones like the 'five guarantees'.

The village instituted various responsibility systems in both agriculture and rural industry soon after the state's call for reform and the issuing of guidelines for rural reforms. Within the national context of market reforms and new opportunities, the economic structure of the village has changed dramatically. A tremendous number of labourers, most of them men, have shifted their occupations away from agriculture, mainly to the construction sector through migration or to rural industry through contracting with collective enterprises. The feminization of agriculture started after the reforms; villagers consequently began to call their village the 'kingdom of women' (*nuerguo*) because most men work outside the village for most of the year. Villagers' living standards have dramatically improved; at the same time, however, increasing social differentiation has been apparent in the village. At a time when opportunities for upward social mobility have increased, following the retreat of the state and the introduction of market mechanisms in the national and local economy, individuals must rely on themselves for social security and share their risks and uncertainties within individual households and families.

The role of village cadres, who enforce the institutional reforms at the local level, has been weakened. They have less control over collective resources and work opportunities; they no longer directly control and determine peasants' income; in addition, they are now busy with their own agricultural lands and businesses. However, although village cadres have lost to certain extent their bargaining power *vis-à-vis* peasant households, they certainly have gained autonomy *vis-à-vis* their superiors. The new economic opportunities and relaxed political environment have also made them flexible in their work as cadres.

The increase in household income and improvement of peasants' living standard have not adversely influenced education and health for the village population as a whole, though cadres' role in education and health has been weakened. However, the increasing social differentiation and weakening role of collective welfare arrangements have created different degrees of vulnerability for differentiated social groups in the village.

Notes

1   Village registration.

2   It should be noted that for the comparison of the official population census with my own population census, the cases of urban household registrations who reside outside the village in my population census need to be excluded. Therefore, the data presented in this chapter and following chapters are made comparable by dropping the institutional numbers who do not usually reside in the village.

3   The more rapid population growth in the village during 1982–90 and the shrinkage of the pyramid base in 1990, which differ from the pattern in the county, are difficult to explain, since the results were combinations of various factors in population structure and fertility, mortality and migration patterns at both the village and the county level.

4   Arrangements varied among different production teams; 60–70 per cent of the collective land was contracted according to the number of labourers in the households, while the remainder was contracted out according the number of dependants in the households.

5   However, all cadres said they have not received the whole amount of 800 yuan for years, because the village has financial difficulties.

6   The weakened role of cadres in different villages might be different, depending in part on the individual ability of cadres, but mainly on how much collective resources are placed under their control. In the villages in suburbs of the county town or in the villages where profitable collective enterprises exist, the cadres have some control over money received when the state purchased land for the development and expansion of the county town, and they may control contracted money through bidding and/or benefits. However, in many other villages where there are insufficient resources under cadre control, the cadres are not able to function well. The county has classified the villages in the county into three groups, one of them being villages with no (or poor functioning) village cadres.

7   Interview with both teachers and parents in the village.

8   Interview with the school teachers.

9   Primary school graduates who did not continue into junior high school education are treated here as dropouts.

10 In early 1972, only half of the production brigades in the county carried out the cooperative health system; among these only 60 per cent were functioning relatively well. In mid-1972, many production brigades stopped their cooperative health system, and I was told that many cooperatives could not collect enough funds for the functioning of the health system (personal communication with county government officials).

11 He was also one of villagers who was familiar with new births of each households in the village, including those extra births outside the family plan. However, he made it known to the public and the village and township family planning cadres, that he would not release any information concerning extra births to anybody else for whatever purposes. The confidence established between him and his fellow villagers also attracted people to see him when they got ill. Knowing this fact, I did not approach him for specific information concerning births, but had only general discussion about health care and childbirths.

CHAPTER 5

Dynamics of Marriage Change

Marriage has been undergoing significant changes in rural Chinese society in the reform period. This chapter will examine what has been changed in the institution of marriage, and identify factors that have influenced the new characteristics of the marriage. Among many changes, this chapter focuses on the following notable ones:

(1) the significant decline in the age at marriage for both men and women;

(2) the increasing number of rural young who marry spouses who live nearby, though there is no significant increase in village endogamy and though some may find spouses from other provinces;

(3) the variation of marriage practices, including the emergence of 'exchange marriage' and 'mercenary marriages', that has resulted from increasing economic differentiation;

(4) the tremendous increase in marriage expenses, and, most importantly, the dramatic equalization of the ratio of dowry to brideprice.

Factors influencing marriage are complex. Marriage, as one element of the family planning programme, is a major concern of the state. In fact, the Chinese government has made continuous efforts to reform the institution (Croll 1981a, Palmer 1995). The state influences the marriage institution either directly, by social engineering to promote purposeful change (the term used by Parish & Whyte 1978) or to obtain certain policy outcomes (in family planning this includes delaying marriage and thus fertility, see Tien 1983), or indirectly, through other macro policies and institutional reforms such as the present rural reforms. As this chapter will show, although governments have made tremendous efforts to reform the marriage institution for purposeful change, many traditional, customary and routinized marriage practices are inherited, and changes and continuities are also related to individual behaviours or actions. Individuals are not passive receivers of customs or tradition or state design. They are agents influencing the change, and their responses to the environment where they work and live will also shape the characteristics of social institutions.

This chapter will argue that changes in the marriage institution in the reform period are closely related to (1) the new contextualization of cooperation and conflicts, and (2) the changing social relations between peasant households and local cadres. The newly-opened opportunities, escalating risks and uncertainties increase the demand for cooperation among some peasant households, while increasing competition and conflicts among others. Individuals respond via changing marital practices, where marriage functions to make alliances and exchange labour among peasant families. Further, the newly-formed relation of peasant households *vis-à-vis* local cadres, where the bargaining power of peasants is reinforced and the role of village cadres is weakened, means that individual marital practices are increasingly mediated by the individual desires rather than by state designs.

This chapter focuses on the most salient changes in a number of aspects of the institution of marriage which have a bearing on fertility. It can in no way deal with marriage institution completely, but it can show the importance of intermediate institutions of marriage which mediate state policies in relation to individual fertility behaviour. To do this it first identifies changes in its structure, in the age at marriage, and in the re-emerging phenomena of 'exchange marriage' and 'mercenary marriage'. It will then discuss the security and mobility marriage means for local people and show how this relates to the fact that people now tend to marry within short distances. It will further show the tremendous increase in marriage expenses and the changes in marital transfer of brideprice and dowry. The final section will show how local cadres and individual households interact in marriage decision-making and how this shapes the features of the institution of marriage in societal practice.

CHANGING MARRIAGE PATTERNS

Changing marriage structure

Early and universal marriage characterized traditional China (e.g. Fei 1939, Gamble 1954, Tien 1983) and this village was no exception. Virtually no women remained unmarried throughout their lives, although a few poor men or those with physical problems might never marry. According to government population censuses conducted in 1982, 1990, and my own census in 1993, no women who were over 28 in 1982, over 25 in 1990 or over 23 in 1993 were single; however, there was still a small proportion of men over 30 who remain unmarried.[1] A local saying shows the situation well: there may

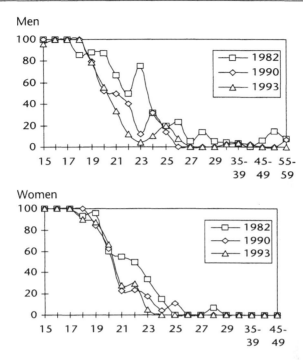

Figure 5.1 Proportion of single men and women by age groups in 1982, 1990 and 1993)
Notes: The number of women aged 15–59 was 388 in 1982, 501 in 1990 and 548 in 1993; and the number of men aged 15–59 was 457 in 1982, 548 in 1990 and 576 in 1993.
Sources: Government population census of the village 1982; Government population census of the village 1990; Research population census of the village 1993.

be handsome men who have no wives, but there are no ugly women who have no husbands.

Age at marriage and proportion of people who are married have experienced significant change since reforms began. For both men and women the proportion in the 20–24 age group who are married has risen sharply in the past ten years. For men it rose from 50 to 62 per cent between 1982 and 1990; it then increased to 76.2 per cent in just 2.5 years in 1993; for women, the proportion increased from 60.6 per cent in 1982 to 74.5 per cent in 1990, and to 73.7 per cent in 1993 (again, according to government population censuses and my own census conducted in 1990, 1982 and 1993 respectively). The graphs of proportion of both men and women single in different age groups in 1982, 1990 and 1993 (Figure 5.1) shows clearly that the proportion of single people in the 20–24 age group declined significantly during the reform period.

Men

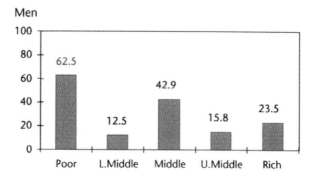

Women

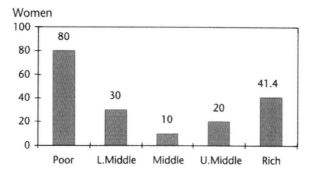

Figure 5.2 Percentage of single men and women aged 20–24 by household wealth in 1993[2]
Notes: (1) The numbers of individuals in the 20–24 age group was 105 for men and 99 for women. (2) L.Middle = Lower Middle; U.Middle = Upper Middle.
Source: Research population census of the village 1993.

Men who marry at the youngest ages may come from richer households and women who marry at the youngest ages may marry into richer households. In early 1993, for both men and women aged 20–24, the proportion that were single was higher in poor households than in better-off households (Figure 5.2). Also, the proportion of single girls in better off families was higher than in other families except the poorest ones. It was likely that girls in richer households may be reluctant to marry out at earlier ages and their parents may be also reluctant to marry their daughters out.

The proportion of divorced is essentially zero for women, and very small for men. Firstly, there still exist social pressure against divorce. Secondly, it seems easier for divorced women to remarry than it is for men, especially since the reforms. Notably more young people have divorced recently, though numbers are still limited. Five young men in their 20s had divorced in the past five years. One young woman divorced in 1982 when she was only 21. One young man who had remarried soon after the dissolution of a first marriage was planning to divorce again during my fieldwork in 1993. One girl from the village who had married and lived out of the village for two years divorced and came back to her natal family in late 1993. There were no extraordinary circumstances for divorce except that the young couples simply could not 'get along' with each other, which could not be the basis for divorce in the past. Some young couples divorced mainly because mothers-in-law and daughters-in-law could not get along and this damaged the husband-wife relationship. In this respect, some women said that young daughters-in-law are no longer as obedient as wives of former generations and did not want to follow the dictates of their mothers-in-law. Divorces could be initiated by wives after reforms; in the past, usually only men initiated the divorce. One woman from another village divorced her husband in the village in 1992. This was initiated by her just after the marriage ceremony, fuelling a rumour that the woman wanted to make money out of the marriage by taking away the brideprice after the divorce. Women should return the brideprice if the woman breaks off the relation before marriage. This is not a requirement if they divorce, although Parish & Whyte suggest that in the collective Guangdong villages women and their natal families were sometimes requested to repay part or even all the brideprice after divorce (see Parish & Whyte 1978: 196).[3] Divorce is gradually being accepted in the society, especially among the young from rich families, who were able to pay the increasingly high marriage expenses and easily find another wife.

Changing age at first marriage

Traditionally villagers married at very young ages. Age at marriage was around 16 or 17 years old in the village before 1949. A man aged 60 in 1993 married at age 12 in 1945, but this was an extreme case. My sampling survey shows that the mean ages at marriage was 18.2 years for men and 17.5 years for women, and the median ages at marriage was 18 years for both men and women in the 1950s.[4]

Figure 5.3 shows clearly the trend in age at first marriage for both men and women in recent decades. Changes in age at marriage have been tremendous since 1949. There was a dramatic increase in the collective period, and then a sharp decline in the post-reform period. The median age at marriage increased 4 years for women (from 18 to 22), and 5 years for men (from 18 to 23), from the 1950s to the 1970s. It then declined 2 years for women (from 22 to 20), and 3 years for men (from 23 to 20), in the 1980s and early 1990s. Women's mean age at marriage rose more sharply than that of men during the 1960s and 1970s. However, men's mean age at first marriage declined more sharply than that of women in the 1980s and early 1990s. This meant that the gap between the mean age at first marriage for men and women was reduced throughout the 1960s and the early 1970s, and became even smaller in the late 1970s and the 1980s. The trend was reversed in the early 1990s; mean age at first marriage for women is

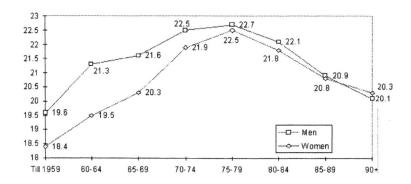

Figure 5.3 Mean age at first marriage for both men and women by year of marriage[5]
Source: Research sampling survey: ever-married women 1993.

even higher than that for men. As men's age at marriage becomes younger, many start looking at older women as potential wives. This is reinforced by the fact that parents of young girls are reluctant to allow their daughters to marry too early.

Ages at marriage for men and women vary by economic background. Figure 5.4 depicts the age distribution of husbands and wives married in 1985 or later, by household wealth. It shows that men from wealthier households married at younger ages; and that women who married into wealthier households also married younger. This differs from the pattern of western societies (and probably also from contemporary urban China) where 'marriage age tends to be later among high status or upwardly mobile groups' (cf. Parish & Whyte 1978: 165). People approach rich families with children of marriage-able age much earlier and more frequently to initiate a marriage. Poor families usually have difficulties in acquiring sufficient money to pay the brideprice and other marriage expenses, thus delaying their children's marriages.

Re-emerged 'exchange' marriage and 'mercenary' marriage

'Exchange' marriages (*huanhun*) and 'mercenary' marriages (*maimai hunyin*) have also re-emerged since the 1978 reforms. 'Exchange' marriages refer to situations where parents in two or even three families exchange daughters: their sons marry the daughter of the other family. 'Mercenary' marriages refer to instances where families purchase women as wives or daughters-in-law from traffickers in women. There have been at least three cases of 'exchange' marriage and seven cases of 'mercenary' marriages in the village since 1990. Women bought as wives were from poor regions of Guangxi, Guizhou, and Sichuan provinces.[6] Two women from Shaanxi were 'introduced' to the villagers during my fieldwork in 1993. The govern-

Husbands

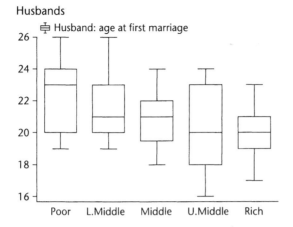

Wives

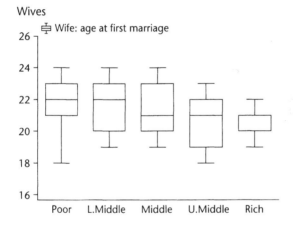

Figure 5.4 Box plots of age at marriage for husbands and wives married since 1985 by household wealth
Note: L.Middle = Lower Middle; U.Middle = Upper Middle. For husbands, $F=13.63$, statistically significant at $p<0.01$; for wives, $F=4.01$, statistically significant at $p<0.05$.
Source: Research sampling survey: married couples 1993.

ment strongly prohibits *maimai hunyin*. The practice nearly disappeared during the collective period, but has re-emerged and, in the 1990s, the incidence increased.

Exchange or *huanhun* happens in the poorest families, which face extreme economic difficulties. It serves as an alternative to meeting marriage expenses, which have become extremely high since the reforms (discussed below). Families in the same situation negotiate the exchange. Looking for potential families is not easy, and daughters are not always willing to marry out for purpose of exchange. Yet parents tend to feel desperate when they are incapable of having their children appropriately married. Villagers believe that 'exchange marriage' is not desirable, although such an arrangement is acceptable when there are no other alternatives. The exacerbation of social differentiation after the reforms may further promote 'exchange marriages'. The difficulties are well illustrated in the following case:

> One poor couple in their late 50s had four sons and a daughter. They managed to have their first two sons married. However, they did not have money to arrange the third son's marriage. The youngest son was seriously ill for some time, and the resulting debts meant they could not borrow money since they did not have the ability to repay. The mother spent months looking for a candidate for an exchange marriage. Finally in 1992 they found a family in the similar situation, and both sides agreed for an exchange of the daughters for having the sons married. The daughter did not agree with the arrangement and threatened to commit suicide. The parents also threatened suicide if the daughter did not follow the arrangement and at the same time begged for her approval. After days of negotiations between parents and daughter, the daughter agreed to go to the other family with desperate tears. The marriage, which was believed as the most important and supposedly the happiest moment for the couple in their lives in Chinese society, was arranged with a quiet exchange of daughters. There was no celebration but desperation, of daughters, and of other family members.

'Mercenary' marriages usually happen in poor families that can manage to borrow money, or families where sons have physical problems and thus have difficulties in finding appropriate wives among the locals. They will be 'introduced' to women who are brought from poor regions in southern or south-western provinces. If they think a woman is appropriate, they pay the 'introducers' two or three thousands *yuan* and take the woman home. They also perform a marriage ceremony to validate the customary 'marriage':

> Aling and Ahong are wives of the typical 'mercenary marriages' which occurred in the village in the 1990s. Aling, as a member of *Zhuang* nationality, comes from Guangxi province. She is 'married' to a man who had physical difficulties in the village in 1990. She was introduced to the villagers by a middle-aged man, who brought her from Guangxi by train with the promise of 'looking for a nice job for her'. Three years after marriage, she had not yet visited her natal family, though there were letter communications. She could not even go back by train herself since she was illiterate and did not know the way. She gave birth to a baby girl and learnt farming and local dialects quickly. She

felt resigned to her situation, since her husband treated her well, and the life here was easier than in her natal family. Ahong was brought from Sichuan to 'marry' a poor man in the village in 1992. She tried several times to escape but failed. The family watched her carefully and the husband beat her when she tried to run away. In 1993, the county government had a campaign to wipe out the illegal marriages, deeming it criminal activity and saving the concerned women. She managed to contact the government and get away from the family. The husband and one man involved in the mercenary marriage were detained by the police. However, the man who had trafficked the woman from Sichuan was not caught since nobody knew his whereabouts.

CHANGING MEANING OF MARRIAGE

Traditionally, marriages were a means for forming families and giving birth to children and for the continuation of family lines. Ensuring that one's children married was the responsibility of parents. Married children, in turn, gave birth, maintaining family lines, and supported their parents in old age. Confucian ideology that the most unfilial thing for children to do is to have no children to continue the family line (*buxiao yousan, wuhou weida*) has influenced Chinese perceptions of marriage and childbearing for more than two thousands years.

The meaning of marriage goes beyond the continuation of the patriarchal family line; it is closely related to family welfare. The main purposes of marriage include establishing alliances and exchanging labour advantageous to the interests of the families concerned (though not symmetrically) as means for their socio-economic and political security and mobility (Parish & Whyte 1978, Croll 1981a: 3–4, Greenhalgh 1988: 648). Exchanging labour does not necessarily mean that women are exchanged between men or groups of men as posed by Levi-Strauss (Croll 1981a: 3), where little room is left for women's own initiatives. It is rather one of many interactional possibilities in which both men and women participate, though asymmetrically, for their security and mobility (cf. M. De Bruijn 1996: 3).

Traditionally, setting up alliances through marriage was more meaningful among the rich than among the poor (Wolf 1985: 226). The rich and the poor may follow different strategies. Rich families would like (and had the means) to strengthen their social, economic and political positions through marriages. Poor families, however, would focus more on the exchange of women's labour. In the past, women were often said to be worthy of a certain amount of money as brideprice received by bride's family. Dowry was more significant for the rich than for the poor. Parents in poor families would like to ask for a high brideprice and to keep most or even all of it, partly as compensation for the lost labour of their daughter and partly as the daughter's contribution or 'filial piety' (*xiaodao*) to her parents. However, as mentioned, the role of marital transfer of brideprice as a payment for the right to the woman's labour in the strict sense is limited (see Goody 1990), especially at the present time when women themselves are increasingly involved in the decision-making of their own marriages (as discussed later in the chapter).

The Chinese government started marriage reform in 1949. Its redefinition of marriage challenged the assumption that marriage is a private affair concerning only individuals and domestic groups. The government promotes free-choice marriage based on interpersonal relations between equal partners of the opposite sex, rather than arranged marriage based on the interests of and exchange of women between these groups (Croll 1981a). It tries to eliminate 'feudal' elements of marriage like brideprices, which the Party sees as 'marriage by purchase'. Some traditional customs like child marriage have been essentially eliminated.[7] However, the meaning of marriage for social, economic, and political security and mobility for families has persisted and continues to dominate in society, and parents continue to be involved in their children's marriages. Brideprice and dowry customs are still observed in the Chinese countryside. Much of the marriage process consists of interaction processes among household members; further, marriage rules, whether inherited tradition or newly defined by the state, make marital processes much wider interactions not only happened between family members, but also between families and states.

In the collective period, when the number of family labourers was closely tied to family wealth, young unmarried women were extremely valuable. Unmarried daughters could earn more work points than other women, especially those married with children who were bounded by household chores. A married woman had to shift to her husband's family and earned work points in her husband's production team, and she could no longer work and earn work points for her natal family. In fact, married daughters could not easily visit their natal families. They had to ask for leave from collective leaders and they were also obliged to get approval from their husbands and parents-in-law. For a woman's parents, a married-out daughter meant the immediate loss of their labour. Parents thus used to be reluctant to have their daughters marry at very young ages. Also, since parents could not gain much from their daughters after marriage, they usually asked for a high brideprice, and offered small dowries. Women were also reluctant to marry young; they were disadvantaged because they usually did not know their husbands well, had to shift their living places to new, and probably also strange families, and could not easily visit their natal families after marriage.

After the responsibility system was introduced, married-out daughters could come back to their natal families and gave as much help as they wished. The shift of women's household registrations from their natal villages to their husbands' villages has become less meaningful, except when contracted land is readjusted. Children's schooling and health care are paid by parents themselves. The collective essentially has no welfare provision for individual families. Many married women only have their household registration shifted when contracted land is adjusted. At present, most young brides stay in their natal families rather than in their in-law's families if their husbands migrate. This became possible only after the shift of labour arrangements from the collective to the household, which also increased the bargaining power of young women. Newly-married brides often do not want to work in their husbands' families under the supervision of their parents-in-law. Some young brides stayed in their natal families as much as ten months in a year when their husbands stayed outside; they went back to their husbands' families only when their husbands returned home and during important festivals like the Dragon Boat Festival (*duanwu*) and Mid-autumn Festival (*zhongqiu*). They come back to their marital homes during the Spring Festival (*chunjie*) when their husbands also come home. Parents-in-law can do little about this. Poor families in particular are happy if the marriage continues, since getting their sons married has, after all, cost them a lot of money and energy.

The phenomenon of newly married wives living in natal families rather than in their husbands' families when husbands are absent, appeared only after the 1978 reforms.[8] It challenges the presupposition that wives belong to husbands' families before they belong to the husbands, and that they must be daughters-in-law before they can be wives (see Watson 1991: 351, on her observations in Cantonese villages in rural Hong Kong during 1969–70 and again in 1977–78). The new feature in the reform period shows that young brides do not belong to their parents-in-law as their property, as obtained in the past; nor are they their husbands' property.

This is in contrast to the situation of wives in former generations, who were obliged to stay mostly with their husbands' families after their marriage, whether or not their husbands migrated out. Some women said that young brides, who occasionally visited their natal families during the collective period, were reluctant to go back to their husbands' families; some even cried on the way back to their husbands' families. As discussed, wives during the collective period did not initiate divorce, because divorce was not socially acceptable and getting remarried was not easy for divorced women. Further, divorced women had far fewer alternatives during the collective period than they do in the post-reform period. Previously, women were not always welcome to return to their natal families. Villagers reported that women in their 40s or 50s, who married before reforms, are not lucky cohorts. When they married, they were under the severe supervision of their mothers-in-law. However, when they became mothers-in-law, their daughters-in-law were not deferential, as women had been towards their mothers-in-law in the past. As will be discussed in the next chapter, the power which the young women gained from the rural reforms balanced the customary power of their mothers-in-law.

Since the introduction of reforms, households have had to rely on their own networks rather than on the collective for their security and social mobility. Alliances among families have become much more meaningful and important, and at the same time more conflicts among households have become possible, for example in production process (e.g. watering crops) and in safeguarding crops and agricultural products. Mediation of these emerging conflicts by village governments has become less effective than before. There is increasing demand for cooperation in agricultural production, in accessing important market information and seeking paid jobs, or in investments. Information, channels through which they get information, and channels for participating in certain economic activities, have become important, and mostly involve kin, friends, and neighbours.

There are two main institutionalized ways to extend and strengthen social and economic ties. The first is setting up marital ties through marriage; the second is the creation of kinship ties through swearing. The priority is given to marriage, and the increasing demand for cooperation and competition among peasants' households in the reform period also explains, to some extent, the declining age at marriage after the 1978 reforms.[9] Families with children of marriageable ages will rush to have their children married to set up alliances, even before the children have reached the minimum legal marriage age. When there is no chance to set up marital ties, they may arrange for their children to become sworn brothers or sisters. Sworn brothers and sisters have the same responsibilities and obligations as blood brothers and sisters. They need to attend important family activities like marriages and burials; they should help each other wholeheartedly to guard against risks. Since reform, the number of cases of sworn relations in the village has increased. Traditionally, sworn relations took place between adults in the village, mostly based on intense emotional bonds. However, the present form may even involve children who do not know the meaning of sworn relations and have been brought into the relationship by their parents. Youngsters might find such arrangement funny; however the parents are serious. Through setting up sworn relations among young people, the families concerned are bound to each other, mainly for security concerns and sometimes for the purpose of doing businesses together. The poorer families, and a few families with only a single son, are more inclined to set up sworn brothers or sisters with other families, mainly within the village.

The basic reference group for villagers comprises their kin, neighbours and their fellow villagers in the same village. Families like to be strong enough to protect themselves against risks firstly from inside the village. Therefore, families in weak positions are inclined to set up marital ties or sworn relations with other families from the same village. Families with only daughters will marry off one or more of their daughters within the village. Thus parents can easily access help from the daughters, if they could not arrange a marriage in which the husband joins his wife's family. The latter arrangements are rare. There was only one case of uxorilocal marriage in the village in the early 1970s and another in the 1990s. However, it seems that the idea of uxorilocal marriage is increasingly accepted in the village. Some people expressed their willingness of having one married-in son-in-law in the household if possible, even when they had sons themselves. This may also reflect their dissatisfaction with their present sons and stronger motivation for having daughters. Further, as will be discussed in Chapter 9, adoption of infant girls by infertile couples, in the hope of having sons-in-law in future, has become increasingly popular, although this practice was rare in the collective period.

Marriages within the village occur among people of different surnames. While there is no strong sense that marriages within the same surname are incestuous, it simply is not the tradition. There was only one such case in the 1960s. Small surnames (*xiaoxing*), i.e., surnames with a small number of households whose family clans are usually weak, try to have marital ties with households of big surnames (*daxing*) in the same village.

Villagers believe that intra-village marriage is more popular than before. Intra-village marriage is more frequent between the poor or families of small family lineage. There were ten cases of intra-village marriage between 1985 and 1993. Only one man came from a rich and strong family and that marriage resulted from free choice and was not arranged by the parents. Setting up social networks (*shehui guanxi*) with families outside the village does not necessarily help with social affairs inside the village. If conflicts occur inside the village, it is considered inappropriate for members from outside to interfere. However, this restriction is not applicable to families within the same village who are linked by marital ties. There are other advantages for parents to marry their daughters in the same village. They can easily access their daughters' labour and other forms of support. Parents with daughters but no sons tend to have their daughters married within the village, though they could also have married-in sons-in-law. This ensures that parents are not left without care in their old age. Parents who marry off all their daughters in the same village may, if they also have sons, stimulate gossip that they are too ambitious to occupy superior positions inside the village.

The results of my sampling survey (see Table 5.1) show that there have been no clear changes in the proportion of village endogamy over time, though the absolute number of cases of intra-village marriage has increased along with the increase of population.

However, an increasing proportion of families tends to marry their daughters out to neighbouring villages, rather than those far away.

The farther out their daughters were married, the less contact there would be between daughters and their natal families and between husband's and wife's families. This would eliminate the possibility that the marriage could set up alliances. Women themselves do not like to marry far away; they prefer to keep close contacts with their natal families, in order to support each other (Cheng 1992), or do business together. Table 5.1 shows that there are significant changes in the distribution of wives' natal villages since the 1980s. There is a higher proportion of men with spouses originally from the same township and a lower proportion of men whose spouses come from outside the township. Since reforms began, most rich families have found spouses in the same township or in other townships within the county; only a few have married women from within the same village and none married women from outside the county. The few men from poor families whose wives come from outside the prefecture engaged in 'mercenary' marriage practices.

Variations in village endogamy and exogamy do exist in various villages in rural China. Some scholars suggest that the collective institution encouraged intra-village marriage following the growing isolation of village communities during the collective period, and this was the case in many villages, for example, Wugong village in Hebei (Selden 1993), Zenbu in Guangdong (Potter & Potter 1990), Chen Village in Guangdong (Chan et al. 1984), and Guangdong villages in general (Parish & Whyte 1978). Some scholars predicted a decline of village endogamy and reinforced village exogamy in post-reform

Table 5.1 Wives' natal origin by year of marriage (per cent)

	Until 1959	1960–64	1965–69	1970–74
Same village	5.9	11.1	16.1	6.3
Same township	31.5	22.2	29.0	28.1
Same county	56.3	55.6	41.9	46.9
Same prefecture	6.3	11.1	9.7	18.8
Other places	0.0	0.0	3.2	0.0
Total	100.0	100.0	100.0	100.0
Cases n	15	9	31	32
	1975–79	1980–84	1985–89	1990+
Same village	17.9	11.4	11.1	15.4
Same township	20.5	36.4	46.3	42.3
Same county	53.8	40.9	29.6	38.5
Same prefecture	7.8	9.1	9.3	3.8
Other places	0.0	2.3	3.7	0.0
Total	100.0	100.0	100.0	100.0
Cases n	39	44	54	26

Source: Research sampling survey: married couples 1993.

villages, especially where endogamy was formally frowned upon (e.g. Harrell 1992, Selden 1993). However, in places where village endogamy was a traditional pattern, the pattern continued (e.g. in Sichuan villages studied by Harrell 1993). This was also the case in this multilineage village where intra-village marriage was the tradition. The increasing contact villagers had with the outside world after market reforms and the increasing social differentiation among the households predict two opposite trends: rich households can set up marriage alliances with households from a distance for business, investment, or other economic purposes; poor households usually set up alliances with households within short distances and especially with households from the same village, for their security demands in village society. This issue is very complex, and closely linked to the local context, taking into account the prosperity of the village in relation to its neighbouring villages, the extent of social differentiation in the village, local segmented market, etc. (see Lavely 1991 on spatial hypergamy in rural Sichuan during the collective era). Clear patterns still remain to be seen in the village, where there are not only few entrepreneurs but some of these have migrated out of the village with all their family members (thus being disqualified from my sampling survey). As of 1993, only poor men had spouses who came from even poorer regions outside the county, and this is because the costs of such marriages are lower. This is consistent with Lavely's findings in Shifang, Sichuan during the collective period, where the poor generally draw brides from further down the spatial hierarchy (Lavely 1991).

The meaning of marriage differs among household members. Parents appear eager to get their children married. The old generation preferred their sons to marry earlier, relieving them of their parental burden and allowing them to retire earlier. They could also have grandchildren and get help from them earlier. Sometimes it is the grandchildren who provide their elders with the most help, when the adult sons and daughters-in-law are busy, or as the elders have less control over family labour along with the changing family relations (see Chapter 6). Unmarried sons do contribute economically to their families. However, what they earn before marriage is far from sufficient for their marriages. One frequently hears complaints from parents in their 50s that they still have not completed the 'task' of getting all their sons married.

The older generation's eagerness to marry off the young does not suggest that the young resist early marriages, nor are daughters necessarily reluctant to marry into a new and unfamiliar family at early ages (cf. Potter & Potter 1990). In fact, the young currently seem willing to marry at earlier ages than former generations. The young have more frequent contact, and get to know each other better before they marry, and relations between young couples have become more intimate than ever before. Further, young married women have more frequent contacts with their natal families. For many, marrying young has also become simply a norm. If they did not marry young, they would be left out of the marriage 'market', and this delay would make them more difficult to find 'appropriate' spouses. The alternative of becoming engaged and delaying marriage is more expensive for the grooms' families, that they are reluctant to pay.

MARRIAGE FINANCE AND MARITAL TRANSFERS OF BRIDEPRICE AND DOWRY

Increasing marriage expenses

Marriage expenses usually require years of total household savings. At present, the expense is so great that most parents must borrow a portion of the money needed to arrange their sons' marriages. A rough estimate of the cost to a groom's family of the complete marriage process includes the following items: building houses; gifts or money for small meetings (xiaojianmian or introduction); gifts or money for large meetings (dajianmian, or engagement); gifts sent to the bride's family during important festivals; brideprice; expenses of the young for social contacts; marriage ritual money; and expenses for the marriage ceremonies. The three largest categories of expenses are building houses, brideprice, and expenses for the marriage ceremonies.

Marriage expenses have been on the rise in recent years, and it is not only because people are getting richer and thus have more money to spend on marriage. Increasing marriage expenses for grooms' families includes brideprices which are requested by brides' families and must be paid (not always willingly) by grooms' families. My informant helped me calculate roughly the marriage expenses at present and those incurred ten years ago (see Table 5.2). Ten years ago, villagers spent 3,000–4,000 yuan to arrange a son's marriage, while at the time of my fieldwork they needed to spend 15,000–26,000 yuan. In 1984 prices this would be 8,500–15,000 yuan, which is three times the cost, net of inflation. This estimate assumes that the prospective groom successfully marries his first prospective bride. If the prospective groom has several small meetings of introduction, or becomes engaged and later the marriage does not proceed (this does happen more often at present than in the past), this would cost the boy's family much more. In cases where the woman's family breaks off the engagement, the young man's family can get all or part of the brideprice back; however, his family loses the entire brideprice if they want to prevent the marriage. Losses for a groom's family would be even more serious in the case of divorce, since they have spent so much on marriage.

Ten years ago, house-building was not a necessity for arranging a marriage, and the new couple could live either in a new house or in a decorated old house. At present, one house with five rooms and a yard is a basic necessity (which is also the case in rural Guangdong studied by Siu 1993). Table 5.3 indicates that a large percentage of the population that married in the 1950s went to live in existing (older) houses. It is only in the past ten years or so that more than half of the

Table 5.2 Normal marriage expenses circa 1984, and in 1993

Items	Circa 1984	1993
Building houses	No special request for house; cost for building five rooms: 2,000–3,000 *yuan.*	Five room house required; cost of the house-building: 10,000–15,000 *yuan.*
Small meeting	10 or 20 *yuan*	100 or 200 *yuan*
Big meeting	200 *yuan;* or clothes, shoes, sheet, etc. of 200 *yuan* value;	500 *yuan;* or gifts of value 500 *yuan*
	Banquet in the county town for 50 people or so 200 *yuan.*	200 *yuan*
Gift to bride's family in Chinese festivals	20–30 *yuan*	200 *yuan* or so
Brideprice	500 or 600 *yuan*	2,000–5,000 *yuan*
Marriage ceremony	400–500 *yuan*	2,000–5,000 *yuan*
Gift of money to the bride getting into the wedding car	20, 40 *yuan*	100, 120, 140, 160 or 200 *yuan*
Gift of money for sending dowry	None	100 *yuan* or so
Total (8,500	3,000–4,000 *yuan*	15,000–26,000 *yuan*
		14,705 *yuan* at 1984 price)
Average amount borrowed by groom's family	500 or 600 *yuan* in average; maximum 1,000 *yuan*	3000 or 4,000 *yuan* in average; maximum: 7,000 *yuan*

Table 5.3 Percentage of couples living in new or old houses after marriage, by year of marriage

	New house	Old house
Until 1959	7.1	92.9
1960–64	0.0	100.0
1965–69	16.7	83.3
1970–74	25.8	74.2
1975–79	23.1	76.9
1980–84	33.3	66.7
1985–89	52.7	47.3
1990+	70.4	29.6

Source: Research sampling survey: married couples 1993.

Table 5.4 Percentage of couples married 1985–93 by age of first house and family wealth

	New house	Old house	Sample size
Poor	31.6	68.4	19
Lower middle	55.6	44.4	18
Middle	68.8	31.2	16
Upper middle	73.3	26.7	15
Rich	75.0	25.0	12

Source: Research sampling survey: married couples 1993.

population have had new houses provided for them when they married; 70 per cent of those married in the 1990s live in new houses. A higher proportion of the young from richer households lived in new houses after marriage while the proportion of the young from poor families who lived in old houses after marriage was higher than that of couples from other categories (Table 5.4).

Rural people are getting richer and most families spend most of their money on building new houses. Building houses is also becoming very costly. Villagers must hire and pay construction teams to build houses, a task which used to be supported by their neighbours and friends. Further, they must pay for housing plots that had previously been provided free.[10] New houses are seen as symbols of their social status, and some better-off families even build new houses and will destroy houses less than ten years old, simply because the originals are deemed 'old fashioned'. During the collective period, new couples would live in available rooms when parents could not build new houses. However, these rooms did not belong to new couples, and some time after their marriage they would have to shift elsewhere, since the rooms would be needed for another son's marriage. Parents would live in the best rooms available. Married sons only got rooms or houses when households were divided. Since the reforms, brides' families have been able to request specifically, in oral or even written contracts with fingerprints, that new houses will be the property of the new couples after marriage, to avoid confusion and conflicts afterwards (something which is more likely in families where there are many sons or in families with economic difficulties).

Marital transfer of brideprice and dowry

Brideprice is usually negotiated between brides' and grooms' families through matchmakers. After xiaojianmian, when both members of the prospective couple consent to develop their relationship, the young woman's family usually requests an amount of money as brideprice. Dowries are also negotiated between the two families, for practical reasons; for example, the groom's family will not buy a cassette recorder if the bride will bring one as dowry. Part or even all of the dowry is purchased using the money received as brideprice. In the village, once the engagement has been formalized and the young woman's family receives the brideprice, they will usually request more money to purchase the dowry before the marriage ceremony. For example, they may add a television set to the dowry and ask the groom's family to pay for it. Thus if they request 4,000 *yuan* for the brideprice upon engagement, the final brideprice before the marriage ceremony may well reach 5,000 *yuan*. The groom's family will bargain by offering a much lower brideprice than what could be accepted. The bride's family, however, will not request a very high brideprice from a rich family. Villagers believe that the poorer the family, the higher the brideprice must be. Poor families often specifically request new houses for the marriage, while since good housing can be assumed in rich families, it is usually not mentioned. The brides' families know that their daughter will never receive much property from poor parents-in-law, and thus finds it better to request more before marriage, when the daughter has alternatives and more bargaining power; this is considered the proper occasion to ask for material or monetary transfers from future parents-in-law.

The sampling survey data shows that richer households pay higher brideprices, but also that it is not the poorest who pay the lowest brideprice (Figure 5.5). The poorest group pays a higher brideprice than the middle-lower group, though less than the rest. The poor pay less betrothal money than the rich, simply because they cannot afford to pay so much. The richest have the biggest range, but not the highest mean (see Figure 5.5). Rich families have more options; they can provide more betrothal money if they wish, and the brides' family does not need to worry much about their daughter's finances after marriage.

Poor families also request high brideprices because parents usually retain a part of it for themselves before using the rest to provide dowries for their daughters. At present, many families also give brideprice money to their daughters for buying bicycles, watches, etc., as dowries, something termed 'indirect dowry' by Goody. Rich families may add money for part of the dowries of their daughters. Figure 5.5 indicates that women marrying into richer families also bring more dowry with them on the day of the wedding. They most often bring dowries whose monetary value is higher than that of the brideprice. Some even provide dowries worth two or three times the brideprice (Figure 5.6). This confirms Siu's statement that higher status groups tend to stress direct dowry and lower status groups brideprice or indirect dowry (Siu 1993: 167).

Unfortunately, I have no time series data on peasant income and thus cannot ascertain whether marriage expenses now require a greater share of peasant income. However interviews with villagers give the impression that this is the case. Although variations among families may well exist, complaints about escalating marriage expenses were frequent. Many said that it was less difficult in the past

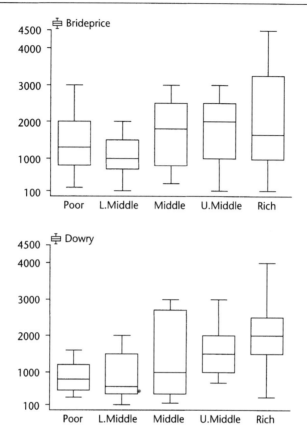

Figure 5.5 Box plots for brideprice and dowry for marriages since 1985 according to household wealth (current prices)
Note: L.Middle = Lower Middle; U.Middle = Upper Middle. For brideprice, F=2.12, not significant; for dowry, F=16.97, statistically significant at p<0.01).
Source: Research sampling survey: married couples 1993.

to arrange one's son's marriage than at present. Parents did not experience serious difficulties even when they had to arrange marriages for three or four sons. At present, however, one has to be extremely rich to have three sons married.

In general, both the value of the brideprice and the value of the dowry from the bride's family have been increasing over time. In the pre-reform Maoist period, both brideprice and dowry were strictly prohibited; this was especially so during the Cultural Revolution. Brideprice and dowry still existed throughout the pre-reform period although they differed in value in different years. As Figure 5.7 shows, there was little dowry before 1980, and since 1980 the value of dowries has seen a significant increase. In the 1960s, dowry included

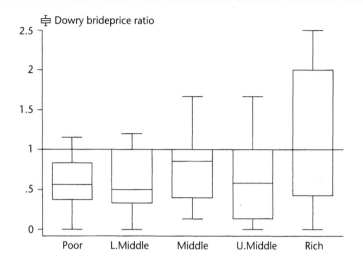

Figure 5.6 Box plots for dowry to brideprice ratio for marriages 1985–93 according to household wealth
Note: L.Middle = Lower Middle; U.Middle = Upper Middle. F=4.49, statistically significant at P<0.05)
Source: Research sampling survey: married couples 1993.

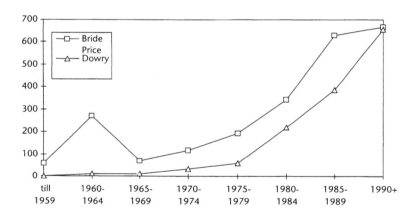

Figure 5.7 Mean value of brideprice and dowry over time (at 1950 prices)
Source: Research sampling survey: married couples 1993.

only basic living necessities like washing basins, small tables and bedding. In the 1970s, bicycles, sewing machines, and watches became part of the dowry. In the 1980s, the brides' families started to send black-and-white televisions, cassette recorders or even colour televisions as dowry. Wooden chests and wardrobes, luxuries in the

1970s, have in the 1990s become so commonplace that brides' families usually no longer send them as dowry. Instead, over half of brides' families sent watches and black-and-white televisions as dowry, while a few sent colour televisions for their daughters.

The value of dowry has increased not only because rural families have become richer and thus have more money to invest in social status, but also because daughters themselves now can control most or all of the brideprice. Before the reform, the value of the dowry sent by the bride's family was small compared with the value of the brideprice. Until recently, parents retained most of the brideprice and might spend some of it to arrange marriages for their sons. This practice has become difficult, if not impossible, since daughters may not agree to have their money (brideprice) spent on their brothers' marriages, especially when their brothers can earn money themselves. Part of the brideprice-dowry fund may be saved and controlled by daughters themselves. Many young girls, after graduating (or leaving) school, prefer working in brick kilns, local factories and the like, where they can earn salaries, rather than working in the household responsibility fields where their contribution may be obscured and where they do not directly control the income earned. Young women's incomes are mostly managed by their parents, though they can retain some pocket money to buy new, fashionable clothes. However, in principle all of the daughter's income specifically belongs to her, and it is mainly saved toward her dowry. Parents are not to use it for other purposes and especially not for covering the marriages of sons. However, in some poor families, of course, parents pool all possible incomes together and also retain part of the brideprice they get when marrying out their daughters.

Figures 5.7 and 5.8 show the increasing value of the dowry, and the gradual trend toward balance in the ratio of dowry to brideprice. In

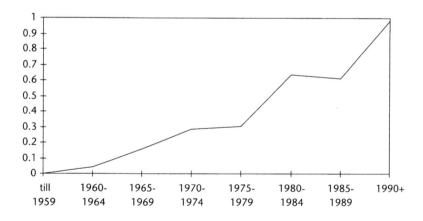

Figure 5.8 Ratio of mean value of dowry to brideprice over time
Source: Research sampling survey: married couples 1993.

the 1980s, the value of dowry was half of the brideprice while in the 1990s, the value of dowry almost equals brideprice. Before 1980, most women brought dowry with a lower value than the betrothal money they received. In the 1980s, one fourth of the women brought dowry of equal or higher value than the brideprice (betrothal money) they received, and this was true of half of the women who married in the early 1990s.

The increasing dowry and the balancing of the dowry-brideprice ratio may have been even more significant in practice than these figures suggest. For instance, the brides themselves may have controlled some of the brideprice retained by brides' natal families. This share of the money, taken from the brideprice and belonging to and controlled by the brides without their husbands' (or public) knowledge, can be termed 'hidden dowry', and is also part of the 'indirect dowry' to which Goody refers. One young man married in early 1993 was sure that his wife (rather than his wife's parents) kept at least 1,000 *yuan* of the 5,000 *yuan* given as brideprice. The emergence of 'hidden dowry' is a reasonable response to the security concerns of wives. Unlike normal dowry, which is shared by both wives and husbands, hidden dowry is only controlled by wives, and wives can use their own discretion as to how 'hidden dowry' might be used. Women with such personal funds have more leverage to bargain with their husbands and they also have money of their own if they divorce. It is reasonable to believe that the 'hidden dowry' is differentiated among different social groups. The significance and the implication of this new phenomenon in the reform period needs to be further explored.

The trend toward balance in the dowry-brideprice ratio over time has been substantial since the reforms. Prior to the reforms, the bride's parents were likely to keep part of the brideprice as an 'old-age pension' (*yanglaojin*) provided by daughters, or as compensation for the loss of daughters' labour. At present parents usually send most or all the brideprice back to their daughters as dowries, with 'no gain, and no loss', since they claim that their living standard has improved tremendously. The rich may send their daughters more dowry of higher value than the brideprice, as shown in Figure 5.5. The increasing balance in the dowry-brideprice ratio shows that the sharp rise of brideprices in the reform era is not always in response to demands from the brides' households for compensation for the loss of daughters' labour (Croll 1994: 169), although compensation for the loss of a daughter's labour may be valid for some, especially poor, households. Other families provide substantial dowries to their daughters upon marriage partly to show their high status, and partly to create alliances; in this case, the larger dowry serves in part to improve their daughters' situations in their new families after marriage.

In other places where dowry exists, for example in northwestern India (see Sharma 1980, cited in Watson 1991), substantial portions of the dowry are given, not to the bride, but to the groom and his family. However, in the case-study village, dowries are women's property and belong to women, even though the dowries come indirectly from the husbands and parents-in-law. The dowry would be taken fully by the woman if the couple divorces. The increasing dowry, and especially the balancing trend in the dowry-brideprice ratio (increasing the share of indirect dowry relative to brideprice in some families) reflect changing familial relations, especially between daughters and their parents. Clearly, young women have gained some power in their natal families since reforms began. This change also affects familial relations between husband and wife and between daughter-in-law and parents-in-law in the newly emerging family. A woman with a substantial dowry may have status and power other women do not (Watson 1991, Ebrey 1991: 8). Thus, the rich will provide substantial dowries, and other parents will vigorously request higher brideprices in order to send more dowry to their daughters; daughters find this satisfying, and the relationship between daughters and their husbands' families, and between daughters and their natal families, are strengthened. In short, the value placed on affinity has increased with the reforms because cooperation is much in need, both in agricultural and non-agricultural activities among rural families.

DECISION-MAKING CONCERNING MARRIAGE

Decisions concerning marriage include interactions at two levels: at the family level among family members, and at the community level among families and the local administration (Croll 1981a, 1981b). At the family level, children's marriages were traditionally arranged by their parents, and even after liberation when the government started to promote free-choice marriages, many men and women still had no say in the choice of their marriage partner. This situation has been changing rapidly, and increasingly both men and women have been able to decide their marriages. At present, although parents initiate most of the marriages, they will consult with their children to get their approval. However, children still can not decide their marriages completely, independently of parental involvement, because they need their parents to pool the household income to finance the marriages. While both men and women have been increasingly involved in decision-making, the changes for women are not precisely on par with those for men. Though women do not need to save money in order to marry, they would make themselves vulnerable if they were to marry without the consent of their parents. Losing ties with their natal families means the loss of one of their security resources, namely the ability to return to their natal families if their husbands did not treat them well, or wanted divorce. Despite this, some women do decide by themselves to marry, and the number of such cases have been increasing since the reforms, now that young women and men have more alternatives. This is different from the collective period, when women had little option but to return to their natal families if divorced.

Interactions concerning marriage also occur between families and the state in many areas, including age at marriage, marriage rituals and marriage expenses. Three major laws and policies regulating age at marriage have taken effect in different periods since 1949. The marriage law of 1950 set the legal minimum age for marriage at 18 for women and 20 for men. In the 1970s, family planning programmes stipulated later marriage, sparser births and fewer births, and set the minimum age in rural areas at 23 for women and 25 for men. The marriage law of 1980, which went into effect on New Year's Day 1981, lowered the ages: 20 for women and 22 for men .

In assessing the impact of changes in state marriage laws and policies on the rural population, or the roles of local-level cadres in the implementation of these laws and policies, one should be aware that many young people married below the minimum legal marriage age permitted either by state laws or by government policies (see Table 5.5; figures in bold indicate marriages below the legal age or age standard set by policies in each reference period). From liberation through the 1970s, the percentage of men and women who married below the minimum marriage age declined. More than half of men married were

Table 5.5 Percentage of ever-married men and women married below the minimum legal marriage age and policy requirements during different periods

	Until 1959	1960–64	1965–69	1970–74
Men below 20	**52.9**	**31.3**	**22.0**	**18.2**
Women below 18	**26.5**	**0.0**	**0.0**	**3.0**
Men below 22	76.5	56.3	68.3	37.9
Women below 20	82.4	68.8	43.9	12.1
Men below 25				80.3
Women below 23				62.1
	1975–79	1980–84	1985–89	1990+
Men below 20	12.9	24.3	36.4	41.1
Women below 18	0.0	0.0	3.4	7.1
Men below 22	32.3	**56.8**	**64.8**	**75.0**
Women below 20	6.5	**17.6**	**30.7**	**32.1**
Men below 25	**77.4**	77.0		
Women below 23	**50.0**	64.9		

Source: Research sampling survey: married couples 1993.

below age 20 in the 1950s, while this was true for just over one in ten in the late 1970s. However, in the late 1970s, the government had stipulated 25 as the minimum age for marriage, and three-fourths of men and half of all women married younger than this. In the 1980s and the beginning of the 1990s, the percentage of men who married below 22 years old increased from over half to three-quarters, and from less than one-tenth to one-third for women. Clearly, individual marital behaviour has never been totally led by state laws and government policies. This raises the question of whether government policies on marital practices in rural China are at all effective, or whether individuals and families behave with no consideration for state laws and government policies.

In the late 1970s, the percentage of men and women who married below 20 for men and below 18 for women was at its lowest, and the minimum marriage age stipulated by the government was at its highest. Whether this actually implies that higher target ages set by the government will reduce the percentage of people who marry young (because individuals and families in rural China respond to government pressure) depends mainly on the practical implementation of state policies by cadres at local levels.

As discussed previously, cadres have lost much bargaining power. For example, they may not themselves initiate efforts to press their fellow villagers for compliance with state policies. Village cadres complained if overly pressured from above, saying that village cadres would stay in the village 'forever' (*yongjiu*), while the township cadres could fly away sometime in future like 'pigeons' (*feige*). The implication is that they cannot press their fellow villagers too much since they would live in the same village for life, while township cadres are usually formal state employees and they can shift to other places if necessary. Furthermore, village cadres, as members of the same society with their fellow villagers, may also prefer to deviate from state policies. For example, in 1991 one of the village cadres arranged for his son to marry at age 17, far below the prescribed minimum legal age. Obviously, this made it extremely difficult for him to promote compliance with the state policy.

In addition to the bargaining process between village cadres and families, there exists a bargaining process between village cadres and township cadres. Sometimes village cadres work together with their fellow villagers to resist pressures from above. They might disguise the real situation, for example, by reporting a lower number of marriages below the legal marriage age than actually took place, thereby making it easier to 'realize' the assigned target (this aspect of the implementation of family planning programmes is discussed in Chapter 8).

At present, the marriage registration procedure is complex. The couple needs to get a letter from their appropriate village government representative to prove that they are unmarried and have reached the legal marriage age. The township cadres need to ascertain that all conditions for marriage have been met. If they do, the marriage is approved with one marriage certificate given to each couple; the recently introduced registration fee was 28 *yuan*.

The way in which cadres check the marital status and age of the couple has changed. During the commune system era, the village government kept the agricultural registration books. Township cadres gave approval for marriage based on the certification letter from the village government. Since the reforms, the township government keeps a copy of the registration book, and checks the marital status and age of the candidates. If the certification letter is consistent with the registration book and the couple fits the conditions for marriage, then the marriage will be approved. Through this means, the problem of falsifying age to facilitate early marriage can be to a certain extent avoided.

However, as Table 5.5 shows, in the past 15 years or so most men and many women married before they reached the legal minimum marriage age. They usually approached the village cadres to get the certification letters, then simply went ahead and performed the marriage ceremony. Villagers still regard the marriage ceremony, rather than the registration, as validating the marriage. Village cadres may attend the marriage ceremony to congratulate the parents for their sons' marriage, even when the couple has married below the legal age.

In the collective period, most people registered their marriages before they held the marriage ceremony. At that time, as we know, married out daughters were no longer assigned work or allocated grain by their original production teams. They usually joined the production team of their husbands and had work assigned there. In this situation, couples had to report to their corresponding production brigades for registration of marriage as well as for migration, so marriages enacted without previous registrations were rare.

In the post-reform period, however, many people in customary marriages without legal registrations did not even register their marriages later when they reached the legal marriage age. They could see no reason to register and pay the registration fee, since the lack of registration caused no problems in their lives. They can divorce legally even without the legal registration for marriage, and property could be divided through the mediation of relatives, friends, or the village and township cadres. Registration also has no apparent effect on access to contracted land. At present, one important factor influencing family income and welfare is the size of household-contracted land, and this is based in part on household size. However, newly married wives would not get their contracted land for some time if land contract had taken place just before their marriages. The families in which wives did not come from the same village, consisting of husband, wife and usually two or three children, that have been formed since the land adjustment in the village in 1987 have only one person's contracted land to work on to feed the whole family. The re-contracting of land to rural households is no trivial undertaking, and village cadres had no incentive to do it on their own initiative if there are no new guidelines from above. When another re-contracting takes place, these wives will already be merged with local society and able to receive contracted land, whether or not their marriages are registered. Their children, even including extra births outside family planning, can also get contracted land. Children of unregistered marriages can go to school, and receive a piece of housing plot without problems. In practice, mothers and their children are treated as members of the community according to the local custom of marriage ceremony, in which formal official registration is irrelevant.

Since 1992, in an effort to avoid early marriages, the government has levied a 300–*yuan* fine on those who marry below the legal marriage age. Collection of the fine is combined with family planning campaigns. During the campaign, the cadres will counsel those families identified as early marriages, requesting they pay the fine. Usually cadres need to go to families quite a few times before they can collect any portion of a fine, and generally only part of the fine is paid, in a process of bargaining between cadres and families.

Meanwhile, cadres have not been able to make much headway in their efforts to reform a number of marriage customs along state-determined lines, even though there is some demand for the reforms from inside. It is not the customs *per se* which cannot be changed; it is the power structure that maintains or deviates from the customs which cannot be easily changed. Villagers complain that it is now too costly for parents to get their sons married. Most parents would like to have these marriage customs reformed and to reverse the trend of increasing marriage expenses. However, forces that would promote marriage reforms from inside do not seem to be strong enough. Though the government still makes great efforts to influence marriage practices through television, radio and other media, this is not as effective as it had been during the commune period, when local people were requested to follow marriage guidelines under the supervision of the village cadres. If local people deviated from the guidelines, they might be criticized over public loudspeakers; cadres also requested them to attend a study group to be educated to follow the 'new way for new marriage' (*xinshi xinban*); or cadres could deduct work points from their account books directly as economic punishment.

Based on the above discussion, some features with respect to age at marriage and decision-making on marriage can be summarized. Firstly, the earlier age at marriage for rural Chinese in the earlier years of the People's Republic reflects a greater degree of parental control over the marriages of young people. Secondly, stricter state control during the collective period may have increased the marriage age of rural Chinese. Thirdly, following the retreat of the state in the post-reform period, power-regulating marriage decision-making has not totally returned to the older generations; such authority is now also shared by the younger generations. Finally, the shift of some decision-making power from the old to the young does not mean the young will automatically delay their marriage.

The institution of marriage is undergoing significant changes in the village and so are the intermediate variables of fertility concerning marriage. The social, economic, political and demographic forces behind the changes are complex. Changes in the marriage institutions are closely related to the institutional reforms which have changed the context within which rural Chinese live and work, and adaptations and responses of individual farmers to the changing context. Rural reforms which emphasized economic efficiency by introducing responsibility systems and importing market mechanisms, open up available opportunities, but also increase risks and uncertainties. Increasing demand for cooperation among some peasant households and competition and conflicts among others inevitably induces peasants to try to arrange early marriages for their children, in order to set up alliances and exchange labour among the families concerned. This also motivates peasant families to select spouses or alliance partners within a shorter distance, though there has been no significant increase in endogamy in this village.

The changing marriage institution also has implications for fertility perceptions and motivations. One of the reasons for this is that arranging a child's marriage is largely the responsibility of parents. For example, the recent rapid increase in marriage expenses may well become an important factor in young couples' decisions not to have too many sons. Parental preferences for sons or daughters may also change, since the expenses related to their marriages will in future differ. These issues will be further explored in the following chapters.

Notes
[1] It might be suspected that the difference in marriage structure between men and women could be due to an imbalance of the sex ratio in marriageable age cohorts. However, such difference in this particular village also depends on the changing local marriage market, which is also related to the economic disparities in the surrounding villages. This calls for higher level detail studies.

[2] Households in the village are divided evenly to five groups in this and following figures according to their household wealth (measured as ownership of houses, endurable consumer goods, agricultural machinery, livestock, and grain) as surveyed in early 1993; the five categories are labeled as poor, lower middle, middle, upper middle, and rich, as shown in the figure.

[3] Parish & Whyte (1978), in their study of Guangdong villages in the collective era, argued that the husband's family pays the brideprice for the transfer of rights to a woman's labour (including children). Thus if a woman wanted a divorce she needed to repay the brideprice. However, this is not the case in the Northern village in my study. Unfortunately, I do not know whether divorced women needed to repay the brideprice during the collective period in the village. Thus it is unclear whether this is a regional

difference in which the husband in this Northern village has gained only sexual access to his wife by paying the brideprice, or whether this reflects the fact that the groom and his family have less control of the bride's labour in the Northern village at present than was the case in the past. In any case, the meaning of marriage as a mechanism for the transfer of rights to women may become less significant in modern society than in traditional patriarchal society, where women participated less in decision-making about their own marriages.

4   Marriage in my sampling survey refers to customary marriage by rites and ceremonies (*shishi hunyin*, a *de facto* marriage), rather than legal marriage through registrations in the government civil department.

5   Data used in the figure is from the 1993 sampling survey of women aged 15–59 on their birth histories, which contains information on age at first marriage for both husbands and wives for a larger sample (450) rather than from the smaller sample (254) of couples containing detailed information on their marriages.

6   Three of them were from the poor ethnic areas of Guangxi and Guizhou.

7   I heard during my fieldwork that child betrothal re-emerged in the county after reform; however, I encountered no cases of this, and thus did not pursue the issue systematically during the fieldwork.

8   In three Shandong villages studied by Judd (1989), it seems that women are also staying in *niangjia* (their natal families) after reforms, now that labour arrangements have become flexible and migration much easier. During the collective period women faced much pressure to move to their *pojia* (their marital homes) because once married they were not allowed to work in their natal villages and they were required to shift their household registrations.

9   Changes in age and sex structure have a strong impact on the marriage market and age at marriage. The impacts of dramatic changes in age and sex structure as a consequence of the Great Leap Forward (1958–60) on early marriage in the early 1980s at the national level are discussed in Tien's (1991) work. This issue needs additional study and cannot be easily dealt with here. It needs to be pointed out, however, that the age at marriage in the village continued to decline in the early 1980s to the early 1990s, which cannot be due only to the demographic factors.

10   After reforms, the village government began to charge a fee for the allocation of housing plots. At the beginning of reforms, this was 200 *yuan*; by the early 1990s the cost had increased to over 1,000 *yuan*. This five-fold increase in housing plot fees has generated complaints from many, especially poor families.

CHAPTER 6

Changing Nature of Family Relations

Many scholars suspect that economic reforms which reinstate peasant households as production units reinforce the power of men over women and the old over the young within the household (e.g. Kelkar 1985 & 1990, Davin 1988, Robinson 1985, Aslanbeigui & Summerfield 1989, Summerfield & Aslanbeigui 1992, Summerfield 1994).[1] The underlying assumptions are that collective institutions and egalitarian policies during the Maoist period ensured greater equality between family members, and that the retreat of the state would reinforce or restore the inequalities that existed before the collective period. These assumptions are not necessarily correct. Collectivization did not demolish all economic and social bases for inequality and some of them may be preserved. Economic reforms, which brought about many changes in social institutions, are more likely to reshape rather than to restore characteristics of family relations. Changes in the marriage institution and changes in household economy in the reform period will meanwhile influence social relations within and between households.

As discussed in the last chapter, changes in the marriage institution in the reform period have consequences for social relations between genders and between generations within the family. As the marriage institution has experienced tremendous changes, so too has the family institution. The formation of conjugal couples, the increasing contacts between the young in the selection of spouses, shrinking marriage circles, increasing brideprice and dowry and increasing marriage expenses, etc., all have important implications for the structure of the newly emerged families.

Many economic opportunities released by the economic reforms are asymmetrical and unequal between men and women and between generations. These call for new forms of division of labour as a strategy for peasants' families to take advantage of the available opportunities. The new forms of division of labour redefine familial relations, which can be partly shown in the consequent household divisions. Household division, an important topic for anthropologists (e.g. Cohen 1976, 1992, Parish & Whyte 1978, Potter & Potter 1990), is now increasingly noted by demographers in terms of the post-marital residence of new couples with their parents or in-laws (Dankert et al. 1990, Zeng, Li & Ma 1991, Lavely & Ren 1992). The new productive and living arrangement, which has been shaped by the new economic and institutional context, may determine or mani-fest new familial relations between couples and between generations in quite complex and unexpected ways.

Opportunities in the reform period also vary among households, and this has enlarged social differentiation (see Chapter 4). Reliance by peasants on their households rather than on the collective has increased cooperation, and at the same time, increased competition and conflicts among households. Cooperation along paternal and maternal lines may become equally important. Thus, when the patri-archal family clan is strengthened, relations between husbands' and wives' families may also become important

Family change, as Caldwell *et al.* (1988) argues, is key to explaining other aspects of demographic change. Changes in the family to be investigated in this chapter are, however, not in family size and composition *per se.* The focus is on the social relations between family members, especially intra-generational relations between wives and husbands and intergenerational relations between married children and their parents or in-laws. This chapter will argue that family struc-ture, i.e., these social relations between family members, is changing substantially under the influence of economic transition and that this is closely related to the newly reshaped division of labour which peasant families have developed as an adaptive strategy. This newly reshaped division of labour and the changing social relations between family members are influencing or reshaping the rules for family formation and family division, and this has implications for family size and family composition.

The first section of the chapter will briefly itemize changes in family size and composition in the village, as captured by quantitative surveys. The following section focuses on rules and changes in house-hold division, which manifest changing social relations between family members and determine household size and composition, without discussion of the impact of demographic changes on house-hold size and composition. The third section will discuss the newly reshaped division of labour within the family and the strategy peasant families have adopted to adapt to increasing opportunities, risks and uncertainties. The final section discusses what has changed in intra-household and inter-household relations.

POST-REFORM FAMILY AND HOUSEHOLD: SMALLER IN SIZE AND SIMPLER IN COMPOSITION

Concepts of family and household are ambiguous and flexible (see discussions by Yanagisako 1979, B. White 1980, Harris 1981, Zonabend 1996). In the village, a family refers to a couple with their children living together. A man is said to have set up a family when he marries (chengjia), though the new family is attached to the parents' family to form an extended family. The extended family is considered a stem family if only one couple in each generation is living together, or a joint family when more than one couple in the same generation is living together. A household (hu) usually consists of family members and sometimes non-family members living together (under the same roof and cooking and eating together), or having the same property and budget, or having a division of labour among themselves (cf. Cohen 1976 in his study of Chinese households in Taiwan).

In rural Chinese society, the arrangements of groups of people living together are complex. Nearly all households in the village are family households (jiatinghu) and so I will use the terms family and household interchangeably. Family members usually arrange their lives under the same budget and through a division of labour, though they do not necessarily reside in the same courtyard. People who live in two distant houses but eat and work together and have the same budget are considered as comprising one household. A couple with husband working outside and wife working in the village also form one household. Usually two new independent households are set up after an old one is divided (fenjia).

The general trend in household size in the nation, the province, the prefecture and the county is declining in the reform period, though the decline is not uniform (see Table 6.1). Given the tremendous size of China and its diversity of economic structures, different trends in household size and structure are expected. For example, county statistics in Handan show different patterns of change in household size; between 1980 and 1990 household size in some counties increased, showed little change in other counties, and declined in still others.

Peasants live in small households in this village. The average household size has been declining in recent years, from 4.58 in 1982 to 4.50 in 1990 and was 4.46 in 1993, according to two official population census and my own population census. This trend was not predicted at the initial stage of the reforms (see debates in Potter & Potter 1990, Croll 1987a, 1994, Ikels 1990)[2] and is due to the decreasing proportion of bigger households and increase in single-person households. The proportion of households with more than eight members is declining from 7.2 per cent in 1982 to 4.1 per cent in 1990 and only 1.7 per cent in 1993 (see Figure 6.1). The proportion of single-person households is increasing from 2.4 per cent in 1982 to

Table 6.1 Household size in 1982 and in 1990 according to state population censuses

Region	Household size		Difference
	1982	1990	
China	4.41	3.96	−0.45
Hebei Province	4.14	3.89	−0.25
Handan Prefecture	4.39	4.33	−0.06
The studied county	4.49	4.48	−0.01

Sources: CASS (1988, 1994), HDRPB (1985, 1992), CSBPCO (1982, 1990).

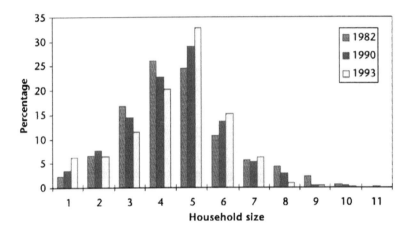

Figure 6.1 Distribution of household size in the village in 1982, 1990 and 1993 (per cent)
Sources: Government population census of the village 1982, Government population census of the village 1990, Research population census of the village 1993.

3.6 per cent in 1990 and 6.4 in 1993. In the village, all single-person households in 1993 consisted of elderly in their 60s or 70s, most of them widows and widowers.[3] Most have children who live separately. A few have only daughters, who married out and lived in husbands' households.

Nuclear families form an increasing proportion of households in the village. In 1982, the proportion of households with one couple or one couple with their unmarried children comprised 60 per cent of total households. In 1993, this proportion increased to over 68 per cent (see Table 6.2).

The proportion of households with only one couple and the proportion of households with one couple and their children have both increased. Households with only one couple consist of two

Table 6.2 Household structure in the village in 1982, 1990 and 1993

	1982		1990		1993	
	Cases	%	Cases	%	Cases	%
Single	8	2.4	15	3.6	30	6.4
Couple with or without unmarried children	201	60.2	265	63.4	316	68.2
Widowed parent & unmarried children	14	4.2	12	2.9	8	1.7
Couple & 1 married son & other unmarried children	9	2.7	12	2.9	15	3.2
Couple & 1 married son & unmarried grandchildren	14	4.2	12	2.9	18	3.8
Widowed parent & 1 couple with or without unmarried Children	42	12.5	49	11.7	35	7.4
Couple & 1 married son & unmarried children & unmarried grandchildren	11	3.3	11	2.6	15	3.2
Others	35	10.5	42	10.0	34	7.2
Total	334	100.0	418	100.0	471	100.0

Sources: Government population census of the village 1982, Government population census of the village 1990, Research population census of the village 1993.

groups: young couples in their 20s whose household separated from their parents before they had any births, and older couples aged over 50 whose children have set up their own separate families. The latter type account for the majority. Of the 25 households in 1993 consisting of only a couple, four were newly married couples in their 20s, and the rest are couples in 50s or over.

Changes in the proportion of stem families are complex. Some forms have declined significantly, some have slightly increased and some remain essentially unchanged. The proportion of families of widowed parents and one couple with or without unmarried children had a significant decline from 12.6 per cent in 1982 to 7.4 per cent in 1993; the proportion of families with one couple, their married son and other unmarried children increased slightly; the proportion of households with one couple, their married son and other unmarried children plus their small grandchildren changed little in the period (see Table 6.2).

Demographic factors like marriage and remarriage, widowhood and divorce, life expectancy and number of children (especially number of sons) influence household size and household composition (Zeng 1991, Harrell 1993). Zeng (1986) has demonstrated that there will be an increase in the incidence of stem households and a decline in the incidence of nuclear households when fertility and mortality decline. Other factors being equal, the lower age at marriage and longer life expectancy will result in higher proportion of three generation or four generation households, because earlier marriage would also mean earlier childbearing and longer life expectancy means a greater chance that three or four generations will be alive at the same time. The number of brothers might also affect the proportion of household of different generations, because if most households are divided before the death of the parents, more brothers would mean more nuclear households for each stem family.

In the village, as shown in Chapter 5, the age at marriage for both men and women has declined tremendously since the reforms. Parents are also increasingly younger and are having fewer children (see Chapter 9). Also, it is most likely true that life expectancy is increasing.[4] However, the proportion of three-generation and four-generation households has declined sharply. In 1982, three-generation households accounted for 25.5 per cent of the total households, in 1990 20.6 per cent and only 16.8 per cent in 1993 (see Figure 6.2).

The continuing increase in the proportion of nuclear families in the village contrasts with the prediction of Zeng (1986, 1991), based on his family status life table model, that the proportion of nuclear families will decrease 'when young people born after the tremendous fertility decline reach the age of family formation, given that certain proportions of parents will wish to live with one of their married children' (Zeng 1991: 166). The difference in this particular village may be

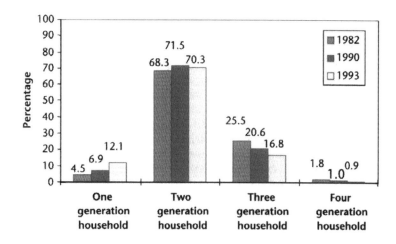

Figure 6.2 Change of household composition over years
Sources: Government population census of the village 1982; Government population census of the village 1990; Research population census of the village 1993.

because its fertility decline in the 1970s may not have been dramatic (see Chapter 9) and the young born in the first half of the 1970s are just reaching their family formation age. Most importantly, the difference relates to the complex set of rules of family formation and family division, living and production arrangements not captured by models. For example, a large number of widowers, widows and old couples live alone in separate households although they would prefer to live with their married children.

Demographic factors alone cannot easily explain household size and composition, and their impact on household size and composition is not the primary concern here. The next section focuses on changes in household division which manifest its rules and, importantly, the social relations between family members. It discusses the reasons for household divisions, who initiates household divisions, how family property is divided, who participates in household divisions, what forms household divisions take, and the underlying principles involved.

EARLY HOUSEHOLD DIVISION IN THE REFORM PERIOD

In the traditional family system, parents keep their married sons living with them; however, this ideal pattern may only have existed in elite families in the past (see Fei 1939, Lang 1946, Levy 1949). In Cohen's terms, a gap exists between 'ultimate aspirations' comprising ideals commonly held in traditional times and 'practical management', tied far more closely to actual economic management and family reproductions (Cohen 1992). Household division is inevitable when a household becomes large and the social conflicts among its members have increased to a degree that remaining together does not benefit all or some of its members. It may become difficult to manage economic activities and daily life, or interests among household members may diverge greatly that serious 'free rider' problems emerge. For the villagers, household division not only reduces social conflicts within the household but also clarifies the interest relations among family members, and is also the occasion for children to inherit part of household property and to clarify their responsibility towards their parents.[5]

In the village, division mostly happens in households where there are two or more sons. In theory, parents with a single son never divide their households. However, in reality parents may separate their eating and living arrangements from those of their son while maintaining close ties, or parents and child may split up due to animosity between the two generations. For example, I observed one married son who did not treat his widowed mother well during my fieldwork in 1993. His mother ate and lived alone, and the son did not provide the needed care to his mother. The neighbours gossiped, but the son ignored social pressure and the mother's situation remain unchanged.

In fact, most elderly parents who could still take care of themselves cook and lived alone. Villagers said that life-style differences make it difficult for parents and their married children to get along while living and eating together. The young prefer separate households, in which they have more personal autonomy. Only after the parents become too old to take care of themselves do they again reside and eat together with their children.

Household division not only divides household property and clarifies each son's responsibility to his parents, but may also include dividing credit or debt. Parents' debts need to be paid by their sons even when parents pass away. Detailed information on how to divide the house, furniture, agricultural machines and tools, credits or debts, and contracted land, etc. is discussed and written into a contract, including the responsibility of children to their parents, and sometimes grandparents, concerning food, pocket money, provision of daily needs, health care, and funeral and burial expenses. The household division contract is kept by the relevant parties.

Although land is still collectively owned and contracted to individual households, in this village the contracted land is also divided during household division. The rule for dividing household contracted land is simple and seldom challenged: land contracted to a household is contracted out on an individual basis, so each person takes his or her share upon household division. Wives who marry soon after land contracts are arranged are in a disadvantaged position because they would not yet have any land entitlement to take with them after division.

Household division is a process rather than a threshold event. Households may be divided, but not always clearly or completely. Some household property, like houses, furniture and personal belongings, might still be controlled by parents and only divided among sons after the death of both parents. Certain property could be specified to be inherited by certain sons in the household division contract. Sons must fulfil their obligations for caring for their parents in order to get the inheritance, since failing in their obligations to care for their elderly parents may deprive them of their rights to inherit further household properties, and those who provide more care would get a larger share of the remaining household property.

During the collective period, newly married couples used to live for some years with the husbands' parents, and villagers believed that parents at that time had the authority to hold the household members together. There were also practical difficulties for earlier household division in the collective period because there was a shortage of separate houses. Living together in a big household also had offered certain advantages. For example, childcare was incompatible with their work in the fields, and women could be important work points earners because in a large household the grandparents could provide childcare. If a young couple lived by themselves, the wife would stay at home taking care of household chores, which meant the loss of one labourer. Married children and daughters-in-law would work in the collective while their parents did the cooking and other household chores, including taking care of the children. The grandmother could take babies to their mother (who worked in the fields) to be fed. Villagers said that in the collective period household members took care to avoid conflicts among themselves and sometimes endured incompatible relations in order to remain together instead of prematurely splitting up the households.

Villagers feel strongly that since reform, newly married couples are separating from their parents much earlier; this is supported by the data collected in the sampling survey (see Table 6.3).[6] For the 1985–89 marriage cohorts, one-fifth divided their households from their parents within the first year of their marriage and over three-fourths divided their households from their parents within five years of their marriage. The increase in the incidence of household division within five years started in the late 1970s and the increase within one year started in the 1980s. It should be noted that some households do not divide because they are stem families in which the sole (married) son remains with his parents until their death.

Reform is also linked to earlier household division elsewhere in rural China, such as Zengbu in Guangdong province (Potter & Potter 1990) and in several Hebei, Sichuan and Shanghai villages (Myron Cohen 1992). Potter & Potter (1990) show that in Zengbu earlier household division has become desirable both because the joint family household offers no economic advantage and because it is not used as a form of status display, as was the practice among the traditional gentry. However, in the western part of the Pearl River delta, Johnson (1993) found that local people, mostly those with connections to overseas relatives, favour delayed household division. In three Sichuan villages studied by Harrell (1993), the proportion of family divisions in which brothers wait until the joint family has existed for a few months or years has increased in one of the villages (Renhe) in the years since the economic reforms. This type of family division has always constituted a significant proportion of all divisions in Yishala, and essentially all family divisions come piecemeal at the time of each

Table 6.3 Proportion of married sons living separately from their parents within the first and the fifth year of marriage, by marriage years

	Until 1959	1960–64	1965–69	1970–74	1975–79	1980–84	1985–89
S1	0	11.1	12.9	6.3	12.8	17.1	20.4
S5	31.3	33.3	22.6	25.0	59.0	60.0	77.6
Cases	16	9	31	32	39	44	54

Notes: S1 = proportion of sons' household divided with their parents' household within the first year of marriage; S5 = proportion of sons' household divided with their parents' household within the fifth year of marriage.

Source: Research sampling survey: married couples 1993.

brother's marriage in Zhuangshang. Different studies (e.g. Potter & Potter 1990, Johnson 1993, Harrell 1993) have shown that the timing of household division may vary according to the different economic incentives of the local economy. It seems that in villages with a subsistence farming economy, where there are no economies of scale, households tend to split apart earlier, while in villages with many entrepreneurial families household division tend to be later. This is closely related to the household strategy of pooling material, monetary, and labour resources within the new economic context, which is reflected in household division of labour (discussed in the next section).

Using large-scale sampling survey data from both two phases of the *In-Depth Fertility Surveys* (IDFS) conducted by State Statistics Bureau of China in cooperation with the Netherlands Demographic Society in 1985 and 1988 respectively, demographers like Dankert *et al.* (1990), Zeng, Li & Ma (1991), Lavely & Ren (1992) show that the duration of co-residence of couples with parents (mostly patrilocal residence) after marriage has declined substantially. The duration of post-marital co-residence is closely related to the timing of household division, and Dankert et al. (1990) show that the duration of co-residence has shrunk over time in both urban and rural areas of Shanxi, Hebei and Shanghai. Furthermore, the IDFS data and the data from survey conducted by Population Institute of Beijing University in rural Hunan and Shanxi, Zeng Yi & Li Xiaoli (1990) show that for these rural areas the percentage of co-residence five years after the marriage in the 1980s is smaller than in the 1970s, and also smaller than in the previous decades. Note that while demographic studies have shown the pattern of post-marital co-residence on a large scale, they fail to explain why the married young with their parents are co-residing for increasingly shorter periods since reform.

Within the village, one task in studying this household division process was to identify the principal decision-makers, and then to consider whether it is economically beneficial for married children to stay with their parents in extended households. Also, as discussed below, increasing participation of young women in decision-making regarding household divisions has instigated earlier household division since reforms. Daughters-in-law usually wish to live apart from their parents, to escape parental interference, especially when generation gaps in ideology and attitudes are large, as has been the case since the introduction of open door policies. Daughters-in-law are said to have *waixin*, acting like centrifugal forces trying to split the original families.

In the village, household divisions can be initiated either by parents or by the married sons or daughters-in-law. They usually do so in different ways. The father (or sometimes the mother), may clearly request household division. The young seldom asked directly for household divisions in the past but would intentionally create problems, pushing the parents to request household division. Parents and married sons (and sometimes also unmarried sons) will be present at the household division meeting. Daughters-in-laws may be absent from the meeting, and their role in the division is mostly through their husbands. They can, however, veto the decision if they consider it unfavourable. Some daughters-in-law are present in the meeting, but usually act as observers and express their ideas to their husbands (who speak on their joint behalf) and only in a few cases do they speak for themselves.

The proportion of women participating in decisions regarding household division has been increasing in the village. The data from the sampling survey shows some (though not a linear) increase in the proportion of daughters-in-law participating in household division decision-making. As Table 6.4 shows, the proportion was high during the Cultural Revolution period (1966–76) and also in the 1990s. From my interviews, it is clear that women have much more say in household division than before. Women also have more leverage in speeding up household division. It is frequently heard that daughters-in-law are clearly initiating the division, which was rare in the past. A daughter-in-law can bargain with her parents-in-law for an earlier household division by not working in her husband's undivided household and staying most of the time in her *niangjia*, her natal family, until the parents-in-law agreed to a household division (see also Judd 1989). This seldom obtained during the collective period. This strategy, namely staying in natal families and not working in their marital families, may well be supported by their natal families, which otherwise would request their daughters to remain with their marital families. Some brides even asked for immediate household division, and living and working separately from their parents-in-law

Table 6.4 Participation of wife and mother in household division for different marriage cohorts

	Until 1959	1960– 64	1965– 69	1970– 74	1975– 79	1980– 84	1985– 89	1990+
Wife								
Yes %	40.0	42.9	58.8	54.6	51.5	58.3	47.7	85.7
No %	60.0	57.1	41.2	45.4	48.5	41.7	52.3	14.3
Cases	10	7	17	22	33	36	44	7
Mother								
Yes %	50.0	80.0	100.0	85.7	100.0	97.1	92.7	83.3
No %	50.0	20.0	0.0	14.3	0.0	2.9	7.3	16.7
Cases	10	5	17	21	33	34	41	6

Source: Research sampling survey: married couples 1993.

upon marriage, and this may be set as one condition for the final marriage ceremony. As discussed, marriage has become extremely costly for men's families, divorced women have become much more accepted, and women after divorce have more alternatives in their living arrangements and work opportunities than previously. Women also may initiate divorce procedures if they are not satisfied with living and working arrangements. Thus women can and do use threats to divorce as a lever in the bargaining processes.

Many parents in the village believe that household division is inevitable nowadays. Parents-in-law mostly follow the wishes of their married children regarding household division, and consider it wise to divide the household early in order to maintain close ties with their sons and daughters-in-law. The older generation also reported that earlier household division saves them a lot of trouble (*shengxin*). Furthermore, daughters-in-law work much harder after they set up their own separate households. They manage their finances much more carefully, and even get support from their natal families.

However, not all sons or daughters-in-law want to have the household divided as quickly as possible. Setting up their own individual households might make the interest relations clear, but the young then must rely on themselves to take care of their agricultural land, find non-agricultural employment and meet their responsibility to provide grain and money to their parents. Though their parents may continue to provide help in the form of field labour and childcare after household division, they are acting only as helpers rather than as principal labourers. For couples where both engage in non-agricultural activities, and especially where these activities are outside the village, an undivided household would be beneficial, since parents would farm their contracted land and care for their children, freeing them for their non-agricultural activities.

The emergence of entrepreneurial families has tended to slow family divisions, despite the growing strength of forces for earlier household division. Such families usually need to pool their labour, material and financial resources to invest in their non-agricultural enterprises. Also, the economic power which the entrepreneurs have gained since the reforms facilitates their ability to keep their married children living with them. Their skills in work, investment and management, their social network, etc. are of benefit to their children; even when married, it is in the couples' interest to stay and work with their parents, who would also have much say in decision-making around household divisions. In the village, the only extended family in the village in 1993 consisted of a couple, their two married sons and their families. The father contracted the village kiln in 1992–93 and the mother and both married sons worked alongside the father.

Household division is closely related to the demand for division of labour, and also to household security and to mobility strategies for making the possible best of family resources and local economic activities. As discussed, households do not necessarily divide until social conflicts within the household becomes too apparent or serious. On the contrary, most households would rather have the household divided before too many conflicts emerge, because the household division clarifies the interest relationship between them, and makes the advantages of cooperation clear. This cooperation in turn, is linked to the reshaped division of labour, which is increasingly demanded for cooperation among family members.

DIVISION OF LABOUR: *NANGONG NUNONG*, WOMEN IN AGRICULTURE AND MEN IN NON-AGRICULTURE

The changing pattern in the household division in the reform periods reflect changing familial relations closely related to the division of labour. The division of labour within peasant households is influenced by past pattern, new opportunities released by structural transformations, strategies adopted by individual households for their security and social mobility, and interwoven traditional and modern ideologies around gender roles in work and life.

Traditionally, women in northern China might do less farm work than men.[7] The idea that 'men take care of the outside world, while women take care of the family' was popular before the Revolution. Some women said that men would feel ashamed if they allowed women to work in the field, because it implied that the men had no capability to feed their wives and children. Women were also socialized to think that they could not and should not work outside the home, as home responsibilities were their only destiny (Chai 1995). Most of them held the idea that '*jiahan jiahan, chuanyi chifan*', meaning that they had to rely on men for their living. Taboos also existed which prohibited women from engaging in certain agriculture work. Women in the past did not plough, till or hoe in the fields, though they were needed to harvest wheat and maize and to pick cotton in the busiest season.

In the collective period, women were encouraged to participate in collective work outside the household. The government continuously stressed the Marxist ideology that women's involvement in social production was of utmost importance to women as a precondition for their liberation and for improvement in their social position. Many women were encouraged to work together with men, under the popular slogan that 'anything a man can do, a woman can also do'.[8] In the village, women did regular work in agriculture which outstripped their previous involvement. Young women in their 20s and 30s worked daily with their male counterparts. Young married women would participate in collective work before they got pregnant. When men were mobilized to contribute their labour outside the village in a big project (e.g. an irrigation project), women were expected to work in the collective to fill the gap created by the withdrawal of men's labour.

However, this did not mean that women had equal access to work possibilities in the collective period. Women were expected to work during harvest season when their labour was much in demand, but not during agricultural slack seasons. Village cadres would not arrange women's labour when there was surplus male labour to be arranged. Women also retired from collective work much earlier than men. Women in their 40s, with children to care for and households chores to do, would quit collective work. Men, however, continued work in their 50s and 60s, to the extent their physical strength permitted. However, retired women still worked intensively in household chores, while men seldom contributed to domestic work.

In the reform period, as discussed in Chapter 4, the available opportunities for husbands and wives and for the old and the young are by no means equal. More husbands than wives, more young people than older people, work in non-agricultural paid jobs, mostly obtained through migration. More young women than older women are working in rural enterprises. The primary agricultural labour force now is comprised mainly of married women, along with the old and the young (Table 6.5).

Since reforms, most new opportunities are in non-agricultural activities. With an increasing level of agricultural technology and

Table 6.5 Work status among husbands and wives

Status	Age				
	20–29	30–39	40–49	50–59	Cases
Husband					
Non-agricultural job out-side for over 1/2 year	58.6	60.6	51.3	26.7	130
Non-agricultural job in or near the village	18.6	25.8	20.0	20.0	52
Agriculture	11.4	6.1	13.7	33.3	33
Others	11.4	7.6	15.0	20.0	31
Total	100	100	100	100	246
Wife					
Non-agricultural job out-side for over 1/2 year	4.2	3			
Non-agricultural job in or near the village	5.6	6.2	4.7	12	
Agriculture	87.3	92.3	91.7	87.5	220
Others	2.8	1.5	3.6	12.5	9
Total	100	100	100	100	244

Source: Research sampling survey: married couples 1993.

declining per capita arable land, there is less demand for labour in agriculture. Villagers employ less manual labour for agricultural work, and some paid jobs have emerged in agriculture. For example, villagers usually obtain the services of the owners of big agricultural machinery like tractors and threshing machines, to plough their fields, and to plant and thresh their wheat; and they pay for both the labour and a 'machine depreciation charge'. All providers of such services are men whose families either own the machinery, or co-own the machinery with other families.

Although the proportion of women ever having had paid jobs is still lower than that of men for every age group from 20 to 59, the notable change is that the younger women have increasingly had some sort of paid job. Women's increasing involvement in paid work is mainly due to the rapid development of non-agricultural enterprises in the village or in near-by villages. The gap between women and men involved in non-agricultural paid jobs is becoming smaller. As Table 6.6 shows, at present nearly 60 per cent of women in their 20s have had paid work, as had nearly 78 per cent of their male counterparts. Among those in their 50s, many more men than women take advantage of available paid job opportunities. These proportions do not, however, reflect another critical difference, namely that paid jobs for men are normally their primary activity, while paid jobs might be secondary activities for women. Thus men spend much more time in their non-agricultural paid jobs than women do. Though some young women may work on a long-term basis, other women may work temporarily, mostly in agricultural slack seasons.

One consequence of the new forms of division of labour in the reform period is the intensification of family labour. While male labour, especially unskilled labour (e.g. in construction) must engage daily in 10 or 12 hours of intensive work outside the household, women take every opportunity available to work. Though household

Table 6.6 Proportion of husbands and wives who have ever had a paid job

Age group	Yes	No	Cases
Husband			
20–29	77.8	22.2	63
30–39	91.2	8.8	68
40–49	85.5	14.5	83
50–59	76.2	23.8	21
Wife			
20–29	59.4	40.6	64
30–39	37.7	62.3	69
40–49	33.3	66.7	84
50–59	24.0	76.0	25

Source: Research sampling survey: married couples 1993.

chores were still intensive during the collective period, many women say that they are working harder since the reforms. Women must now remain on the contracted land and work intensively in household sidelines, when they are also responsible for domestic labour. Some manual labour which during the collective period was believed to be inappropriate for women and was usually done by men, is presently being done by women instead.

The more intensive labour for women does not necessarily mean they work longer in the fields. On the contrary, women now work in the fields for fewer months of the year than during the commune system. Under the collective system, low work efficiency, lower agricultural input, relatively more land and sometimes the construction of agricultural infrastructure, kept peasants working almost all the year round. Many villagers said labour during the commune system was not so hard but time consuming. Since reform, the absolute time people spend working in the fields is much less, due to higher level of agricultural technology and smaller plots of land available for rural households.

Women spend much of the time saved from fieldwork either on other income-earning activities such as keeping more pigs, chickens, or on providing necessary help to men in their activities, or working temporarily in village enterprises while also caring for the children and the old, and performing household chores. At present, many women can work in the fields while taking care of children at the same time. Though some children can be cared for by mothers-in-law, other women may take care of their children alone or leave them with their neighbours for part of the time. These women enjoy their independence and do not want their mothers-in-law involved in many of their decisions. Women having difficulties taking care of their children by themselves will usually ensure that their husbands stay and work in the village. Men did little domestic work during the collective period, but are increasingly willing to share some domestic work, though not equally with their wives. Men fetch water, clean the yard, play with children and sometimes help in cooking.

In summary, a new division of labour was defined after reform. Women have not quit their participation in the economic activities; they have not returned to the home. They have been exhorted to come out of the domestic sphere and to participate in economic work since 1949, and it would be impossible to push women back into purely domestic labour. In any case, they have become the primary and indispensable force in agriculture. This is a substantive change. Men who wish to pursue non-agricultural activities must rely on women to cultivate the land. At the same time, relying on the grain market for income is too risky and the profit margin too low, and households with both men and women working in agriculture are economically poor. Cooperation among family members is more necessary now than ever before. Such cooperation within the family takes place most often between young couples rather than between young sons and their parents, especially when the parent is less competitive in the labour market because of physical weakness or low level of education. At the same time, cooperation among brothers will mostly be problematic, since traditionally they would form their own families and earn their own separate livings. Long before the division of the household they are already preparing for their future families.

INTRA- AND INTER-FAMILY RELATIONS

Intra-family relations: Continuing shift of core family relations from father and son to husband and wife

The increasingly significant role of women in agricultural and non-agricultural work in the reform period does not necessarily improve women's position within the household, as was shown by Parish & Whyte (1978) in collective Guangdong. Women's position within the household depends also on the nature of the division of the labour and changes in the relevant institutions such as marriage and marital transfers in the reform period.

New forms of division of labour reflect increasing interdependence between husbands and wives rather than between the old and the young. This can be best revealed by looking at what would change for one person's well-being without the cooperation of the others. During the collective period, many functions of the peasant household were largely taken over by the collective. Household labour was arranged by the collective's leaders rather than by the household head. Each individual labourer earned work points and received both grain and cash which was distributed, however, to household heads. The collective policies favoured the least productive and the elderly. Minimum allowance ensured that families with less labour for earning sufficient work points received a monthly quota of grain. The elderly, and those who had lost their ability to undertake labour, were helped by the collective. Others who had difficulties with certain jobs would be assigned appropriate work to ensure their income and basic living security. Each family member, labourer or dependent, were guaranteed a supply of grain through the ration system. In this sense, peasants relied much more on the collective than on other family members in the collective era.

The above principle applied to widows but not always to divorced women. Divorced women would usually not stay in their husbands' villages but would go back to their natal villages, as they had no other alternatives. Whether they were accepted or not depended to a great extent on the initiative of local cadres and the social position held by their natal families. Married women who returned to their natal villages were regarded as outsiders. They would not be welcomed back to share the limited collective resources. Women thus relied heavily on their husbands and on their marital families in the collective period. Further, the household heads, usually the older working males, received the grain and cash distributed by the collective, which reinforced their patriarchal power. The young and young mothers with children, would rely on their mothers and mothers-in-law to take care of children so that they could work in the collective and earn work points.

Since the reforms, the young, who are both more educated and physically stronger, are more successful in finding non-agricultural opportunities through migration than are older villagers. Young migrants receive their income directly from the employers. Whether they remit money to their parents depends on whether they are married and, if married, whether the family has been divided. Parents still have much authority over their unmarried children; parents may arrange their labour and their earnings usually go to their parents. However, this is mainly because children cannot pay the tremendously high marriage expenses by themselves. Once married, they keep part, if not most or all, of the money earned. They would not contribute wholeheartedly to the whole household. Daughters-in-law generally retain all their earnings. Before household division, most sons contribute a share of their income to the household, while daughters-in-law will retain their income and would not hand it over to the household head to be pooled as part of household finance.

Traditionally the primary familial relation is between father and son and the dyadic relationship between mother-in-law and daughter-in-law is subject to, and attached to, the father-son relationship. Many other studies have shown the subordinate position of the daughter-in-law within the family (e.g., Yang 1959). Collectivization eroded the economic basis for the patriarchal power of the father and the old generation, and daughters-in-law ceased to be the family servants (Parish & Whyte 1978). However, it is also true that in the collective period the earnings of the young were controlled by the male household head, women had few independent opportunities, and their claim to collective resources and work opportunities was subject to their attachment to the husbands' family. Furthermore, divorce for women was socially unaccepted and it was difficult to remarry. In this situation, women had to work hard, bear sons, and wait their turn to become mothers-in-law, the main change that would improve their positions within the family.

In the village, the patriarchal power of father over son, husband over wife (also mother-in-law over daughter-in-law) has been further eroded in the reform period. An adult son in the collective period could take either his parents' side or his wife's side in conflicts between parents-in-law and daughter-in-law. Now he is often on his wife's side rather than on his parents'. This is understandable since husbands are more involved in selecting their own wives and since they have frequent contacts before marriage. Older parents complain that the unmarried young, who have paid jobs, do not listen to them as the young did in the past. Older parents also accuse their married sons of being *buxiao*, 'not filial', and *qiguanyan*, controlled strictly by their wives. They complain that even before household division young couples, including husbands, may help the wife's natal family with their harvest, although their labour is much in demand within the husband's family. The old believe that the young no longer know the family rules (*budong guiju*) since the introduction of the open-door policies. Contrary to the traditional situation, parents may find they have to give in when there are conflicts with the daughter-in-law. In the words of an old man from the village, now the old have only 'the empty box without the seal'.

Since the reforms, women became free to move around; it is also easier for them to stay in their natal families. They may now give help in their natal family's responsibility fields, or in household sidelines. As mentioned, if they prefer to have earlier household divisions, they go back to their natal families more often and stay there for long periods, without contributing their labour to their parents-in-law's household economy. The proximity of brides to their natal families among marriages which have taken place in the village in recent years makes going back to their natal families and getting their support much easier. Parents-in-law are annoyed if daughters-in-law visit their natal families too often. However, they have fewer means to prevent them. Further, the increasing bargaining power of women and the young is making earlier household division possible, and the continuing nuclearization of the family is eroding the patriarchal family system. In short, the traditional primary relationship in the family is gradually changing from the father-son relationship to husband-wife relationship.

The continuing shift of the core familial relations from between father and son to between husband and wife is not only due to the increasing demand for cooperation between couples, as the village and region's economic structure is transformed; other factors are also strengthening husband-wife relations and reinforcing cooperation within couples. The young have more open intimate relations than do older generations. They can sometimes show their intimate affections in front of others, which older couples would never have done. The education gap within young couples is also significantly less than in older couples; older women had far less education than men (see Chapter 4). Thanks to their new freedom to arrange their time, their education, and their exposure to urban culture, the young can develop more intimate relations between themselves, than the customary and hierarchical relations between parents and adult children.

A number of recent changes in marriage practices in the village have affected the character of the relationship between spouses and women's positions in their husbands' families. The smaller marriage circle and increasing cooperation between married daughters and their natal families mean that women get needed support from their natal families more easily than they did before. This is useful, since women may still find it difficult to bargain with their husbands' family members, especially when they are newly married and do not know other family members well. Furthermore, the increasing dowry and the trend toward the equalization of the dowry-brideprice ratio also empower women greatly. This levelling of the dowry-brideprice ratio means brides contribute directly and significantly to their newly created family. Part of the dowry is indirect dowry, which is specifically women's property and women can take this with them if they divorce. The brideprice has lost the meaning of exchanging labour between men of two families (as posited by Parish & Whyte 1978 in their studies of collective Guangdong villages). Divorce means a loss of men's rather than women's property. Women are increasingly more able to initiate a divorce.

One consequence of the increasing bargaining power of women is that a higher proportion of family income is controlled by women. The proportion of women managing family finance is higher for young generations than for older ones. Table 6.7 shows that family finance managed either by women or by husband and wife together reached 55.7 per cent for women in the age group of 20–29, while that of age group 50–59 is 40 per cent. Now women do not need to save their private money (*sifangqian*) secretly, without their husbands' knowledge, since they have the needed money at hand for their daily use.

Women are playing increasingly larger roles in household decision-making, and are usually involved in decisions such as how much grain should be sold in the free market, when to build a house, or whether the household should buy a television set or a thresher. They do not need to follow the will of their husbands on these matters. Husbands and wives are inclined to consult with each other on the purchase of expensive durable consumer goods, input of money in agriculture, building houses and in other major investments. Some

Table 6.7 Financial management in the family

	Age group			
	20–29	30–39	40–49	50–59
Husband	23.0	34.3	34.9	51.4
Wife	29.5	43.3	32.5	31.4
Husband & wife	26.2	14.9	28.9	8.6
Father	6.6	3.0	1.2	2.9
Mother	11.5	0.0	0.0	2.9
Others	3.3	4.5	2.4	2.9
Total	100.0	100.0	100.0	100.0
Cases	61	67	83	35

Source: Research sampling survey: married couples 1993.

young husbands find they would be in trouble if they have made decisions alone, especially when they send money to their elderly parents without first consulting with their wives.

Macroeconomic reforms vary in their influence on women in different families. With the improved post-reform situation of women and their increasing bargaining power in the household in general, two other trends coexist. One concerns women in the rich, usually entrepreneurial households; and the other concerns women in poor households. In these families, where resources tend to be controlled by men and the division of labour favour men over women, patriarchal power of men over women in the household seems to be reinforced.

Chinese society is still a male-centred society. Not only do the macro structural transformations and changing labour market bring more opportunities for men, inherited tradition keeps most women at home or at least within the village, even when opportunities for women become available. The most economically successful households, are those headed by men with non-agricultural investment and management skills and a strong social network, who have taken advantage of the new opportunities to run their own enterprises, contract collective enterprises or find well-paid non-agricultural work. The family representatives who contract the village kiln, or run shops or small factories are usually men. Women entrepreneurs are few. Only one woman had primary responsibility for her enterprise, a charcoal kiln; temporary employees called her (instead of her husband) 'jingli', the manager. In the rich families of the village, where men are the household heads, women's living condition has improved; however, their bargaining power has not increased accordingly. The young, including daughters-in-law in the family, cannot possibly challenge the position of the elderly males.

Most poor families work only in agriculture, lacking the labour or necessary social connections to engage in non-agricultural activities. Families with many children to care for also lag behind others economically, because wives have difficulties combining agriculture and childcare; they rely on their husbands, who then cannot migrate out for work. As mentioned, poor families cannot even borrow money to get their children married, since they simply have no power to repay. They resort to a kind of 'exchange marriage' (huanhun), to escape the burden of high brideprice and marriage expenses (see Chapter 5). In these families, daughters who have already formed romantic attachments elsewhere either must follow their parents' arrangements or run away. However, young women who elope or marry without proper introduction are looked down upon and face many difficulties if they encounter problems with their parents-in-law and their husbands later on. Young women who attempt to elope are usually caught and persuaded to return to their natal families. The situation of these young women has not improved in the reform period.

Women purchased as wives from other provinces through 'monetary' or 'mercenary' marriage also face quite challenging situations. Without any social network in the locality and no access to support from their natal families, they have little decision-making power within the household. Sometimes their free movement is restricted because families try to prevent them from running away. As mentioned in Chapter 5, though the government has tried hard to eliminate mercenary marriage, it has nevertheless re-emerged in some rural areas. Many women purchased as wives are also illiterate, and are thus restricted in many ways from getting support.

Inter-family relations: Conflicts, competition and cooperation

New forms of division of labour and intra-family relations partly explain earlier household divisions and family nuclearization processes. The simplified family structure seems not to correspond with the increasing security demand in the reform period. However, kinship relations and family clans have been reinvigorated. Such reinvigoration is also a result of the increasing demand for cooperation that will lead towards social mobility. Cooperation happens not only among households of close patriarchal kin (though this is the major form of cooperation) but also increasingly between husbands' families and wives' natal families. Also, other cooperation systems have developed between households of neighbours or friends. Some of these might set up sworn kin relations to strengthen their ties. The close kin, like brothers' households and parent's households, cooperate by pooling their labour, land, capital and other resources, to form what Croll (1987b, 1994) termed aggregate families: new forms of association or cooperation based on economic and socio-political links and exchanges. It is this aggregate family that enables the household to meet security and mobility demands. Households meet part of security and mobility demands, with other needs provided for by close kin, neighbours, friends as well as formal governmental institutions. The new arrangement for security and mobility makes it possible for people to maintain useful ties while living in small, nuclear families.

New forms of cooperation between households of close kin have many advantages compared to remaining within big and complex households. In small households, conflicts among members are minimized, and interest relations are easily clarified. Management of household economy is also much easier in small households. Economic cooperation is based on voluntary participation, rather than the obligatory participation required in joint households. Thus the pooling of resources is usually partial and considers the capabilities of each unit and the likely benefits.

For example, in the village, several married brothers, who have formed their own households, may contribute money to purchase one or two pieces of agricultural machinery like a thresher, tractor, or water pump. Agricultural machinery is so costly that it is inefficient a machine is purchased and used by a single household. Households also pool their labour, mainly in planting and harvesting during agriculture busy seasons, when many labourers are needed and it is more efficient to work together as a team. Even in the daily management of fields, labour from different households might be exchanged among themselves and people might work together to resolve the loneliness of working separately. When young mothers are too busy to keep an eye on their small children and there are no other household members available to take care of the children, they leave their children with their close kin like a grandmother, aunt or cousin who might be free. Agricultural products and outputs from their separate responsibility fields is the entitlement of individual households, though they might work together from plantation to harvest and from one household's individual responsibility field to the other's field.

Other forms of household cooperation includes pooling capital for certain investments in rural non-agricultural enterprises, like running department stores, transportation, brick kilns, etc. This ensures sufficient funds for investment and also spreads the risks. While running a department store or purchasing vehicles and engaging in transportation usually involves two or three households, cooperation for contracting brick kilns would involve many more households. The village brick kiln was contracted by two groups in 1993. Each group comprised over ten households, divided by subgroups. Management, production, and distribution in such an arrangement are complex.

Some households of non-close kin would like to strengthen their relations to insure better cooperation by set up informal kin relations, by arranging for the sons or daughters to become sworn brothers or sisters. Setting up sworn relations is not new. However, the significant changes are that the proportion of sworn brothers or sisters is increasing, while the ages of the people involved are decreasing. Sworn relationships formerly involved adults, and now involve children and are increasingly arranged by parents.

In addition to increasing cooperation, competition and conflicts among peasant households are also increasing. For example, the two department stores located side by side in the village centre compete with each other. The two groups of households who contract the same collective kiln must cooperate by using the same kiln and sometimes employing the same expert for managing the kiln. At least one serious conflict occurred between the two groups during my fieldwork, and this was mediated through village cadres and through strong men in the village. Conflicts can easily arise in production processes, and these are more noticeable since decollectivization and are especially likely when groups are making use of collective resources. Crops and agricultural products, which belong to individual households, are easily damaged or stolen, and this creates tensions and conflicts among peasants households; such problems were uncommon during the commune era, when crops and products were collectively owned and managed.

Conflicts also arise among households in cooperation, and can occur among households of close kin, within aggregate families or within same lineage and same family clans. For example, the plastic factory was set up after the owner had disagreements with his kin, who cooperated to run the enterprise in the county town. Several households who contracted brick kilns outside the village broke their relations after the unfair distribution of the profits.

Households and families experienced many changes in the village in the move from pre-reform collective to post-reform mixed economy. This is partly manifested in the changes of household size and household composition: households continue to be smaller in size and simpler in structure. Demographic factors may well contribute to other changes in rural Chinese households and families (termed as 'demographic determinism' by Lavely & Ren 1992). Most importantly, socio-economic forces, which determine division of labour within households and patterns of household division, have further influenced household composition and structures.

In general, new economic freedom and newly available economic opportunities, together with limited land resources (relative to China's population), have shaped an economic structure which favours small nuclear households rather than big extended families. Since reform, women and men, and the young and the old, are in different situations and face different sets of opportunities and risks. The new institutional environment and individual responses and strategies to adapt the environment have redefined the division of labour. Women are increasingly responsible for agriculture and its sidelines and men mainly engage in non-agricultural activities. Women's contribution to household economy is increasingly important, partly because of the intensification of labour and diversification of income sources after the reforms. Women's labour has become increasingly indispensable in the household under the new gender division of labour. However, the continuing belief that women naturally belong within or close to the family (e.g. within the village) restricts them from making use of some of the opportunities available. The changing economic structure and social division of labour shape family relations, i.e. family structures, at present.

As households become smaller and nuclearized, inter-family relations, among families in the same clan and among husbands and wives' families have been strengthened. Women have much more contact with their natal families, as they exchange labour and pool capital and other resources for investment. Cooperation among certain families also means competition and conflicts with others. This also goes hand in hand with the increasing differentiation among the households. Changes in both intra-familial and inter-familial relations will influence household fertility decisions within the family and interactions in fertility decisions among families and local cadres.

Notes

[1] Kelkar (1985, 1990) postulates that the greater participation of women in the household contract system after the reforms is insufficient either for women's control over the products of their labour or for a high social valuation to be assigned to their participation, since this is dependent upon already existing structural arrangements for the management of the rural economy which is in the hands of men. Davin (1988) and Robinson (1985) believe that responsibility systems actually reinforce both the role of household heads (who are usually older, experienced men) and male-female inequality. Also, Aslanbeigui & Summerfield argue that the shift to the household as a production unit may affect the division of income among the individual members of the household. They conclude that by reinforcing the traditional arrangements in the Chinese economy, women's bargaining power and hence their entitlements may decrease, affecting their development and capabilities (Aslanbeigui & Summerfield 1989, Summerfield & Aslanbeigui 1992, Summerfield 1994). See Zhang 1998 for more detailed debates.

[2] It should be noted that the object of my population census conducted in the village in early 1993 is *de jure* population which include institutional members of the families in the village (see Chapter 3), which is different from *de facto* population, the object of the official population census. However the gap is small (less than 3 per cent of the village population). The data from my own census and from the official census are presented together here to show the changing pattern (in household size and composition) rather than to compare exact numbers. If institutional members are excluded from my population census, the declining household size and nuclearization of household structure becomes even more significant.

[3] The others include two men, one single and one divorced.

[4] The national life expectancy increased from 68.0 in 1982 to 68.5 in 1990 according to government population censuses in the two years respectively (CASS 1988: 709, SSB 1995: 70).

[5] The following household division contract made in 1988 divided a household that had consisted of parents, two sons and one grandparent. Division of the household was initialized by the father after the first son married but before the second son did so, though the daughter-in-law also intended to have the family divided. The daughter-in-law had a serious disagreement with her mother-in-law on the division of household property, before the father made a decision to call a meeting to arrange household division. Four people from outside the family were invited, all of them respected and powerful men in the village. Relatives from the mother's side, who would normally have been asked to act as mediators in such household divisions, were not called in, because the daughter-in-law disagreed. The text of the contract was as follows:

> People concerned with the contract: father (with red stamp), the first son (name with finger print), and the second son (name with finger print)
>
>> Because of inconvenience of living together, today we discuss and decide the division of household property once and for all in the presence of the invited people. The old house with five *jian* rooms in the east yard in which the grandparent will live until she passes away, and another three *jian* rooms in Huang XX's courtyard, and

one new housing plot with the trees planted there, belong to the first son. The new house with five *jian* rooms in the west yard in which the parents will live until they pass away, three adjacent rooms, and the trees inside the yard, belong to the second son. The two sons, in turn, provide yearly 500 *jin* of wheat, 100 *jin* of maize, 40 *jin* of millet, 12 *jin* of edible oil, 20 *jin* of sweet potato flour noodle, 3,000 *jin* of coal and monthly pocket money of 10 *yuan* to the grandparent, which will be evenly shared by the two sons. Parents are provided with yearly 1,000 *jin* of wheat, 200 *jin* of maize, 100 *jin* of millet, 16 *jin* of edible oil, 4,000 *jin* of coal, 30 *jin* of noodle and monthly pocket money of 12 *yuan*. Expenses on health care, and on burials when the grandparent and parents pass away, will be shared evenly by the two sons. The needed care of the grandparent and parents will be taken by the two sons in turn. After the grandparent and parents pass away, the furniture they used will be evenly divided among the two sons. The above arrangement are clarified and agreed without regret among those concerned, and supervised by the present witness. Contracts are written to be kept by each party, since there is no proof by oral agreement.

Signed by witnesses
Date: 13 April 1988 (Chinese calendar)

[6] The life table technique is used to calculate the proportions of the marriage cohort 1985–89, because some couples would have their household divided from that of the parents within the fifth year of their marriage, which would not have been captured by the sampling survey conducted in 1993 (before the end of the fifth year). The marriage cohorts of the 1990s are not included since there were so few.

[7] Buck (1937: 291–2), investigating the percentage of farm work done by different groups in northern China, estimated that circa 1930 men performed 80 per cent of all the farm labour in China; women, 13 per cent; and children, 7 per cent (quoted in Parish & Whyte 1978: 187). Judd, however, suspects that women might have done more work in the period than the data has suggested. See Judd (1990: 199–200).

[8] Some scholars, however, have argued that the Chinese Communist Party lacked the will (e.g., Johnson 1983) or the theoretical insight (e.g., Stacey 1983) to push through significant gender reforms. The issue is beyond the scope of the study.

CHAPTER 7

Inter-generational Obligations and Fertility Motivation

The context in which people work and live has profound implications on individual fertility perception and motivation. Peasants, whose family and community contexts are rapidly changing, will adapt, and this will include taking available opportunities, covering contingencies, and adjusting childbearing patterns as long-term strategies in their lives.

This chapter will first discuss the changing roles of children shaped by the changing institutional context, and it will then consider family members' changing perceptions of and motivations for childbearing since reform. Many factors influence fertility perceptions and motivations. Family clan, community, family planning programmes, migration, exposure to urban culture, etc., all influence fertility perception in many different ways. However, this chapter will concentrate mainly on the mutual responsibilities and obligations between parents and children, on their social relations, and on how these factors influence fertility perception. Contextual changes in the roles of children, as identified in the fieldwork, concern childbearing and childcare, children's education and labour, children's roles as sources of insurance, security, social mobility, support and care of the aged, and their responsibility for burials. The fertility-related perceptions and motivations can be seen not only in terms of number of children, but also in sex composition and the timing of childbearing.

CHANGING ROLES OF CHILDREN WITHIN THE FAMILY: PRE-REFORM AND POST-REFORM PERIOD

The mutual responsibilities and obligations between children and parents can be divided roughly according to the following life stages: (a) births, (b) rearing and educating children, (c) children's contribution to household economy, risk aversion and social mobility, (d) children's marriage, (e) support of elderly parents, and (f) burial of the deceased parents. In rural Chinese society, the responsibilities and obligations of parents to children are mainly to raise them, get them educated, and get them married; and those of children to their parents are to contribute their labour to the household economy, to provide various kinds of insurance and security, especially when the parents are elderly, and arrange their eventual funerals and burials.

Childbearing and childcare

Childbirths are important events. Pregnant women are referred to as *youxi*, i.e., having happiness. Traditionally a child must be born in the father's family. Women were not allowed to give birth in other homes. It was believed that doing so would damage family property and bring bad luck to the family in whose house the child was born. At present, many women still give birth at home though some give births in hospitals. However, as family planning programmes have intensified, couples desiring 'unplanned births' usually arrange for the pregnant wives to stay in the families of their kin in other villages or towns, where their children are born. The traditional notion of a place where children *must* be born has broken down.

The cost of childbearing and childcare increased tremendously after economic reforms. Having increased their standard of living by earning more income, parents tend to spend more on childbearing and childrearing. They also pay prenatal care and the assistance of midwives or doctors to attend the births of their children (see Chapter 4), and they also spend more when celebrating childbirths.

Further, the increasing cost of having children is not only because parents can afford to spend more for their children's health, food, clothes, and other necessities; it is also because some of the costs of having children which used to be shared by the collective have now shifted to individual households. For example, a part of health care costs for both mothers and children in the collective period were (though less adequately) partly taken care of by the collectives. In the collective era, although the village's health care cooperative existed only for two years at the beginning of the 1970s, a household with a seriously ill member could be subsidised in many ways. The collective might cover part of the cost if it was too much for a household to pay, or the collective could lend money to the household; the collective could also lend grain to a household facing difficulties because of illness. At present, individual families must pay for health care for both parents and children by themselves; the same is true for education.

The care of children is mainly women's responsibility, although men are now willing to help when they stay at home. They say this willingness is because they cannot have many children like before, and children have become much more precious. In fact, and most importantly, men's beginning involvement with the care of their children is an indication of the changing relationship between husbands and wives since reform (discussed in Chapter 6). Men can no longer ignore household-based chores, including childcare, since daughters-in-law, wishing to be independent, may be reluctant to rely on their mothers-in-law for childcare, when they have asked for an early household division.

Education of children

Having children educated is the responsibility of parents. In the late 1970s, the state reiterated that students entering the government's higher education system enrol through entrance examination. This opens the possibility for children to continue their education and has encouraged many parents to invest in their children's education. From statistics collected by the director of the village junior school, there were 34 students (15 male and 19 female) entering into professional school or college between 1987 and 1992. Opening up non-agricultural opportunities also helped peasants realize the importance of education. For utilizing the newly-available opportunities, primary and junior high school education is a must. At present, the highest aspiration for rural children is to get a formal university or mid-level professional education which would lead to a formal and stable job in an urban area. Second choice is a non-agricultural job in an urban area, though this is usually temporary and unsecured. The least attractive option is to stay in the village and work in farming as a field-hand.

However, the education of children is becoming increasingly costly. Students did not pay registration fees in the collective era. The school started to collect registration fees after reforms began, and the fee has been increasing. In addition, students must pay for books and stationary (both much more expensive than before) and must also pay for the school's electricity, coal, pupil's insurance, and so on, all of which were taken care by the collective in the past. Furthermore, junior school students are now required to buy student uniforms. In 1993, the yearly cost for a primary school student was approximately 60 *yuan*, and over 100 *yuan* for a junior high school student.

It seems that a major reason that students drop out of school is their poor performance, or parents' belief that their children cannot enter professional school and continue their education. However, although children themselves prefer to stay in school, students from poor households are more likely to drop out, given the increasing costs of education and the increasing demand for their labour. The cost to educate one child may not be too much, but families with three or more children at school at the same time could find costs overwhelming. Better-off families want their children to finish their junior middle school education. Some rich families whose children have graduated from junior middle school but fail to pass the entrance examination for professional school education or to continue their education in senior high school, expect their children to review their courses and retake the exams. In 1993, there were 18 such students from rich families. Their parents said they would not mind paying money for their children's education if they pass the entrance examination and continue.

Investing in the education of girls has become more significant than before, though there is still strong preference to invest in boys. It is true that at present more girls have dropped out of school, and at earlier ages. However, many girls were not sent to school at all in the collective period (see Chapter 4). The parental attitude toward children's education is now a willingness to support a child for higher and professional education if the child can pass the examination, whether they are boys or girls. This attitude is differentiated among rich and poor households however, with the rich providing as much (or even more) support to daughters as to sons. Among the 18 junior middle school graduates who were reviewing their courses in order to retake higher education entrance examinations in 1993, 11 were boys and 7 were girls.[1] In one case, an economically better-off family sent their daughter to a professional school for education because she passed the entrance examination, but only as self-financed student.[2]

Children as labour

Grown-up children help in the household and contribute to the household economy. Since reform, the duration and intensity of adult labour have increased. Children are needed to help with household chores in order to relieve the burden of their parents, who are engaging in economic activities. Household chores like cleaning the house, taking care of other siblings, taking care of the elderly or the sick, washing clothes, cooking, and shopping, etc., are mostly done by girls. Most boys never cook or wash clothes. Some children, starting as early as age six or seven, also help in the fields, pulling weeds, caring for cotton, tending a few sheep, etc. By age eleven, some children begin to help harvesting wheat. Young children can help a great deal, especially during the harvest season, doing lighter but tedious jobs, saving much of their parents' labour for heavy work, especially when parents cannot get help from others, who are busy with their own work during harvest seasons. Some children can even engage in non-agricultural paid jobs. For example, a few work in the fields or in the streets selling ice cream or soda water in summer and melon or sunflower seeds in other seasons when they are off from school. Many parents reported that children now work in the fields or provide help at home at earlier ages and that child labour intensified after the introduction of reforms. Table 7.1 shows that the youngest to begin work in the field or at home for the 6–14 age group is younger than for cohorts aged 15 and over at the time of the study.[3]

Boys and girls who drop out of school help in household chores, and engage in agricultural or non-agricultural activities (see Table 7.2).

Table 7.1 Numbers of children doing regular work, age of beginning work
(youngest case) and average age of beginning

Age group Activity	No. of children	Mean age beginning work	Age of beginning (youngest case)
6–14 years old			
Watering fields	18	11.6	9
Hoeing fields	20	11.7	8
Cutting wheat	32	11.5	8
Threshing wheat	65	· 9.9	6
Planting corn	37	10.3	6
Applying pesticides	3	12.7	12
Fertilizing	43	10.4	6
Pulling weeds	87	9.6	6
Pulling carts	25	9.0	7
Selling small commodities	6	9.7	7
Fetching water	28	11.0	8
Washing clothes	57	9.7	6
Preparing meals	71	9.9	6
Cleaning yard	116	8.1	4
Taking care of siblings	90	7.3	4
Taking care of the sick	21	9.1	6
Shopping	126	6.6	4
15 and over			
Watering fields	18	12.2	10
Hoeing fields	13	12.4	11
Cutting wheat	15	12.3	11
Threshing wheat	28	12.0	7
Planting corn	18	11.4	6
Applying pesticides	5	12.8	12
Fertilizing	21	12.0	7
Pulling weeds	31	10.6	6
Pulling carts	9	10.3	7
Selling small commodities	1	10.0	10
Fetching water	9	11.9	10
Washing clothes	31	10.8	7
Preparing meals	34	11.1	7
Cleaning yard	57	9.0	6
Taking care of siblings	42	8.5	6
Taking care of the sick	10	9.4	7
Shopping	61	8.0	5

Source: Research sampling survey: the young 1993.

Girls who drop out might work in the village brick kiln, if others can
take care of the household chores and agriculture work in the household. Most of them do the physical job of making bricks. They
transfer the clay to the brick kiln machine, and transfer the ready-
made bricks to be dried and stored. This is heavy physical work;
usually they work about 10 hours and earn 4 or 5 *yuan* per day. Only

Table 7.2 Main activities of children immediately after dropping out of school

Activities	Boys (per cent)	Girls (per cent)
Household chores	4.3	5.0
Care of young siblings[a]	4.3	0.0
Care of the elderly or the sick	0.0	0.0
Agricultural fieldwork	13.0	45.0
Paid job in the village	8.7	25.0
Paid job outside, but live in the village	8.7	15.0
Paid job outside and live outside	30.4	0.0
Other[b]	30.4	10.0

Notes: The sample included 23 boys and 20 girls.

a. One boy and no girls reported this as their main activity immediately after dropping out of school. However, this does not mean that boys are more likely to drop out in order to take care of their young siblings than are girls. Instead, this is a sampling error due to the small sample size.

b. 'Other' includes activities like learning martial arts, travelling, simply doing nothing, and also the lack of clear response.

Source: Research sampling survey: the young 1993.

unmarried young girls or married women from poor households do this work. Boys, whether they drop out or graduate, may also work at the brick kiln, or seek work outside the village in construction in urban areas.

In the past children's labour was less important because there were few labour opportunities within the collective. Child labour at earlier ages was not accepted by the collective, which already had labour surplus problems. Also, work time in the collective was fixed, and children could not easily attend school and work at the same time. Furthermore, children earned so few work points (much less than an adult labourer) that parents were reluctant to send their children to work at earlier ages. The youngest labour allowed in the collective was by 15– and 16–year-olds, and they received only half the work points earned by adults. Only children from poor households, or households with insufficient labourers, worked in the collective while still young.

At present, although children's labour is important, the demand for boys' and girls' labour within peasant households differs. Parents place more restrictions and limitations on girls' labour; parents worry if daughters work alone in the vast area of agricultural fields, especially in the evening. This was not a problem in the collective era, when women and men from the same production team worked together, or at least in groups when men and women did jobs separately. Also, many parents are reluctant to let their daughters work and live outside the village, even when opportunities are available. The sampling survey of the young shows that majority of young girls who dropped out of school did non-agricultural jobs in the village, or in nearby villages but lived at home (see Table 7.2). Nearly half of the girls who drop out do agricultural work at home, and a quarter of them do some paid work, mainly in the village brick kiln enterprise. Very few perform paid work outside the village.[4] Parents not only worry that their daughters might be attacked by bad men, but also worry that their daughters might have premarital sex. Parents make strong efforts to prevent this from happening, because if it did they would lose face, and it could be difficult for the daughter to marry well if the news spread.

The value of the labour of both daughters and sons has changed since reform. Traditionally it was believed that a married daughter, like water poured out on the ground, was useless to her natal parents. As discussed in Chapter 5, in the collective period a daughter's labour was almost immediately lost upon her marriage. However, since the reforms, it is quite easy for a married daughter to come back and help her natal family. Many young brides now stay in their natal families before having their first child, while their husbands leave the village for paid jobs; this was not possible during the collective period. Meanwhile, a son's income is mostly controlled by his parents before marriage. Few sons complain about this arrangement, since they must rely on the whole household to finance their marriages. Earnings from sons before their marriages are insufficient to cover marriage costs; yet after sons marry, parents have much less ability to control their earnings or their labour. A son who marries early means less of the son's labour will be under parental control.

Children's roles as source of insurance, security and social mobility

Children have multiple roles as insurance, security, and social mobility to parents, and these roles also vary in different life stages. Children can increase the share of community resources. They can take up available work opportunities for increasing their security and social mobility. They can share and·spread their risks. They can set up alliances to gain strength and power. They can also provide support to their parents in old ages.

Children's role in sharing community resources and work opportunities

Increasing the number of children may be one way a family can claim a greater share of community resources and work opportunities vital for household security and social mobility. In the collective era, most community resources such as land were collectively owned, and exploitation of community resources was collectively arranged, although limited private plots and housing plots were assigned on a per capita bases. A ration system was used for distribution of basic life necessities like grain, sugar, oil, wine, cloth, coal, and so on. Because the grain ration was not always sufficient for consumption by adults, some couples wanted more children so that they could use the grain ration distributed to children to compensate for the insufficiency of the adult ration, and to get a greater share of other daily necessities. There used to be a saying in the village in the collective period that 'to work is no better than to have a child'. Work opportunities were provided rather evenly among labourers. The number of labourers, and the ratio of labourers to dependants in the household was a major determinant of household income and livelihood. Therefore, though household and family depended on the collective for their security, their upward social mobility depended heavily on the number of labourers available in the individual households.

The ration system was abolished in the reform era, and although land in theory is still collectively owned, usufruct rights are assigned to individuals. The contracting of land, and assigning of housing plots, are still done on a per capita basis (and unplanned births also get their share of 'grain ration land', and housing plot, following modified village policies rather than the formal provincial regulations). After 1987 when land was last adjusted, the contracts were made for a 15-year term, and village cadres have no incentive to make interim adjustments. Per capita land is also declining. Villagers realize that some household with increasing household sizes may not have much increase in responsibility land after future land adjustments. Others could have even less, and it seems that no one now sees having more children as a strategy to gain a bigger share of contracted land.

Children's role in diversifying the household economy:
Spreading risks and achieving social mobility
Having more children (in fact, mainly sons) has given parents more options in arranging their economic activities. Having only one son makes diversification of the household economy, and the increased insurance this would provide, much more difficult. The parents would need to live together with the only son, hoping he is filial. Most parents in the village do not want their only son to live too far away when he grows up. Couples like having at least one married son staying close by. Though the family has become increasingly nuclearized in the village since reform, living alone without care is believed to be a miserable situation.

If a family has more than one son, it is not always ideal for them to live together in the same household, or even in the same village. On the contrary, if one son lives with the parents, it is better for the others to work somewhere outside the village, preferably living in urban areas and engaging in non-agricultural activities; this spreads parental risks. More than one child means more sources of income and security. Some villagers believe that if they have more than one son, they can still rely on the others when one is not filial. If no children are filial, they believe it is their fate and attributable to *tianyi* (willingness of heaven), which is out of their control.

'Not afraid of being bullied if you have many children'
There are other risks, not from nature but from people. Family members and property may be hurt or damaged. Property such as consumer goods, cattle, agricultural machinery, trees, crops, etc. may be stolen, or damaged. There may be conflicts in land issues, watering plants, construction of houses, etc. Villagers believe that one will not be bullied if they have many children. This is especially the case when many conflicts are mediated informally through kin, friends, and neighbours rather than by formal authorities. 'When there are several sons standing beside you, nobody dares to bully you', many people said when talking about the advantages of having many children. Both young and grown-up children could provide insurance against risks in various ways. Grown-up children have both the knowledge and the physical strength to deal with various risks. Young children have potential power and can increase their parents' power to bargain with others.[5]

Parents can easily be bullied if they have only girls. In many matters, couples with only daughters could be put in disadvantageous positions. For example, one women said her husband's brother inherited more of their parents' property at a time when she had not yet given birth to sons. The property rights of girls are not insured, and women who give birth only to daughters may not get the care they might otherwise expect. In household divisions, couples without sons do not get the same amount of household property as brothers who have sons. In general, parents prefer not to transfer their household property to female offspring.

Support and care of the aged

The basic unit for supporting the elderly is the family. If the aged have no children, their support should come from their closest relatives. Neighbours and friends could provide some support, however this is neither obligatory nor automatic. The village's *wubao* system and welfare provided by the township are usually last resorts, and although an insurance company was set up in the county town in the early 1980s, and it provides old age insurance,[6] it seems that no villagers have so far made use of the newly available insurance programme.

Within the family, care of the elderly is primarily the responsibility of sons. Support of parents in their old age is institutionally guaranteed through the formal household division contracts (see Chapter 6) which specify the responsibilities of each son to their parents in the provision of clothes, food, dwelling, health care, and burial. A sons' failure to provide the specified support can be punished. They may be gossiped about. they may face increased transaction costs in their contacts with neighbours, close kin, and other villagers. They may find that people infer that children who do not treat their parents well would hardly treat their neighbours, kin, or friends well. Furthermore, a son who does not provide support to his parents in their old age, or provide insufficient support would be pressured by kin, neighbours, village elders and perhaps by village cadres. In applying moral pressure, there might be recourse to government administrators, or from the courts. At the same time, sons have incentives to comply with social institutions: they will be well received, and it is much easier for them to seek help from their fellow villagers.

Many elderly people believe that 60 is the age for them to relax and 'take a breath',[7] though many believe that they will work as long as they are physically able. Many still look after their grandchildren, cook, wash clothes, clean house, and even help in agricultural work and sidelines. A significant percentage live and cook alone if they can support themselves. In 1993 among those aged people in their 60s and 70s, nearly 45 per cent lived alone or lived only with their spouse, 38 per cent lived with their children, 4 per cent took turns living in the separate families of their sons, and nearly 10 per cent even lived with their daughters' families.[8]

Parents believe that sons in general are much more unreliable and that sons, since reform, are increasingly unwilling to support their parents. However, the quantitative data (Table 7.3) does not prove that sons are much more unreliable than before. In fact a high proportion of both male and female respondents said that sons at present are much more filial towards their parents than those in the past. However, many elderly people presumably would have been unwilling to expose the fact that their own children did not treat them well or as well as they expect. Such a confession might imply that they had no ability to make their children filial, and would incite pity in others. Also, people held the idea that those who did not practice (*xiulian*) well in the past would have a miserable life in their old ages. Thus people who have a pleasant, peaceful life in their old age,

Table 7.3 Responses to question: 'Are sons more filial to their parents at present than during the commune system?'

Respondents Age group	Response			
	More filial before reforms	The same	More filial after reforms	Can't say
Male				
60–69	11.8	29.4	23.5	35.3
70+		44.4	44.4	11.1
Total	7.7	34.6	30.8	26.9
Female				
60–69	7.5	42.5	32.5	17.5
70+	19.2	15.4	26.9	38.5
Total	12.1	31.8	30.3	25.8

Source: Research sampling survey: the elderly 1993.

supported by filial and willing children, are much admired. Similarly, the many people who said that children at present are much more filial than before were not necessarily expressing satisfaction with their sons. Many who answered the question as the 'same' or 'cannot say' in fact conveyed the message that 'children at present are no better than before', which might imply the unspoken message that 'children at present are worse than before'. A small percentage of people did state clearly that they are less satisfied with the children at present than those in the past.

The living standards of the elderly in the family may have improved with the general increase in the standard of living since reform. However, the lost of their power over the younger generation, and increasing reliance on their children rather than the collective, mean that their lives in old age are not necessarily happy. Conflicts happen more frequently between the elderly and the young. As discussed, older couples are increasingly living alone. It is not that the elderly do not want to live with their children and grandchildren together in harmony; it is the young who want to live alone and separate from their parents. Many elderly have to endure this because they have no recourse except moral pressure for the young to respect the elderly. Daughters now play an important role in mediating between parents, sons and daughters-in-law when there are inter-generational conflicts or when sons fail to provide the needed care of the elderly. Village cadres, who used to act as mediators and who pressed sons to provide care for the elderly, now avoid involvement in familial conflicts, since this is time-consuming, provides little economic return, and may damage their relations with one of the two conflicting sides. Some elderly may complain or even quarrel in public with the daughter-in-law they blame for the failure to provide care; a few have even threatened to appeal the court for help. There were few cases of quarrels between elderly parents and married children concerning old age care in the village, and no such cases were heard by the court. Most elderly would rather keep silent and not tell anyone publicly.

Burial of the deceased

When the parents pass away, it is the sons' responsibility to have them buried. The grandchildren, who may have grown up and set up their own financially independent households, may also contribute money for covering the burial expenses. During the Cultural Revolution, many traditional practices for burial were strictly prohibited, and consequently burial expenses were also kept small. After the reforms, however, burial expenses increased tremendously. Major expenditures include purchasing the coffin, providing a feast for mourners, paying for performances of local traditional opera or modern films, setting up a mourning tent, and buying white cloth (for the offspring of the deceased) and other ritual materials.[9]

Traditional opera, or films shown during the ceremony, might be initiated and paid for by friends or kin,[10] and some ritual materials such as wreaths of flowers, paper boys and girls, a paper house, or even paper television sets, etc. (supposed to be used by the deceased), are purchased by others. However, the family must reciprocate when members of the families of their friends or close kin pass away.

Roles of sons and daughters in the ritual of burial ceremony vary. During the mourning session for receiving guest, sons of the deceased kneel in front of coffin in the mourning tent, and return thanks to close kin and friends attending the rituals. Women, including daughters and daughters-in-law and granddaughters, sit in the rear of the tent. Men lead the group to the burial ground, walking before the coffin and women follow behind. The eldest son leads, followed by his brothers. However, when placing the deceased in the coffin, sons carry the body while one daughter carries the head. It is daughters who clean the face of the deceased before the body is placed in the coffin. The person who cleans the deceased could be replaced by another woman in the family if the deceased has no daughter, however there would be a general feeling of regret if the deceased has no daughters to fulfil that ritual.

RESHAPED FERTILITY MOTIVATIONS

Changes in children's roles, and changes in responsibilities and obligations and social relations between parents and children, shape the fertility perception and motivations of reproductive couples. However, fertility motivation and perceptions are difficult to measure. Measurement from survey questions around the desired number of children (see Tables 7.4, 7.5 and 7.6) is subject to deficiencies of validity, reliability, and intensity of the attitudes reported (see Hauser 1967 cited in Wang Jichuan 1990, Hermalin & Liu 1990). Survey data does, nevertheless, provide some hints about fertility motivation concerning the number and sex composition rural couples would like to have, and possibly some differences in motivation between husbands and wives, and between people of different age groups.

Certain problems in the survey must be taken into account to make the best use of the data. First, although the survey was conducted at the very late stage of my long fieldwork and many villagers had confidence in my research, there were still problems. It is difficult to judge the precise extent to which their answers to the questions are influenced by current family planning policies, though the absence of family planning cadres during interviews helped create a quite comfortable environment for the villagers to speak of their true fertility motivations. Second, husbands and wives may have different fertility motivations, but some couples did not like exposing their differences to outsiders. Thus the quantitative data was considered in combination with anthropological observation and interviews in the development of the following summaries of fertility motivations of married couples.

Fertility motivation: Changing notions

The number of children desired is decreasing
As Table 7.5 shows, a great majority of couples (between 51–70 per cent in every age group) had no clear idea at the beginning of their marriage concerning the number of sons and daughters they would like to have in their whole lives. However, it was very clear for them that they wanted to have children. Most respondents who claimed a *laissez faire* approach to the number of children they wanted (*nengsheng jige suan jige*) did not suggest that they wanted to have as many children as possible, though some older couples did have nine or ten children, mainly because no effective contraception had been available at the time.

The idea during the collective period that one would have the number of children that would occur naturally (*nengsheng jige suan jige*) must be seen in context: there was no family planning in the 1960s, and essentially very loose and random family planning in the 1970s. This is not the case at present, and younger families take the family planning programme into account when thinking about the number of children they would like to have. Many people said they would not have many children now, since family planning is so intensive. Years of state family planning programmes have made fertility behaviour increasingly a matter of conscious choice.

Younger generations want fewer children than did older generations. Most Chinese couples want to have both boys and girls (*ernu shuangquan*) though there exists a strong preference for sons. During the collective period, most couples expressing a preference wanted four to six children, generally three or four boys with one or two girls. In the sampling survey conducted in 1993, most rural men and women expressed a desired family size of only one boy and one girl. Most of those who wanted four or more children wanted even numbers of boys and girls. The notable change in fertility aspirations since reform is the desire to avoid three sons, while in the collective era most couples wanted three or more sons, or at least two sons.[11] The desired family size for the majority is one boy and one girl; others said that in the absence of a family planning programme (or if the programme was less intensive) they would like to have two boys and one girl, or even two boys and two girls (compare Tables 7.4, 7.5 and 7.6).

The desire for fewer children is due partly to the ever-increasing cost of having children. Some parents are unwilling to pay the increasing opportunity cost for having children, because doing so means failing to take up available economic opportunities and thus lagging behind. When asked why some women wanted no more children, they said: 'everybody is busy with their work. How can I stop my

Table 7.4 Number and sex composition of children desired at time of marriage by age group

Age group	No children	One child either sex	One boy	One girl	Two children, either sex	Two boys	Two girls	One boy, one girl
20–29		7.9	10.5		4.0			22.4
30–39	3.0	1.5	1.5		7.6			9.1
40–49		2.6	3.9		2.6			15.6
50–59					4.8	4.8		14.3

Age group	Three children, either sex	Three boys	Three girls	Two boys, one girl	Two girls, one boy	Four children, or more	No clear	Total no. of cases (100%)
20–29	2.6					1.3	51.3	76
30–39	3.0			9.1	1.5	3.0	60.6	66
40–49	1.3			1.3		2.6	70.1	77
50–59	4.8						71.4	21

Source: Research sampling survey: married couples 1993.

Table 7.5 Number and sex composition of children that would be desired, if couples were young again and had just married, by age group

Age group	No children	One child either sex	One boy	One girl	Two children, either sex	Two boys	Two girls	One boy, one girl
20–29	2.6	9.2	11.8		4.0			38.2
30–39	3.0	10.6	3.0		4.6	1.5		34.9
40–49	1.3	11.7	9.1		5.2	1.3	1.3	29.9
50–59		9.5	14.3			9.5	4.8	19.1

Age group	Three children, either sex	Three boys	Three girls	Two boys, one girl	Two girls, one boy	Four children, or more	No clear	Total no. of cases (100%)
20–29	1.3			5.3	4.0	5.3	18.4	76
30–39	6.1			12.1	1.5	4.6	18.2	66
40–49			1.3	3.9	1.3	15.6	18.2	77
50–59				4.8		4.8	33.3	21

Source: Research sampling survey: married couples 1993.

work only to have more children?' It is likely that the opportunity cost of having children is lower for those working in agriculture since reform. In the collective, women's ability to earn work points was compromised by pregnancy and childbearing, while in the post-reform period field yields are not much influenced by labour lost to

Table 7.6 Number and sex composition of children desired, if couples were young again and had just married, and no family planning programme existed, by age group

Age group	No children	One child either sex	One boy	One girl	Two children, either sex	Two boys	Two girls	One boy, one girl	Three children, either sex	Three boys	Three girls	Two boys, one girl	Two girls, one boy	Four children, or more	No clear	Total no. of cases (100%)
20–29	4.0	4.0	5.3		5.3		1.3	40.0	2.7			9.3	2.7	9.3	16.0	76
30–39	1.5	4.6	3.0		7.6			30.3	7.6			12.1	1.5	13.6	18.2	66
40–49	1.3	3.9	2.6		2.6	1.3	1.3	24.7	5.2	1.3		10.4	2.6	23.4	19.5	77
50–59		4.8	4.8			9.5	4.8	23.8				4.8		9.5	38.1	21

Source: Research sampling survey: married couples 1993.

childbirth, since other household members or even close kin usually help. The opportunity cost of having children for those engaged in sidelines and non-agriculture activities, however, is tremendous. It is much more significant now than in the collective era, when such activities were heavily restricted. In non-agricultural activities, the opportunity cost is also greater for husbands than for wives. Husbands could migrate for non-agricultural activities during the period of their wives' pregnancies, returning for only a few days around the birth itself. However, since women alone have difficulties when they have several children to care for, husbands then must stay at home, though it is usually economically less profitable to stay in the village where fewer non-agricultural activities are available. The payment for village-based non-agricultural activities is usually low, and young men in particular prefer not to stay in the village, since neighbours, friends, and close kin may ask them for help for which there is little economic return.

Although the cost of children is increasing, the benefits that parents can receive from their children are mixed. For example, one element of the value of children is their labour, but parents must control their children's earnings in order to benefit from rearing them. As discussed, in the collective era children's work points and earnings used to be controlled by their parents until and even after their marriage, because grain and cash were directly distributed to the household heads. At present, control over children's earnings is still certain before their marriage, but is much in doubt after they marry, and marriage and the timing of household division have both become much earlier (see Chapters 5 and 6), implying less parental control of children's labour and earnings.

The purpose of having children is not merely to receive what they can contribute to the family during their childhood. Most importantly, it is the fortune they might bring to the family later in their adulthood, and the security and risk insurance they can provide to their parents. However, households can increase their income substantially in many other ways because of the newly available opportunities released by economic reform. Because land is limited, it can be farmed by fewer labourers than before; at the same time, increasing agricultural inputs and a higher level of agricultural technology have meant that land productivity is increasing and this can substantially increase household income. Having more children can well spread risks and increase sources of income, but this holds only when all of the children can explore their potential under the available opportunities. The new non-agricultural opportunities in the reform era are meaningful only to those who have capacity to make use of them. The capacity to take up available opportunities includes not only physical strength, but most importantly, knowledge, skills, and a social network. There are many examples in the village that parents who have four or five sons all engaged in agriculture and remained poor, and many parents with fewer children who have become better off. Villagers know that the number of children is not the only factor for increasing their security and mobility. Thus the increased demand for labour since reforms is resulting in a much-intensified use of presently available labour in the household, rather than in a wish to have more children who might provide more labour sometime in future.

The changing inter-generational relations, i.e., the loss of the power of the older generation over its adult children not only influences parental control over children's labour, but also influences the old-age support parents receive from their children. There is a growing sense that sons are unreliable, and may not be willing to support their parents in their old age. Parents dislike having sons side with their wives after the parents have spent so much money to get them married. They may seek other alternatives to increase their insurance and security, like strengthening family clan ties, strengthening co-operation between households, setting up alliances through marriage or setting up sworn brothers or sisters, or by making and saving money themselves. Many elderly people said that parents who have saved money would be better treated by their sons and daughters-in-law. The young generation seems to know this very well. Many of them believe that earning more money by themselves is more important than having many sons. In discussing the issue, many young people said publicly that 'you cannot make your children treat you well if you have no money'.

At present a majority of people do not agree with the traditional saying *duozi duofu* (more sons, more happiness), nor with *zinu yueduo, zhifu de jihui yueda* (more children, more chances to get rich). Still, people have a stronger sense that *renduo bupa renqifu* (if one has more children, there is no fear of being bullied), following the increasing competitions and conflicts among peasant households and risks and uncertainties faced by peasant households. At present, many people believe that it is not the number of children but the 'quality' of children that can benefit them economically. For many reproductive couples, the wish is for capable, promising, and filial children who will make their lives happier.

Strengthening of the motivation to have girls, with persistent son preference

The prevalence of son preference in Chinese society is well documented (see e.g., Arnold & Liu 1986, Wang Jichuan 1990, Li & Cooney 1993), and this village is no exception. Many social phenomena demonstrate the strong son preference. Parents and grandparents are extremely happy when boys are born, and celebration of the birth of a son is more important than that of the birth of a girl. Grandparents are more willing to provide post-natal care for a baby boy than a baby girl. It is sometimes more apparent that father and mother compete to invest in their sons (rather than their daughters) through the weaving of emotional ties.[12] Most obviously, no couples voluntarily stop childbearing before at least one son is born (see Chapter 9 and many other studies, e.g., Croll 1994, Wang 1996).

Son preference in the village can also be shown by the survey data. No one said they wanted only girls, and the percentage wishing more boys than girls (e.g. two boys one girl) is higher than the reverse (e.g. two girls and one boy) (compare Tables 7.4, 7.5 and 7.6). The fact that the percentage of couples wanting two or three daughters in the two hypothetical situations was slightly higher than the percentage wanting no girls at the beginning of their marriage probably does not show that the couples wanted only girls. It is most likely an indication that they are not satisfied with their sons.[13]

Since reform, the motivation to have girls has become stronger, although son preference persists. The two hypothetical situations summarized in Tables 7.5 and 7.6 show that couples are not aiming to have as many boys as possible; they find it rather better to balance the number of boys and girls, e.g. one boy and one girl, or two boys and two girls. Some people even said that they would prefer to have more girls than boys. It is clear that preferences changed over the course of marriage, because under the two hypothetical situations, the percentage of couples clearly expressing a preference for two girls and one boy is higher than that for couples at the beginning of their marriage (compare Tables 7.4, 7.5 and 7.6). It should be noted that a stronger wish to have daughters over time does not lessen the existing discrimination against and unfair treatment of girls, which may lead to the imbalance in sex ratio at macro levels.

The stronger wish to have girls is partly because girls are less costly than boys. While parents must spend large sums to cover their sons' marriages, they *receive* brideprices, and can, in theory, keep part or even all of the brideprice if they want to do so. The increasing motivation to have daughters is also because couples have found daughters to be much more useful since the reforms. In many respects, daughters behave much better than sons. Young daughters help much more than boys and at an early age with household chores, agricultural work, and household sidelines. When they marry, the marriage ties can link the two families and set up a useful alliance. Most importantly, an adult daughter's labour is no longer immediately lost upon her marriage, as was the case in the collective period, and she may even bring her husband to give a hand in her natal family. Furthermore, since married daughters have gained more say and control of incomes in their own households, they are also more able to provide better financial and old age support than before. Many of the couples surveyed said that they believe girls are much closer to their parents, and that parent-daughter communication is better. Thus daughters can give much emotional as well as financial and material support.

The increasing value of daughters is reflected in the tendency towards the equalization of dowry and brideprice. However, the increase in dowry should not be taken to be an increasing cost for having girls, in the same way that the increasing brideprice increases the cost of raising boys. Providing dowry to daughters is a matter of choice, while the brideprice must be paid. Parents can provide more or less dowry depending on their own economic situation, while brideprice is traditionally somewhat out of parents' control, and it is not the poorest families who pay the least brideprice. Many men and women now reject the saying *'jiachuqu de nuer pochuqu de shui'* (marrying out a daughter is like pouring out water).

The stronger motivation to have girls reflects usefulness and somewhat higher status of young women in the post-reform household, while strong son preference is closely linked to the low status of women (Arnold & Liu 1986). When young women gain bargaining power in the household, as is the case for many peasant families in the village, one could expect that parents would tend to have a stronger motivation for having daughters. When married daughters have more influence over their husbands and greater control over their household income, and thus are more able to provide needed care to their natal parents, parents are more likely to find one or more daughters acceptable (providing at least one son is born). Parents worry if they have three sons, but do not worry if they have three daughters. Thus with the higher status of young women, though son preference will persist with the existence of gender inequality, parents now tend to prefer a more balanced number of boys and girls.

Stronger motivation to have more children in the absence of a family planning programme

Fertility perception and motivation is influenced by the presence of family planning programme. In the two hypothetical situations, when no family planning programme is included, the percentage expressing a desire to have fewer children and a small family dropped significantly, and that desiring more children increased dramatically (see Tables 7.4, 7.5 and 7.6).

The role of family planning in fertility perception can be better understood in the context of an analysis of local family planning policies and its practical implementations. The local implementation of family planning policy (which does not follow precisely the state family planning regulations) concerns couples' fertility motivations, and at the same time influences couples' fertility perception. For example, if newly married couples know that they can have two or more children, only when their first two children are daughters are they likely to worry about having a son by any means possible.

One way in which family planning policies are changing fertility perception is by making childbearing of higher parities too costly, e.g. by imposing penalties on those who deviate from the desired family size. Such penalties not only result in fewer children, but also affect the timing of childbearing. With family planning becoming more and more intensive, couples rush to have the desired number of children earlier.

Different perception of childbearing exist between men and women

As mentioned, in the sampling survey I interviewed both women and men about their perception of childbearing, as well as that of their spouses. I wanted to look at their knowledge of their spouses' motivation to see if there was any difference between them, and whether couples communicate about the issue. I found that both husbands and wives say that they know what their spouses think, and that they also claim that the spouse shares their own ideas, though a few women and some men can explain their differences.

Although it is difficult to judge whether preference for more children was stronger among husbands or among wives, there are differences in fertility motivation between the (69) male respondents and (176) female respondents in the survey. A higher proportion of women than men said they did not think about family size at the beginning of their marriage (also in the two hypothetical situations), although this does not mean that women are taking a *laissez faire* approach to family size. It is most likely an indication that women have less fertility decision-making power in the household, or at least that wives would not indicate to an outsider whether they were the main decision-makers on this issue. From Table 7.7 one can argue that men are more strongly motivated to have more children, since the percentage of men who said they would like to have four or more children is somewhat higher (except when the option is two boys and two girls). This could simply reflect the fact that it is not men but women who bear much of the burden of giving birth to and rearing children. Women, on the other hand, while they also face more risks and uncertainties especially in their old age, have fewer opportunities to develop themselves and thus to rely on themselves for a better life. Women are in a disadvantaged position both within the household and within the society, and many women said that they would rather have fewer children if they could. For example, they said that if their situation changed to resemble the situation of urban couples, they would prefer to have only one child.

The data suggest that women are more motivated to have girls than their husbands are. In Table 7.7, while the proportion of men who would like to have one or two boys is much higher than that of women, only a few men (and no women) want to have only three sons. Meanwhile, more women than men would like to have two girls and only one boy. The stronger wish for girls among women can be seen in many interactions between husbands and wives where families have sons and no daughters. For example, a woman in her late 40s with three sons and one daughter said she liked having a baby girl after she had the three sons. The husband did not like the idea, and did not want more children. 'What is the use of having a girl?' he said. The wife however wanted to have a girl because she believed that boys could not give much help in household chores, while a girl would help her with laundry, cooking, cleaning the house, and with agricultural work. As the only woman in the household, she felt it was too much of a burden for her to fulfil all her responsibilities and obligations.

Many other examples from my interviews and observations reveal differences between husbands and wives in fertility motivation, not much in the sense of desired family size at the beginning of marriage (though this is also probable), but at the point where sex preferences enter into the question of having additional children. A women in her 30s, with one boy and two girls, reported that she would like to have another boy, although the husband wanted no additional children since this would make him too busy to concentrate on his charcoal-making business; this business also required that his wife do the household chores and agricultural work, care for the children, and assist in the charcoal production by purchasing the raw wood sent by their customers. He said to his wife: 'Do not expect me to even hold it for a moment if you have another baby'.

Changing fertility perceptions: Life-cycle perspective

Fertility perception also concerns the timing of childbirth. Whether and when to have another child depend a lot on the number and sex composition of children already born. Normally almost everyone expects a new couple to have children soon after marriage. Only in mber and sex composition of children desired by men and women

	No children	One child, either sex	One boy	One girl	Two children, either sex	Two boys	Two girls	One boy, one girl	Thr…e
	1.1	4.4	4.4		4.4	1.5		23.2	.
		4.6	5.1	0.6	4.6			13.6	.
	2.9	14.5	13.0	1.5	2.9	2.9	1.5	31.9	.
	1.7	9.7	6.8	2.3	4.6	1.1	0.6	33.5	.
	2.9	4.4	4.4	1.5	5.8	2.9		31.9	.
	1.7	4.6	3.4	2.3	4.6	0.6	1.7	30.9	.

	Three boys	Three girls	Two boys, one girl	Two girls, one boy	Two boys, two girls	Four children, or more	No idea	Total
			2.9			4.4	50.7	100
			2.8	0.6	1.1	1.1	63.1	100
	1.5		2.9	1.5	7.3	1.5	13.1	100
			8.0	2.3	6.8	1.1	21.6	100
	1.5		11.6	1.5	10.1	4.4	13.1	100
			9.1	2.3	13.1	1.7	21.7	100

sex composition of children desired at time of marriage.
sex composition of children desired if couples were young again and have just married.
sex composition of children desired if couples were young again, had just married and there were no family planning program in the
sample survey: married couples 1993.

exceptional cases did women wish to postpone having children, for example, when a woman was unhappy in the marriage and considering divorce.[14]

Grandparents like to have grandchildren soon. Paternal grandparents expect grandsons to continue their family line. Younger grandchildren can also provide much support to grandparents, especially when the intervening generation is busy with economic activities. They can provide much needed care, like making tea, bringing food, assisting in walking, keeping the grandparents company. Most importantly, grown-up grandchildren could give financial help, or provide help with food, medicine, facilities for daily use, etc., and as a result many parents want their children to marry and have children as early as possible, so that when they are elderly their grandchildren will already have grown up. Since economic reform, grandchildren have become the main supporters of their grandparents in attending to their daily needs, because other adults in the family have become much more busy than before, and may even be absent from the village or the household most of the time. Elderly parents also use their grandchildren as leverage to bargain with and influence their own children, in the sense that their own children must set up a model to be filial and responsible to their parents for the grandchildren to follow. If children are not filial to their own parents, their children will not be filial to them in the future. Also, with the intensification of adult labour in economic activities, elderly parents are losing their power in the family, so it is reasonable for them to expect to want grandchildren earlier.

Newly married couples may also prefer to have children earlier rather than later, since grandparents can take care of the children. Having children prior to household division can reduce the opportunity costs of children tremendously. Also, a young wife needs to give birth to sons not only to continue the family line, but also to improve her situation in the new family by not disappointing their parents and husbands, and, importantly, to have someone she can rely on in future. After giving birth to children, she can get help with childcare from her parents-in-law; this means that a few years later, when the households are separated, she will be able to concentrate on contributing to household earnings, the children will be older and less dependent.

Increasingly intense family planning programmes also push reproductive couples to have children earlier. Without the programmes, parents found it better first to have one or two children, then try to have more children if they are dissatisfied with the sex composition of previous parities. When family planning programmes intensified, the desire that the first child be a boy also became stronger. If the first or second child is a boy, they feel more at ease, since they would have at least one boy even if they could not manage to defy government policy for having more children.

Almost no one wants to stop after having only one child, though the desire to have a second child also depends on the sex of the first child. If the first child is a girl, the motivation for having another child is strong, and most couples will try to have another child without delay. If the first child is a boy, couples still find it better to have another son, to insure that at least one son survives and grows up to be filial. Parents worry about the accidental death or incapacity of sole sons. For example, in the village one bright young man in his 20s, seriously injured in a truck accident, was incapacitated by his head injuries. Another five-year-old boy was lost during a village fair in the late 1980s, and it was believed that he had been kidnapped and most likely sold by a 'population trafficker' (renkou fanzi). One mother in her 30s with one son and two daughters, who could not find her nine-year-old son one day,[15] said (as a verbal expression of her desperation while searching her son) that she would try to have another son.

Couples wanting more children usually prefer to have their children born close together. In fact, most couples are trying to reach their preferred number and sex composition desired sooner rather than later. Having children all together in a short period means intensive care of children, but for a shorter period, allowing couples to concentrate on economic activities later on.

Having the third (or additional) child is a more complex decision. The cost of having an additional child is no less than having the first or second child (of the same sex), yet the benefit of the additional child might add little to what they can expect from children they have already have.

In fact, cost differences associated with different parities are changing. For example, in the past a younger brother could wear his elder brother's clothes, and an elder brother or sister would help parents to care their younger siblings. In this respect, the marginal cost for having an additional child seemed to decrease (again, differentiated by sex). At present, children of higher parity are much more costly than are first and second children. This is not simply because no children wear their elder brother's or elder sister's clothes any more. Increasingly intensified family planning programmes have made having children of higher parity more costly. Other direct and indirect costs are also increasing: It is more costly to get a third son married, since he will marry later and marriage expenses are increasing. Some parents whose first two children are sons may adopt a girl as their third child, rather than risk having another son (see Chapter 9).

Officially instigated institutional reforms, which change the context in which villagers work and live, have reshaped the responsibilities and obligations between parents and children within families, the role of children within households, and the social relations between generations. This changing context (brought about by economic reforms) plus new elements in the implementation of family planning at the local level (discussed in the next chapter), have reshaped individual fertility perceptions and motivations in the reform era.

Among the many changes in the roles of children and the perception of childbearing in this period, the most notable are that: (1) rural families tend to have fewer children; (2) villagers' motivation for having sons has weakened, such that peasants tend to avoid having many sons, and their motivation for having daughters has strengthened; (3) villagers are tending to start having children at earlier ages, to reach their desired number and sex composition of children sooner, and to stop their reproduction younger. These changes are not simply related to changes in the costs and benefits for parents of having children in the reform period. They are related to changes in the distribution of such costs and benefits among family members. Most importantly, they are related to new forms of inter-generational relations that have developed since economic reform, and changes in the roles of both sons and daughters, in relation to their parents.

Notes

[1] Personal communication with village schoolteachers and parents.

[2] One of the reforms carried out in higher education, is that a certain number of students be allowed to enter higher education institutions as self-financed students. In 1993 there was a rumour around the village that the proportion of self-paid students will increase dramatically in some of the local professional schools.

[3] The focus on the age at which children begin work is inspired by Ben White's work on child labour in rural Indonesia (see White 1976, 1982). It should be noted that the direct comparison of mean age of beginning work between the two age groups presented in Table 7.1 requires care. The mean age at which children in the younger age group (6–14) begin work faces methodological problems; i.e., some who were not working at the time of the survey are likely to begin some work later on, and thus the mean age of beginning work for the sample may be higher than reported.

[4] In the whole village, two girls who dropped out of school had left the village. One was working as a baby-sitter in the county town, and the other went to a neighbouring town to help in a household-run restaurant. Neither was covered in my sampling survey. Opportunities for women to migrate out for a paid job were limited in the region, and it was very rare for village girls to go to the cities for work; in this respect the province is different from Sichuan or Anhui province.

[5] I witnessed a conflict between two households on a land issue in a neighbouring village on my way to the county town. There were quarrels, and when one side finally went away, one woman in her 30s from the other side was still angry and murmured 'wait till my son grows up'.

[6] Couples with a single son or with two daughters can join in the old age security insurance. There were 760 persons insured in the county and 37 persons insured in the township respectively, most of them urban household registration holders (personal communication with staff of the County Insurance Company).

7   In the Chinese calendar, 60 equals five 12-year cycles, and is believed to signal the start of a new life.

8   The proportion of old men living alone with their spouses is much higher than that of old women similarly situated, mainly because that men's life expectancy is lower than women's, and in the past, more men married younger women. Thus the old men are more likely to be cared for by their spouse, in addition to the care they can get from their children.

9   There is not much difference between the burial expenses of mothers and fathers, although in Chinese society, women's position in family and society is still much lower.

10   Payment for local opera was 120–130 *yuan* per day in 1993, and performers were also provided with free meals for the day.

11   In the village, the concept 'number of children' is often conflated with 'number of sons', especially among the old. If they were asked how many children they had, they would answer three if they have three sons and several daughters. Thus, in order to know clearly the number of children and avoid confusion, one must clarify the question by asking how many sons and daughters they have.

12   One woman was not satisfied with her husband and accused him of not disciplining their sons, and of giving the sons money when she did not agree. She accused her husband of competing to have better relations with the sons than she has with them. Every Chinese might remember that the question most frequently asked by their parents or neighbours when they were small children was: 'Whom do you want to treat well when you grow up, your mum, or your dad?'

13   Villagers all know a single son of a widow who did not treat his mother well; he and his wife quarrelled with his mother, and they divided the household. The villagers said: 'what is the use for her to have a son?'.

14   A woman in her 30s with three children told me that at the beginning of marriage she did not want to have any children with her husband, since she did not like the arranged marriage and wanted to get a divorce. She secretly used some contraceptive pills received from one of her classmates from her school time; however this was discovered by her own mother, who had arranged the marriage. Under the pressure of her own natal family to get along with her husband, sometime after her marriage began she had first a son, and then two girls. She said that only after having a son with her husband did she decide that she wanted to live with her husband peacefully.

     In another case during my fieldwork, a young woman who had been married for two years had an induced abortion of her first pregnancy since she and her natal family wanted to seek divorce, and did not want to have any children born for the husband and his family. It was the husband who answered my questionnaire; he also said that he did not want any children at the beginning of the marriage.

15   He played with other children in a neighbouring village and failed to return home. The parents, with other family members and other villagers, searched for them; they were finally found and sent home by an old man from the neighbouring village.

CHAPTER 8

Implementation of State Family Planning Programmes

The last chapter demonstrated that couples' fertility motivation has been reshaped by the changing post-reform context. In most if not all cases, a rural couple's motivation for having a particular number of children, and their desire to space births are not simply responses to formal state family planning policies. Fertility decision-making is an interaction between individual reproductive couples and their families, as well as village and township cadres. Given the tremendous control the Chinese state wields over Chinese society in the domain of reproduction, a study of peasant fertility strategies alone will not be sufficient to understand the forces underlying family formation in rural China today.

Many studies link family planning programmes to the extensive structure of government control in China. Many emphasize the determining role played by government control in Chinese family planning programmes (Aird 1990, Banister 1987, Wen 1993b, Wolf 1986), and many debate its consequences for human well-being, finding it either negative (e.g. Aird 1990, Mosher 1995), or positive (e.g. Hou 1988; Wu 1986, 1994; CSC 1991, 1996), or mixed (Hong & Mandle 1987, Sun & Wei 1987). The rigidity of Chinese family planning programmes has been controversial in China and around the world. There are however very few studies (the exceptions being, e.g., Greenhalgh 1993, 1994a, Potter & Potter 1990, Huang 1989), which consider in detail how family planning policies are formulated and implemented at the *local* level, in a particular social, economic and cultural context.

In this chapter I will demonstrate that the implementation of family planning policies is not uniform but varies with the institutional context. Family planning regulations and the means adopted by local family planning cadres during the collective period may no longer be valid or effective in the reform period. The characteristics of the implementation of state policies at the local level is related to the changing position of cadres *vis-à-vis* the peasantry, and that of village cadres *vis-à-vis* township cadres. Local cadres should not be seen merely as state representatives at the local level;[1] they may mediate state policies and formulate informal local policies (Greenhalgh 1993). Individuals should not be seen as mere victims of state family planning policies (Greenhalgh 1994a); they also play their role in formulating local family planning policies and in shaping the characteristics of the implementation of family planning at the local level. I will show that the implementation of family planning programmes at the village level relies not on the everyday work of grassroots family planning cadres, but on family planning campaigns with specific targets and quotas imposed by higher authorities. Though such authorities try to institutionalize family planning work (*jihua shengyu zhiduhua*), the implementation in practice is still arbitrary, and is dependent on negotiation processes involving village cadres with both township cadres and villagers. Cadres' negotiation with different families also vary, depending on family affiliations to different clans, or their social, economic, and political status. The choice of family member with whom to negotiate will also vary, along with changing familial relations.

This chapter will focus on the characteristics of fertility control reshaped by the changing context, and discuss how state policies are mediated by local governments and families at the village level. It will firstly discuss the new characteristics reshaped under the new institutional settings, comparing these with the old patterns under collective institutions. This discussion concerns family planning institutions at the village level, policy popularization and family planning education, incentives and disincentives, and the provision of contraceptives and family planning services. The chapter will then show how state policies are mediated by interactions between peasants and cadres, and among cadres in local administrations. Finally, four family planning campaigns in 1993 are described, to indicate how state family planning policies are transferred to the village and how family planning programme are being implemented in the reform era.

PRE-REFORM AND POST-REFORM FAMILY PLANNING: OLD STYLES AND NEW CHARACTERISTICS

Reforms have changed the context in which rural Chinese people live and work, and also the context for policy implementation, including implementation of the family planning programme at the local level, the 'most difficult job under heaven' (*tianxia diyinan*). They have affected responsibility for family planning work at the local level, the style of policy popularization and family planning education, and the operation of incentives and disincentives of the programme in reality. They may also affect the provision of contraceptives and family planning services. These changes can be better understood if the new characteristics of family planning at the local level are compared to the characteristics of family planning within the old collective institutions.

Family planning organizations in the village

Family planning work started in the village in mid-1970s. At the beginning, the main responsibility for family planning work rested with the women's federation (*funu lianhehui*), though other cadres were also involved. Family planning used to be less intensive as it is at present, and was far from institutionalized in the 1970s. There were occasional campaigns (like 'family planning propaganda month', *jihua shengyu xuanchuanyue*), which were designed by higher authorities and implemented locally.

Family planning work intensified in the 1980s. Higher authorities required that the Party secretary and the village governor focus on family planning work, and local administrators could not ignore family planning by claiming that there was a greater need to focus on the local economy or other issues. A family planning commission was set up in the village, headed by the Party secretary and consisting of the vice-secretary, village governor and vice-governors. There are two special family planning cadres (*jihua shengyu zhuanzhi ganbu*) (both currently village cadres), though according to the requirement of the County family planning commission, the village should have three special family planning cadres for its population.

Family planning organizations seem to have been created merely to satisfy directives from above. The responsibilities of family planning cadres are not fixed. Certain responsibilities specified for the special family planning cadres are often shared among all village cadres. There were eight village cadres in 1993. Six male cadres hold the position, either in the village Party committee or in the villagers' committee. The two women cadres are in charge of family planning, women, and youth league work respectively (though no activities for women or the youth league have been organized since the introduction of responsible systems). The Party secretary takes the main responsibility for family planning work with the assistance of one special family planning cadre. The other six cadres are responsible for family planning work in each of the six residential groups. The work includes family planning registrations, reports, collecting family planning fines, and completing family planning work quotas. In the early 1980s, leaders of the six residential groups (who were leaders of production teams before the dismantling of the commune system) used to help in family planning works and in the collection of agricultural tax and collective levies. However, the village level cadres said that they all quit in the 1990s since the work were too difficult for the leaders of residential groups, and the village government was unable to pay them a reasonable wage.[2]

One vice-governor of the township government is responsible for the comprehensive work of the village. He is supposed to guide, supervise, and assist village cadres in their work, including family planning work. Unlike the village cadres, he lives outside the village, and works mostly in the township government. He goes to the village for meetings, and to supervise and assist in family planning campaigns, etc. During intensive family planning campaigns, the village cadres and the township cadre responsible for the village's work may request help from a family planning implementation team (*jihua shengyu zhixingdui*) organized by the township government, if they have difficulties completing the family planning work by themselves.

Policy popularization and family planning education

In the initial family planning programmes in the 1970s, cadres' efforts concentrated on raising people's consciousness of the necessity of family planning. Different means were used to make it known to each individual household that giving birth to children was not only a private matter concerning individuals and individual families, but had important implications for the strength and prosperity of the whole nation. Cable radios, loudspeakers, blackboard and wall posters, mass meetings, study groups, etc., were used to spread family planning policies.

In this period mass meetings were frequent, both for political campaigns and for family planning campaigns. Cadres could easily withdraw people from the collective work to attend mass meetings, and those who attended received work points. Some women with children, who usually stayed at home, would also participate in mass meetings. They would sit, chat· with others, have their children around them and some housework in their hands, and earn work points by attending mass meetings. They also liked to listen to cadres about what was happening outside the village, since there were limited channels for accessing news at the time.

Organizing mass meeting has become much difficult since the introduction of the responsibility systems, if not impossible altogether. People are busy with their own economic activities. Further, many men have migrated out for non-agricultural jobs. During the daytime, only a small group of people are available in the village, so mass meetings can only be organized in the evening when people are home from work. There is, however, no longer any economic return linked to the meetings, and people prefer to relax and watch television. Nonetheless, mass meetings are organized during the 'high tides' of family planning campaigns as requested by higher authorities, usually when township or county level cadres are present. In the evening, when mass meetings are to be held, the cadres must attract villagers with some other entertainment, such as popular films. They also usually turn off the electricity to village households, so that villagers cannot stay home to watch television. They then hold the meeting during the intermission in the movie. They also use other strategies to popularize policies, such as slogans, broadcasting through loudspeakers, and population education programmes on television. None is as effective as the collective's mass meetings and study groups, but although study groups had an effective means to spread family planning policy during the collective period, no study group could be possibly organized in the present period. The cadres also distribute posters during family planning campaigns, not necessarily to educate people, but to meet the standards set by their superiors (though officially it is believed that policy popularization and family planning education is most effective way to change people's attitude in favour of small number of children; see Wasserstrom 1984).

Village cadres know that most couples would like to have more children than permitted, and would take no initiative to popularize the policy if they were not required to do so. In fact, village cadres try to make it clear to the public that they are simply carrying out state policies which apply throughout China, and not only in their own village. One frequent claim cadres make over the loudspeakers is that 'we would not press you to have fewer children if we were not required by the government'.

The existence of the family planning programme is known to each individual household. However, understanding the state family planning policy is a gradual progress. Even cadres themselves took some time to understand family planning as a concept. Population policy is spread mainly through interactions between cadres and peasants in the implementation of family planning policies. People learn from their own experiences, or the experiences of their neighbours, friends, and relatives. In the beginning, villagers believed that giving birth to children was something private, and villagers were also shy about discussing contraceptives, abortions and sterilization in public. Women ran away when cadres tried to talk with them about family planning work. Villagers also could not accept sterilization at the beginning; they thought only animals would be sterilized.

After 20 years of family planning, people no longer see childbearing as merely a private, family affair, and understand that it is also a state concern. People talk openly about contraceptives and family planning, even with those of the opposite sex. Abortion and sterilization have gradually become accepted. It seems that many people agree with the arguments put forward by the state about the relationship between economic growth, living standards, and population growth. The state argues that fast population growth means smaller shares of resources (like land), and blocks to further economic growth, and the villagers do not challenge the state policy. At the same time, they want to have more children than permitted, based on the consideration of their own households.

However, peasants do not know the exact details of population policies and specific regulations. Village cadres do not necessarily know specific policies and regulations either, and they do not strictly follow the state regulations. In fact, each family planning campaign may have its own focus and principles, and individual households often find that the requirements of the local family planning cadres during different family planning campaigns will conflict (see later in this chapter). In the process of bargaining between cadres and villagers, cadres do not refer to specific regulations, but follow their own perceptions of what should be right, and try to complete the family planning tasks assigned during family planning campaigns. Many villagers believe that it is not useful to learn the local policies (*xuela baixue*) because these change over time.

Incentives and disincentives

Incentives and disincentives were introduced to promote compliance with family planning policy in the late 1970s. Certain benefits accrued to couples who followed the policy, and punishments to those who deviated. The incentive and disincentive schemes have changed over the years, so incentives and disincentives in one period might not be in force in other periods; the state would shift its schemes, with effort invested in different directions at different times, and with differing intensities.

Under the commune system, incentives to promote compliance included marriage leave and maternity leave, extra work points or grain distributed to the couples, priority in health care, education, and employment, priority in the distribution of housing plot and the provision of certain materials needed for childrearing (birth to age 14 years). Disincentives included parents' loss of a certain numbers of work points and the unplanned child's lack of entitlement to private land and a housing plot. In the late 1970s, when economic incentives and disincentives were introduced nation-wide, the village provided no incentives to rural couples because no couples were eligible for economic awards, though the cadres had control over work opportunities, distribution, and the collective welfare. Only in 1978 were the first group of couples who had female sterilization (some of them being wives of village cadres) provided work points, cash, and some days of leave.

Incentives did not work well during the collective period, and since the reforms there are simply no incentives applied in the village. As discussed in Chapter 4, the 'five guarantee' programme does not function well in the village; contracting more land to individual households provides little incentive since the comparative advantage of agriculture is low. Priority access to education, health care, and employment is also not significant as an incentive for villagers, especially now that health care is privatized and work opportunities are increasingly located through informal networks rather than through the state or the collective. In fact, since no couples pledged to have only a single child, the incentive scheme as it appeared on paper (drafted by higher authorities) simply did not work in the village. Those whose births were unplanned have had no difficulties in getting their housing plot, education, health care, and so on. They also have no difficulty as adults, formalizing their rural household registration or moving around and finding work. As mentioned, contracting out the collective land to individual households is made on per capita basis, and everyone, including the unplanned births receives a share of the collective land; no local policy gives those who pledge to have only one child a larger share. Many couples have not heard of the 'family planning glorious certificate', which is issued to couples pledging to have only one child. Because the village has no economic ability to facilitate a strong and effective incentive programme, cadres simply put no effort into setting up such a scheme. Knowing no one will pledge to have only one child, village cadres do not waste their time and energy on this. The incentives for rural couples having the number of children set by the state as the norm do not exist in the everyday life of the people in the village.

Cadres reported that no disincentives were imposed in the village during the collective period, though they could easily have deducted the work points from the accounts of nonconforming parents. No couple in their 30s or 40s reported having had work points deducted for unplanned births. Villagers said that economic penalties were seen as low in the early 1980s, and after reforms, when people were richer, the amounts of money assessed as penalties needed to be modified. In 1989, the penalties approved by provincial people's congress were set at extremely high levels. According to the regulation, couples will be fined 1,500 *yuan* for the first extra baby, and 3,000 *yuan* for the second extra baby, and an additional 1,500 *yuan* for each extra child. However, village cadres collect the fine in installments, and not all at once. Also, they cannot simply deduct work points as penalties from those deviated family planning policies; now they must go door-to-door to collect family planning fines. Because village cadres cannot stop their fellow villagers from marrying early (their own children may also marry young) they may only collect fines for early or illegal marriages when this is demanded by higher authorities. And because they have no way to stop rural couples for having children early and with short intervals, they put no effort into regulating the timing of childbearing, nor do they impose economic penalties, since there are no specific regulations from above on how much the fines should be.

The increased social differentiation makes family planning work difficult. Normally, individual families try to avoid the fine or to pay as little as possible. The rich do not necessarily pay higher fines than others do, though they are more able to pay. The poor, in contrast, find it difficult to get fines reduced, because they have little leverage with which to bargain with cadres, except their complaint that cadres are unjust in their family planning work. The increasing differentiation has made negotiation between cadres and peasant households more difficult. The standard fine may be too low for the rich but it is also too high for the poor, and this may make economic penalties less effective as interventions in the reproductive behaviour of individuals. The specific economic penalties attached to the formal family planning policies, and how village cadres impose economic disincentives to individual households in practice will be discussed in detail in the last section of this chapter.

The incentive and disincentive scheme for village cadres performing family planning work does not necessarily improve their family planning work and nor achieve the designed purposes. Villagers believe that cadres sometimes do not stop certain couples for having extra children, in order to have more couples from whom to collect fines, an activity which is rewarded as part of completing their family planning tasks. When it is too difficult to collect enough fine to meet the quota, they are believed to have used certain collective funds to fill the gap and 'complete' the job, receive their incentives and avoid punishment.

Provision of contraceptives and family planning services

Before the village health clinic was privatized in the early 1980s, contraceptives were distributed by barefoot doctors, who took care of family planning services. The delivery of contraceptives was closely tied to the provision of basic health care, and contraceptives were to be provided to individual couples without charge. The privatized health clinics do not have an official function in providing family planning services. Village health clinics are unlikely even to have contraceptives available, because there are simply no rural couples willing to pay for contraception.

In the late 1980s, each township set up its own family planning service facilities, where couples who would like to use certain contraceptives can receive help.[3] Village cadres are assigned the 'hard' task (*yingrenwu*) of ensuring a certain number of IUD insertions during each campaign. They have no incentive to work on the other, 'soft' tasks or indicators (*ruanzhibiao*) such as the distribution of contraceptives, or spreading propaganda on state population policy through household visits, both of which are difficult for superiors to monitor and evaluate. Cadres believe that condoms and contraceptive pills are seldom used by reproductive couples, and would not bother to distribute contraceptives even if they received them from the township family planning commission.[4] Further, cadres believe that when couples are strongly motivated to have more children, the distribution of condoms, pills, etc., which they will not use is both ineffective and a waste of resources. This is also why local cadres heavily rely on IUDs, abortions and sterilization for family planning; all are much more effective and easier to monitor than other contraceptives.

MEDIATION OF FORMAL FAMILY PLANNING POLICIES

The new characteristics of the reform-era family planning programme are shaped not only by interactions among individuals, individual families, and family planning cadres, but also by interactions among local cadres both at the same and at different administrative levels. The ways in which state policies are mediated both by families and by local government administrations can be seen as resistance to some policy elements and as acceptance of others. Village cadres do not follow family planning regulations exactly concerning provision of contraceptives and the carrying out of incentive and disincentive schemes, the collection of family planning fines, or meeting require- ment for abortion, sterilization, etc. Village cadres see that the strict implementation of formal family planning policies is impossible, and instead implement a modified version as village policies. The modi- fied version changes to follow the shifts in state population policy, and is intensified or relaxed according to the intensity of family plan- ning pressure imposed from above.

Mediation through interaction: Among villagers and cadres

The interaction between cadres and villagers has a part in almost every aspect of reproductive behaviour, from marriage itself to the number of children born, the timing and spacing of childbearing, as well as contraception, abortion, sterilization, and so on to the end of a couple's reproductive life.

One element of the provincial population policy is to encourage couples to delay their marriages (see Chapter 5), although cadres cannot stop people marrying below the state-specified minimum age, and do not interfere much on the timing of marriage, except by collecting fines from those married below the legal minimum marriage. Village cadres also do not bother to make newly married couples postpone their childbearing. According to provincial family planning policy, reproductive couples who would like to have a child should be approved and given a birth permission certificate (*zhun- shengzheng*). Every couple should have a birth permission certificate before the wife becomes pregnant. Village cadres actually do not carry out this regulation at all. In fact, the township family planning cadres do not even provide the certificates to village cadres.

After their first child, couples are supposed to use an effective contraceptive measure, such as IUD. Couples whose first child is a girl are also expected to use such contraceptives, though they are allowed to have another child after a four-year interval. Couples are requested to go to the township family planning service station (*jihua shengyu fuwuzhan*) to have an IUD inserted. However, no couples with a single child voluntarily opt for IUD contraception.

In principle, village cadres should request all couples with one child to use an IUD. However, as mentioned, village cadres initiate family planning work only because they are requested by their superiors to do so. After 'village cadres receive their tasks during a family planning campaign, they go to the couples concerned and discuss (or bargain) with them about contraception. However, the villagers reported that cadres do not press for compliance from the powerful, from friends or relatives, or from those who send bribes. Instead, they said that the weak and the poor are usually approached. Those approached can ask a friend or relative who wants no more children to have the IUD insertion in their names, and the same friend or relative would agree have the IUD monitored later on. In any case, both village and township cadres know that every couple would like to have more than one child, and they do not press the villagers too much, even when they know that the couples cheat.

It is formally requested that couples with unplanned pregnancies should have an induced abortion. Abortion is again divided as two categories: first trimester abortions (*liuchan*), and second trimester abortions (*yinchan*). Pregnant women are encouraged to have *liuchan*, but *yinchan* is permitted. Couples with an unplanned pregnancy can avoid this, however; many couples move outside the village during family planning campaigns so that their child will be born elsewhere, and later come back to the village. Neighbours in other villages do not inform on such cases to cadres. Even when cadres in other villages know, they do not concern themselves, since family planning work for couples from other villages is not their responsibility. They do not even inform the relevant cadres.

Village cadres receive, as a family planning task during family planning campaigns, a quota (of abortions) that should be met. The quota is not difficult to meet, since only the number of abortions is specified, but not which households. The actual number of women who should have abortion according to formal family planning policy would be much higher than the task quota. Village cadres usually pressure most strongly those pregnant with higher parities. Some pregnant women who do not want more children also volunteer for abortion.

According to formal family planning regulations, couples with unplanned births should be fined, should have an abortion if another pregnancy occurs, and either the husband or the wife should be sterilized. Cadres implement a somewhat different policy, which is based on the sex composition of the children already born. When children born are all girls, village cadres usually do not pressure a couple to have an IUD insertion, nor to have an abortion. However, these couples do need to pay a certain amount of money (not a fine in the sense of the formal regulations), and this money can be used by cadres to pay fines to the township for 'fulfilling' their family planning tasks.

Village cadres do not differentiate between couples whose first child is a girl and second child is a boy (which is allowed by the formal regulations unless the birth interval rule has been violated) and those whose first child is a boy and second child is either a boy or a girl. Cadres give couples who have two children the option of either (a) paying a fine, or (b) having one partner sterilized. Cadres know that no one will accept sterilization after having only two children, so the two options are offered to make couples agree to at least pay the family planning fine. As noted, the 1500 *yuan* fine for one extra child is usually not paid immediately. In the village, the usual fine for the second birth is 300 *yuan* during each family planning campaign. Village cadres return during every family planning campaign to collect a payment towards the family planning fine until (in theory) the accumulated fine reaches the amount set by the provincial regulation. However, as of 1993 no couples had been fined enough times to actually reach the full amount. In order to convince couples to pay towards the fine, cadres sometimes pledge that they will not return to collect the next installment during the following family planning campaign(s) even if the full fine has not yet been paid.

If women with two children is again pregnant, in one family planning campaign she might be expected to have an abortion, but in another campaign she might simply be fined. During each family planning campaign, couples who deviate from the policy are fined, *or* required to have an abortion, *or* one member is to be sterilized; the sanctions are seldom if ever applied in combination.

Most couples oppose sterilization after only two children. However, there exists some differentiation between the poor and the rich in this regard. The rich can pay the fine and avoid being sterilized. However, the poor, who have difficulties to pay the fine, and cannot easily avoid mandatory abortion, might agree to sterilization. The village pays all costs for sterilization, plus some subsidies. Some couples choose sterilization after the wife is pregnant but before this becomes readily apparent; thus they can have the child without paying any fine for this extra baby. As a rule, couples having sterilization are believed to 'have passed the barrier' (*guoguan*), and village cadres no longer approach them once they have the operation.

According to official regulations, no couples should be allowed to have more than two children under any circumstances. Couples with three children are to be fined for the extra births, and if the wife becomes pregnant again she is to have an abortion and one member of the couple is to be sterilized. Village cadres, however, again depart from official rules, requiring that these couples either pay the fine or undergo sterilization. If couples agree to having sterilization, all costs concerned rest with the village, and cadres charge no fine if sterilization has been done. Again, a share of the fine would be collected during each family planning campaign. Couples with three girls and no son are not pushed to have abortions or sterilization, although they also must pay the fine. In 1993, there were two couples in the village which had each managed to have five girls without being sterilized.

The strategy village cadres use in implementing family planning is to complete the assigned family planning task during family planning campaigns and ignore regular family planning work at other times. Village cadres, as mediators between township cadres and their fellow villagers, feel it is difficult to maintain a balance that can satisfy both sides. They try to complete the tasks, providing the tasks are not too much of a burden and provided they can seek support from their superiors. At the same time, village cadres will not implement a strict policy toward their fellow villagers; they bargain with their superiors for lighter family planning tasks, and will implement more sensitive, less restricted, modified version of population policy. To appease the villagers, they blame the policy on outside forces, such as the township, the county, the province, or even the state. Although higher officials make efforts to institutionalize ongoing family planning work, cadres take no initiative in this area, and only complete such tasks during the family planning campaigns, when they receive specific quotas and are monitored by their superiors.

Though it sounds absurd given the official regulations, village cadres may well allow couples to have unplanned births, and they usually do not intervene except during family planning campaigns. The more unplanned births one village has, the easier it is for village cadres to complete the family planning tasks assigned during the family planning campaigns, because they have more couples from whom to collect fines, and they have more couples 'eligible' for IUD insertions, abortion or sterilization than the quota assigned as their family planning task. In this way, village cadres show that it is not village cadres but higher authorities who request the villagers to regulate their fertility behaviour, and they can also bargain more effectively with villagers, i.e. in return for helping the village cadres meet their quota in this campaign. The cadres may allow reproductive couples to have children at other times, and thus reproductive couples should cooperate with cadres in return.

Villagers want to achieve their desired family size at the minimum cost. For some, this means that during pregnancy and childbirth they live outside the village, without revealing the extra births to cadres, and even to their neighbours or other villagers, in order to avoid abortion, sterilization, and economic penalties. Women who cannot hide their pregnancy and childbirth will 'adopt out', sending the newborns to relatives or friends during family planning campaigns, and having them back at home in other times. They may even claim that the pregnancy resulted in a stillbirth, or that the infant died after birth, in order to avoid penalties.

Mediation through interaction: Among cadres

Cadres in the village Party committee and village government are usually treated analytically as a homogeneous and conflict-free group. In fact, positions and levels of cadres are different. All village cadres come from the same village, and live and work with their fellow villagers for almost their entire lives. Township cadres, however, come from other localities. The main township leaders usually come from different townships, their lack of local attachments is meant to insure a fair and good job completed. Township cadres receive salaries as government employees. They usually hold urban household registrations, and can shift their jobs to other townships or counties.

Village cadres have different responsibilities and interests. They are attached to their family clans. At the same time, village cadres have more in common with each other than with township cadres, and this has important implications in the implementation of family planning policies. Interaction between village and township cadres and among village cadres happen in each step of family planning campaigns and in almost every aspect of family planning work, from assigning tasks to practical implementation and the evaluation of performance.

Village cadres simply receive and try to complete their tasks. Population projects are mostly conducted at the provincial or prefecture level, and local family planning work is assigned on the basis of these larger projects. After receiving its work from Handan prefecture, the immediate superior, the county adjusts its tasks according to local conditions. The county usually adds a 'cap' (daimao) to the task, i.e., makes a higher quota than the prefecture requested, to ensure that the assigned task will be completed. This task, in the form of quotas, is then distributed to the township according to population size and past performance in family planning. Township cadres then assign work to individual villages.

In assigning family planning work to village cadres, the township also want to add a 'cap' to the task received from the county. Village cadres, however, want the tasks to be lighter. The task assigned to the village depends mainly on its population numbers, fertility level and village cadres' past family planning performances. The larger the population, the larger the family planning tasks/ quotas. The poorer past family planning performance has been, the larger the task will be, since township cadres would expect that unexplored potential for family planning work exists. Village cadres may reduce their work burden by falsifying demographic reports and family planning statistics, like household and population size, number of couples of reproductive ages, number of children per couple, number of pregnant women, and so on. At the same time, they keep their own accounts, and based on which they fulfil their assigned tasks. It seems that this system of 'double accounts' is not rare in villages.

Village cadres may seek help from township cadres for the implementation of family planning policies in the village. Township cadres can give effective pressures, since for villagers, the township represent the state, and township cadres have more power than village cadres. Township cadres are unfamiliar to some villagers, come from outside the village and are unafraid of offending someone within the village. However, although township cadres can be used to pressure villagers, village cadres cannot easily escape blame for this, and village cadres may also try to influence township cadres toward less strong measures, as illustrated by the following case:

During the first family planning campaign in 1993, a woman with two children intended to avoid economic penalties and sterilization; this was not acceptable to the village cadres, though so far she had managed to escape all penalties. This time, village cadres tried to push her either to pay the fine, or to be sterilized. Her husband was working outside the village. Her mother-in-law tried to persuade her to pay some money so that the cadres would not bother her for a sterilization. The woman did not agree and insisted on trying to delay, hoping the cadres would give up their efforts. After the failure of many visits, village cadres decided to ask help from the township cadres at a late stage of the campaign. The woman simply ran away to her natal family. Village cadres followed her there, but without success. Township cadres wanted to go to her natal family (in another village of the same township) by themselves to pressure for compliance. However, the village cadres hinted that such an action was not appropriate. Without seeking consent from the woman, her husband, and their parents, village cadres would not use force to push them for compliance. Finally, the woman had not been sterilized, and she did not pay any penalties. However, I was surprised later to learn that in the report on this family planning campaign she was counted toward the quota for sterilization, and no one knew whether this was true or not.

In family planning work, the state always calls upon cadres and communist party members to take the lead and set up good models to be followed. This is usually supervised by higher authorities, though an 'accusation letter box' (*jianjuxiang*) is set up for villagers to register problems in cadres' family planning work. Since cadres are usually older (the youngest in their late 40s), most no longer plan to have more children, and 'cadres taking the lead' has mutated into their children and close kin 'taking the lead', in demonstrating that village cadres can implement strict and fair policies.

In 1993, county cadres, together with township cadres, chose the village for an on-the-spot family planning mass meeting (*jihua shengyu xianchanghui*), together with promotion for cotton production. The director of the county government office, two vice-directors of the county family planning commission, the Party secretary and governor of the township, accompanied by all village cadres, attended the meeting.[5] It was organized in the evening, in the intermission of the public screening of a film. In the mass meeting, the first issue was to consider the family planning work of village cadres and their married children in the village (their responsibility for family planning work does not extend to their daughters who married out of the village), and of their brothers and sisters together with their married children in the village. Villagers were told that they could point out right away if village cadres did not tell the truth; they were also told that they could inform the higher authorities by anonymous letter. The six male village cadres spoke in turn. Villagers did not speak out, but made some noise when they heard false stories. Some made *sotto voce* jokes that one daughter-in-law of a village cadre had been sterilized twice, implying that at least the first sterilization was a false one. Everybody believed that this was only a performance for the villagers (*zouguochang*), which had little effect on village cadres. They believed that higher authorities could not be too serious, and that cadres at higher levels may pretend ignorance so long as no one exposes them, and that when failures are exposed they would just punish a few cadres who seriously violate the family planning regulations, to want to 'kill the chicken to show to the monkeys' (to set an example).

Evaluation of family planning performance is conducted at the end of each family planning campaign. The village is given a certain number of points according to the work completed. There is a certain benchmark, and villages below the benchmark will be punished, and those over the mark rewarded. This is referred to as 'family planning reaching the standard' activity (*jihua shengyu dabiao huodong*). The standard can be comprehensive, involving almost every aspect of family planning work. For example, the evaluation set by the county for family planning work in each village concerned the following six aspects: organizational set-up (having the relevant institutions or not), publicity and education around population policy, policy implementation, measures adopted, quality of services, and scientific management.

'Reaching the standard' is meant to create an incentive and disincentive structure for grassroots level cadres. However, its effectiveness is difficult to assess. One consequence is that cadres cheat when they cannot meet the quotas. There are many different ways of cheating. Village cadres unable to meet the quotas may fool their superiors by using part of the collective fund to cover the gap between family planning fines due and those collected. They also may use collective money to buy false sterilization certificates to cheat and show they have done a good job.

Unlike the interactions between village and township cadres, in which the bargaining process is more obvious, conflicts among village cadres are much more disguised. It is difficult to detect and observe the conflicts that exist among village cadres. In the distribution of family planning tasks, they share the task evenly. In family planning work in the residential groups for which they are responsible, no cadre appears more enthusiastic than others, to avoid censure from fellow villagers in their residential groups. In unified actions, when village cadres make joint family visits during the family planning campaigns, cadres will play the main role in negotiating with a family in their residential group. Other cadres will help, but in a passive way.

Usually, village cadres cannot complete their jobs through individual visits. They do not want to show that they intend to press a couple for compliance, and usually wait for unified action, so that all village cadres are making the family visits together, and they can press a couple to comply helped by the Party secretary and other village cadres. The Party secretary, who is ultimately responsible for the family planning work of the whole village, is dissatisfied with the passive roles that other village cadres assume in family planning work.

THE 1993 FAMILY PLANNING CAMPAIGNS

Mediation of state population policies through interaction between cadres and villagers and among cadres can be better understood from actual family planning campaigns, since cadres rely heavily on such campaigns for carrying out family planning policies. Who cadres negotiate with, and how they negotiate (both with higher authorities and with villagers), differ for different households; this can be best shown by analysing family planning campaigns which have been carried out in the village.

In 1993, there were four family planning campaigns carried out in the village, called for by the county family planning leaders' group. Each family planning campaign had three stages: preparation, imple- mentation, and evaluation. Each campaign had its particular focus; these would depend on guidelines from above. For example, the major focus in the summer of 1993 was to collect family planning fines, and in the autumn the focus was on family planning surgery (including abortion and sterilization). Village cadres are usually called to a meeting with the township government during the preparation stage of the campaign. They are assigned their task, mobilized, and informed about the principles of the work. A family planning task is always very specific. It includes the amount of money to be collected in fines, the number of IUD insertions, the number of first trimester abortions, the number of second trimester abortions, and the number of sterilization.

The Party secretary will then organize a meeting for village cadres. They will discuss their strategy and methods of the work. The six cadres will distribute the fines, numbers of IUD insertions, abortions, and sterilization among themselves. In the meeting, they will refer their own accounts, identify the target couples, and discuss their specific aims for each of the couples concerned. At the same time, the village Party secretary will use the loudspeaker to broadcast the beginning of the family planning campaign. This usually takes place in early morning or late evening, when most villagers are at home. Cadres will then begin to make household visits within their residential groups.

The cadres cannot complete their job through individual household visits, because the households will try all means to bargain, attempting not to pay the fine or to pay as little as possible; the household also may simply run away to escape punishment. Village cadres will set aside one or two days for unified action, going door-to-door together to collect fines, or to persuade couples to accept abortion or sterilization. Finally, at the end of the family planning campaign, the village cadres will report to the township about the campaign and its accomplishments. The township government will evaluate the campaign, and provide awards or punishments according to the village cadres' performance.

The first family planning campaign

The first family planning campaign in 1993 started on 27 March, when the Party secretary announced a meeting for the village cadres (through the loudspeaker, in the early morning). No cadres were allowed to excuse themselves, for any reason. Villagers knew that the meeting concerned family planning. No other work is treated as seriously as family planning.

The meeting among village cadres lasted the whole day. In the evening, the Party secretary informed the villagers about the family planning campaign, again through the loudspeakers, around suppertime, when most people are home from work. He said that reproductive couples who had not had their regular check-up (pregnancy and contraceptives) at the township family planning service station would be considered as being pregnant, and (if the pregnancy was unplanned) they would need to have abortions; that a woman with one child who had not yet had an IUD insertion should do so; that those who reject IUD insertion would be fined 100 *yuan*; and that women with unplanned pregnancies who rejected abortion would be fined 800 *yuan*. The Party secretary said the township cadres and a family planning implementation team of around 40 persons would arrive in a few days, after finishing their family planning work in neighbouring villages, and that they would stay in the village until the family planning task was completed.

The words used by the Party secretary were strong. However, villagers appeared calm, and acted as if nothing special had happened. My host told me that they had become accustomed to it. 'This is only a strong wind, nobody knows if there will be rain or not.' Villagers, especially couples who had family planning problems (e.g. unplanned pregnancies and extra children), would watch carefully to see whether the cadres were going to take the family planning work seriously this time, and they would take appropriate measures accordingly. At this early stage, no women with family planning problems left the village.

The Party secretary did not broadcast to the villagers about the specific quotas assigned. He did not specify which couple should be fined or for how much, nor who should have IUD insertion, abortion or sterilization. Village cadres never spread this information in public. I later learned that the family planning task for this campaign was the following: a lump sum of 7700 *yuan* of fines for extra births and illegal marriage (marriage without registration and early marriage before legal marriage age), 21 IUD insertions, 7 first trimester abortions, 2 second trimester abortions, and 15 sterilizations. Village cadres said that the township government requested a 700 *yuan* fine for each illegal marriage, but the village requested 300 *yuan*;[6] the township requested 1500 *yuan* for a couple's first extra baby, 3000 *yuan* for the second extra baby, and 4500 *yuan* for the third extra baby, but the village requested 20 per cent of this during this particular campaign, i.e., 300 *yuan*, 600 *yuan*, and 900 *yuan* respectively. Those fined before would be fined again if the accumulative fine collected in previous campaigns had not reached yet the full payment (according to provincial regulations). Village cadres believed that it was not practical to collect the fine all at once as requested by provincial regulations. They said villagers did not have sufficient money in hand, especially because there had been no income from cotton in the previous year.

For the next four days, the Party secretary broadcast each morning about the family planning regulations, requesting that couples comply with state family planning regulations, prepare money to pay family planning fines, and be ready to go for IUD insertion, abortion or sterilization. At the same time, other village cadres responsible for family planning work started to make family visits, to collect fines, and to persuade couples and arrange for abortions and sterilization. In this period, some township cadres came to the village to discuss with village cadres about the progress of the family planning work.

On the first of April, village cadres took unified action for family visits. They gathered in the early morning (6:30 a.m.), and started to visit those households with family planning problems, moving from the west of the village to the east along the main street in the village. Most households in the west belong to the sixth residential group, mostly to Guo family clans, the second most common surname in the village. The cadre who was responsible for the family planning work of the residential group also came from the Guo family. Most households in the east belong to Huang family clans, the most common surname in the village. The cadre who was responsible for the family planning work of this residential group comes from Huang family clan.

The decision to starting from the west rather than the east was decided by the Guo cadre and the Huang cadre, who drew lots. This was necessary to avoid complaints of unfair (dis)advantage. Couples with family planning problems liked to be visited much later, when cadres were tired after bargaining with many households, and thus had little strength or enthusiasm to continue making efforts to make couples comply. Cadres usually put in more effort at the beginning, and tried hard to achieve their aims, in order to avoid the discouragement that comes with too much difficulty and too little return on their efforts. Further, they knew that if they failed to persuade one family to comply, it would be extremely difficult to persuade the following families to comply.

From 6:30 a.m. until 6:00 p.m., with a one-hour lunch break, the village cadres visited 15 households. They collected 700 *yuan* in family planning fines, and took away as in-kind payments 100 *jin* of wheat and 600 *jin* of maize; some household property such as an electric fan, television set, and bicycle, all converted into certain cash amounts according to their value, and stored in the village government site as collateral to be returned whenever the owner paid the fine. A few households locked their doors and no one was at home. Two township cadres joined in the family visits later in the morning and left in the afternoon. The family visits were mainly for collecting fines this time, and the cadres tried to negotiate for either the fine, or sterilization. Cadres did not make family visits to request IUD insertions. No first or second trimester were requested during these family visits. In fact, during the whole period of the year's first family planning campaign, I heard of no cases of IUD insertion or abortion.

Each family visit lasted between 30 minutes to an hour. No household paid the fine immediately as requested, and each bargained to pay the least possible amount of money. No households argued that they should not be fined for their extra child. They did not challenge the state policy; they agreed with its principles, and they knew the fine requested by village cadres was much less than requested by provincial regulations. They also knew that they would not satisfy the cadres if they paid no fine and let cadres leave empty-handed, especially when all village cadres were present. They thus usually agreed to pay a partial fine, and might pay an additional amount if pressured. However, none paid the entire amount as requested. Most households who paid the fine during the family visits paid the equivalent of 200 *yuan*, no matter whether this was as a fine for illegal or early marriage, or first extra birth, or second extra birth, or even extra birth of higher parities (see Table 8.1).

Village cadres also knew well the situations of individual households, and had a bargaining strategy in mind to achieve the possible best results. For households which had more money, they would push to collect more. For households with no money but a sufficient amount of grain, they would push by requesting them to borrow money to pay the fine, or to use grain as payment. For those households without cash, who had difficulty borrowing money since they had no capacity to repay, or had insufficient grain for subsistence, cadres would take away an item of family property to be held as collateral; this item would be returned to them as soon as they paid the fine. The amount of money, grain, or household property taken away also varied from case to case; there was no unified, clear-cut standard, and much depended on the bargaining processes. All households visited were poor or average-income households, and, as Table 8.1 shows, there was consequently variation and flexibility in the implementation of state policies at the household level during this campaign.

Because there was an annual market fair in a neighbouring village

Table 8.1   Family planning fine collected in the first family planning campaign in 1993

Household	Reasons for penalty	Penalty imposed	Final outcome
I	illegal & early marriage	300 *yuan*	100 *yuan*, with guarantee from a cadre to pay the rest
II	illegal & early marriage	300 *yuan*	100 *yuan*
III	illegal & early marriage	300 *yuan*	600 jin maize
IV	illegal & early marriage	300 *yuan*	200 *yuan*
V	illegal & early marriage	300 *yuan*	One black-white TV, one handcart, three quilts as collateral
VI	illegal & early marriage	300 *yuan*	100 jin wheat
VII	first extra birth	300 *yuan*, or sterilization	100 *yuan*, with guarantee from a cadre to pay the rest
VIII	first extra birth	300 *yuan*, or sterilization	one bicycle, one electric fan as collateral
IX	first extra birth	300 *yuan*, or sterilization	no payment, & apparently no sterilization, though registered as sterilization
X	first extra birth	300 *yuan*, or sterilization	sterilization after pregnancy, no fine, but later had another child
XI	two extra births	600 *yuan*, or sterilization	200 *yuan*

the following day, and most villagers (including cadres) were attending the fair, the family planning campaign stopped for a day. On 3 April, village cadres planned to continue family visits; however, their plan changed because the new township governor came to the village to check their family planning work.

The following seven days was a period of silence. There were no family visits, and no broadcasts. On 10 April, the Party secretary resumed the broadcasts, saying that the family planning campaign had not reached to its end, and called on cadres to have a meeting. I later learned that the county family planning leaders' group believed that the family planning campaign was insufficiently thorough and had called on cadres at lower levels to continue the campaign. However, no actual action was taken in the following two days. On 13 April, village cadres informed villagers that cadres from the county and the township had chosen their village for a family planning meeting, to push the family planning campaign to a new 'high tide' (see above). After township and county level cadres left the same evening, however, there was only one broadcast the next morning. The village became quiet again, and nothing happened until the second family planning campaign was initiated by higher authorities.

In the first family planning campaign, it was said village cadres had collected 3,600 *yuan* (I calculated this figure to be 2,000 *yuan* at most), and that the cadres used money from collective finance to fill the gap of 4,100 *yuan* to 'complete' the family planning task of 7,700 *yuan*. Village cadres said that there were two cases of sterilization, which everyone suspected was untrue. I heard of no cases of IUD insertion. No abortions were even mentioned by any cadres or villagers throughout this campaign.

The second family planning campaign

On 16 July, three months after the first family planning campaign, the village started the second campaign of the year. This campaign focused on the collection of family planning fines. The task assigned was the collection of 19,250 *yuan* fine, much more than the quota for the first campaign; in addition, the family planning quotas called for five first trimester abortions, three second trimester abortions, and three sterilization.

According to the requirement from the township government, the village needed to pay 80 per cent of the 19,250 *yuan* fine, i.e. 15,400 *yuan*, to the township. The remaining fine collected could be retained by the village. Village cadres planned to collect 10,000 *yuan* from households with extra births, and have the village fill the gap of 5,400 *yuan*, to 'complete' the task. They planned to collect the fine from around 70 households with extra births, and hoped to collect 100 *yuan* fine for first extra birth, and 150 *yuan* for second or third extra births. Couples with one child could pay 50 *yuan* if they chose not to have an IUD insertion.

The township issued specific regulations for this campaign. Firstly, couples with extra births after the promulgation of provincial family planning regulations in March 1989 would be fined 3,250 *yuan* for the unplanned birth of the second child, and an additional fine of 1,625 *yuan* for each additional extra birth, based on the criteria of a per capita income of 650 *yuan* in the township. Secondly, reproductive couples who had male or female sterilization but had not paid enough of their fine would have to pay the remaining fine. Thirdly, cadres must rescind promises they might have made to the villagers if these were inconsistent with the regulations.[7] Fourthly, cadres and Communist Party members should take the lead in the family planning campaign. Fifthly, state employees, cadres, and contract workers must abide by family planning regulations and act on family planning measures accordingly; those who deviate from the regulations would be dismissed from their positions and their contracts cancelled. Sixthly, concerning households with members working outside while their spouses staying in the township, the township would inform the relevant working units about their family planning performances and taking appropriate measures. Seventhly, the family planning court and family planning implementation team use whatever tactics they deemed appropriate to force those who opposed family planning regulations to have operations (including abortion and sterilization) or pay their fine. And finally, those who insulted or assaulted family planning cadres or obstructed family planning work could be fined, punished by administrative disciplinary measures, or legally sentenced according to the seriousness of the incident.

As usual, the township family planning regulations were broadcast almost every morning, starting with the beginning of the campaign. The words used by village cadres were harsh, to show the determination of cadres to complete the work, and the environment was intense. There were more frequent broadcasts, even during the daytime when most people were away at work. Villagers again were observing, trying to determine which actions would be taken this time.

In the first few days, village cadres made individual family visits in their respective residential groups. During most of the beginning of the campaign, the vice-governor of the township, who was responsible for the village's family planning work but could not attend the first family planning campaign in April, together with a young woman cadre from the township, stayed in the village.

In the early 1990s, the county had set up a family planning court, and three days after the start of the campaign, two personnel from the county court came to the village to assist in family planning work. This was the first time the township had requested help from the court in family planning work. Since the county court lacked personnel, its two staff members could stay in the village for only two days, before moving to other villages. The two court personnel arrived during the afternoon of 19 July. They were given a list of 16 couples (not 70 as planned) by the village cadres; all 16 had had extra births for which cadres were finding it difficult to collect fines. The couples were told to come to explain their situation to the court employees, and those who failed to come before 8:00 p.m. were told they would have to pay a doubled fine. The village cadres did not inform couples in public through the loudspeakers, but told them individually. It should be noted that the two court personnel did not follow the township regulations, but worked within the village cadres' original plans, i.e. helping to collect 100 *yuan*, 150 *yuan*, and 300 *yuan* from couples with one, two, or three extra births (instead of the 1,625 *yuan*, 3,250 *yuan*, or 4,875 *yuan* respectively set by the township).

On the first day, four individuals came over to meet the court personnel, all from the poorest households. Three women and one man came before the deadline. Two of the women had serious discussions with the court personnel. Another woman and the man discussed something for a shorter period with the village cadres, then left, most likely to collect money to pay their fine. It is possible that those who failed to appear might simply have decided to pay the fine, or they might have decided to resist a bit longer. On the next morning, the first woman from the previous day was called again, since she had only paid 50 *yuan*, instead of the 100 *yuan* minimum. Later she bargained this down, and was told to pay only another 40 *yuan*. Village cadres revealed that they would accept lower amounts: couples with one or two extra births could pay 90 *yuan* or 135 *yuan*, instead of the 100 *yuan* or 150 *yuan* which had been publicly announced. The court personnel pressed the first woman to pay the further 40 *yuan* by saying that otherwise they would request the village cadres to take a suitcase from the household as collateral (no other more valuable items could be taken as collateral). The women insisted on not paying another 40 *yuan*, the village cadres did not take the suitcase, and I later discovered that she had already been sterilized and that village cadres had promised her that they would never come back and bother her with family planning work. However, in this campaign, village cadres said that they were wrong to have made such a promise, and that the township had left them no alternative but to rescind it.

After another two days of individual household visits, village cadres together with the vice-township governor, and some other township cadres (13 people in total) met for a unified action on household visits to collect fines. They started at 6:00 a.m., and village cadres employed one person with a horse cart to transport wheat, maize, or other household property taken as collateral.

The process was extremely quick; households with few members present found it difficult to bargain with so many village and township cadres. Knowing that there was no way to avoid the fine this time, most paid the money, or its equivalent in wheat or maize, or let cadres take property as collateral. Although several households had again locked their doors and run away, the cadres did not break in to take away household property as their broadcast had threatened.[8] Family visits were brief, and took place only in the morning; approximately 15 households were visited. In the afternoon, village cadres met to see how much fine they had collected so far. Nothing happened the next day, and the day after that I learned that the second family planning campaign was over. I was told that the village had paid 154,000 *yuan* and completed the family planning task. Village cadres said they spent another 1000 *yuan* to buy two falsified second trimester abortion certificates, which were also applied towards their quota.

The fine was not much of a burden for most households when compared with their annual income, or with the thousands of *yuan* spent on house-building, marriage, or burial expenses. Cadres actually collected only 55 *yuan* (not 100 *yuan*) for extra births, whether the birth was the second, third, or later child. However, households did not want to be fined and tried to get avoid paying. Most were dissatisfied with the cadres over the collection of fines, but mainly because they believed the cadres were not even-handed in carrying out the policy, i.e. that cadres collected fines only from them but not from others. Cadres, of course, did not accept this accusation, and answered with the request that villagers specify which couple with extra births had escaped being fined (or scheduled for abortion, or sterilization); however villagers were reluctant to speak out. Further, cadres argued that they could not know whether a case for extra births, or other violations of family planning policies existed. They argued that the village was so big that the omission of a few cases was inevitable, and that with the introduction of the responsibility system, labour was no longer collectively arranged, making it difficult to detect unplanned pregnancies.

Township cadres were less patient than village cadres in bargaining and arguing with individual households. Because they lacked background information about each household, and were unafraid of complaints, they pressured each household equally. Each family visit was brief, and the work style was simple compared with the family visits involving only village cadres. Neither household members nor village cadres were always satisfied with the ways the township cadres implemented family planning work. Household members could be upset with the village cadres because they had led the township cadres to them in order to collect fines. The village cadre responsible for the households' family planning work usually stayed a bit longer after other cadres left, trying to appease the couple, and trying to repair any damage to their relationship with the family arising from the visit. Township cadres were, however, themselves dissatisfied with the way village cadres participated in family planning work. Township cadres believed that village cadres were too soft, that they were usually more interested in avoiding conflict than in doing their work, and that without the help of township cadres, few village cadres could work completely on their own. However, I have no knowledge of how this family planning campaign was formally evaluated.

The third family planning campaign

The third family planning campaign started one month later and followed the same general pattern. On 2 September the main village cadres had a meeting in the township, and the next day all village cadres had a meeting in the village. The quotas assigned to the village for this campaign included five sterilizations, one first trimester abortion, and one second trimester abortion of pregnancy over three months. Village cadres said that the third campaign carried over some of the quota from the last campaign, which had not yet been met.

On the third day, the Party secretary made a morning broadcast requesting villagers with family planning problems to approach cadres and arrange for sterilization or abortion. For the first time that year, he mentioned that family planning needed to be implemented because rapid population growth and the decline of the arable land created problems. He warned that couples whose situation fit the state criteria for sterilization or abortion should not run away this time, and that if they did so they took full responsibility for the consequences. He said that while a family might run away once, this could not be a repeated action, and that it was better for them to take appropriate action sooner than later. He then called on village cadres for another meeting.

However, nothing happened in the days that followed. Township cadres did not appear. It seemed that no one knew whether the cadres had made family visits, nor whether anyone had had a sterilization or abortion. However, when I visited the township family planning commission at the end of the year, it was reported that the village had completed its task as assigned. To me, and probably also to villagers, this campaign was comprised of 'wind but no rain', that is, words but no actions.

The fourth family planning campaign

The final family planning campaign of the year started on 24 October, and focused on family planning surgery. The assigned quotas were one first trimester abortion, three second trimester abortions, seven IUD insertions and 17 sterilizations. No family planning fines were assigned. The township government requested that the tasks should be completed within seven to ten days. The work would be evaluated at the end of the campaign. Each cadre would be awarded 100 yuan if the task was completed within seven days, or 50 yuan within ten days, but no award after ten days. Punishments would be meted out if the family planning task was not completed.

In the first three days, village cadres made family visits; they later said that the first trimester abortion and the seven IUD insertions had been settled. On the afternoon of the fourth day, the campaign started to intensify. Township cadres came to the village to check and assist the family planning work. For the first time that year, township cadres used the loudspeakers, broadcasting to villagers about the family planning campaign as follows:

XX village (the researched village) has been so far listed as the third from the bottom in the performance of family planning work among all villages in the township. XX village need to complete its tasks within a short period. Village cadres must work hard and take full responsibility. No matter what, those couples who should have family planning surgery must have their operations tomorrow afternoon. Family planning has been carried out for many years, and it is not a new thing. After the broadcast, women [note: not men] with two or more children should be sterilised. It is better for you to have sterilisation sooner than later. The women concerned should prepare to have the operation today, and you are not allowed to go outside the village. No village cadres are allowed to ask for leave.

The cadres also made frequent broadcasts the following day; they broadcast that there had not been a single case of sterilization in the village in this campaign, which was the worst performance of all villages in the township. Those who claimed that they had had no unplanned births could make this statement to cadres, and made a 300 *yuan* deposit. If the statement was revealed to be false, the 300 *yuan* would be forfeited, and they would face serious punishment. Women who could not have sterilization on this day must make a 200 *yuan* collateral; if they have not been sterilized by the next day, the 200 *yuan* would be forfeited.

The township family planning implementation team arrived in the village to assist in the family planning work. A family planning propaganda jeep (*jihua shengyu xuanchuanche*) also moved around in the village to broadcast state family planning regulations. The jeep was also supposed to be used as transportation, to bring women who were to be sterilized to the county hospital.

At about 11:00 a.m. a young man was taken by a group of township cadres to the office of the village government. It was said that he refused to be sterilized and threatened the implementation team members with a dagger. The police was called immediately. The young man was in his early 30s and had one boy and one girl. The couple belonged neither to the Huang nor the Guo family, but to a small family clan. The couple was requested to pay the fine for one extra birth, or to be sterilized. However, the man rejected both options, arguing that his second child suffered from infantile paralysis, could not become a normally capable adult and that he should therefore not be fined.

Villagers knew that he would be seriously punished, and neighbours, friends, and other family members tried to ask for leniency (*qiuqing*) on his behalf. His father appeared to have no way to influence his son, but, instigated by others, tried to scold and even beat his son, hoping that punishment from the family would make it possible to avoid punishment from the township. The township governor, however, did not accept this, knowing that if this case was resolved softly the job would never be completed. Village cadres, normally mediators between the township and villagers, now stepped aside so that the confrontation was directly between villagers and township cadres.

After three hours of negotiation between the families, their neighbours and friends, police, and township cadres, the following decisions were made: firstly, the young man had to apologize to the township and village cadres; secondly, he had to admit his mistakes in public; thirdly, he had to pay the family planning fine;[9] fourthly, he had to pay the procedural cost of 350 *yuan*;[10] finally, one member of the couple must be sterilized that afternoon. The young man was not taken away by the police; he admitted his mistakes in public through the loudspeakers, reading out the written self-criticism twice. The day ended with the sterilization of the young man's wife.

The township governor returned to the village the next day. Village cadres reported that they had tried to persuade four couples to undergo sterilization. Two agreed to have female sterilization; of these, one wanted to have the operation on some other day, saying that the day was not a good day for surgery, which was probably not superstition but an excuse for delay. The other two women were reported to have run away to escape sterilization. Township cadres sent three village cadres and two other cadres to the neighbouring villages to find the women to persuade them to undergo sterilization. The village cadres left before noon, and returned in the evening after the township cadres left the village.

The following day, five township cadres again came to the village. It was reported that the village cadres had failed to find one of the women the previous day; they did meet the other woman for a short while, but she ran away again. Village cadres decided to search for them again; if they failed, they would break into houses and take away household property as collateral. Village cadres again left, and the township cadres waited in the village. Again nothing happened. In the afternoon, other township cadres arrived with the propaganda jeep. They had just finished their work in a neighbouring village, and came to offer help.

Again village cadres did not return until after the township cadres had finally left. Township cadres complained that village cadres did not complete their job well this time, and they were thinking about ways to put much more pressure on village cadres in future. This was the last time the township cadres came to the village that year. It was said that the two women had successfully escaped being sterilized. The final family planning campaign of the year ended on 1 November. The next family planning campaign did not take place until sometime after the Chinese new year (February).

The changing context for policy implementations after the 1978 reforms, together with changing social relations between rural households and local cadres, have reshaped family planning work in the new era. Within the new institutional context, a number of methods used in the collective period are no longer effective. For example, study groups for policy popularization and family planning education, which were frequently organized during the collective period, have become impossible. Mass meetings for family planning work have also become difficult to organize since the introduction of the responsibility system and market reforms. The system of incentives and disincentives was ineffective in the pre-reform period, and remains ineffective today; rural couples simply have never accepted state-imposed limits on their childbearing in return for economic incentives. With respect to the disincentives, although the economic penalties have become much heavier since reform, and may put certain limits on the childbearing of rural couples, this cannot stop rural couples from having more children than permitted by formal state family planning regulations. Further, cadres must now approach the relevant households individually to collect the fines; they can no longer impose the fine by simply deducting work points or assigning no labour opportunities to couples who defied state policies, as they could during the collective era. They also find it difficult to oversee the reproduction of rural couples, because labour is no longer organized by the collective, and pregnant women are not as easily discovered as during the collective period, when men and women worked together. The provision of family planning services has also had to shift from health clinics (in the collective period) to a special family planning service centre at a higher (township) level.

Within the changing context cadres have found strict adherence to state policies ineffective; they instead implement 'softer' local policies, and they do not implement some policies at all. For example, the village has never implemented the so-called 'one-child' policy; the double contract system exists only on paper; incentives for meeting the norm for family size have simply been abandoned; many couples with two or three children have never seen a 'birth permission certificate' before they decide to cease childbearing; cadres do not regulate the timing of marriage and childbearing, and thus birth spacing; cadres have never collected fine for unplanned births as a lump sum as demanded by provincial family planning policies; cadres essentially allow couples to continue to have children until a boy is born, and so forth.

Conflict and cooperation among cadres and peasants seems to be leading to a compromise between individual childbearing and state family planning. Village cadres did not put much effort into delaying the age at marriage, delaying pregnancies, increasing birth intervals, or limiting couples to the one or two children permitted by formal family planning regulations. Couples deviating from the formal policies do face certain penalties, though these are the informal rules shaped by interaction between rural households and local cadres, and not those stipulated by formal regulations. Village cadres tend to allow villagers to have the number and sex composition of children they desire. At the same time, villagers have to cooperate with cadres and let cadres 'complete' their tasks reasonably. This is not to deny the conflicts that exist between cadres and villagers in the bargaining processes over reproduction and family planning; the conflicts and interactions between villagers and cadres are the main mechanisms through which compromises are reached and an informal local family planning policy formed. Village cadres are more programme-oriented than policy-oriented. That is to say, they are handling the tasks assigned to them during each family planning campaign rather than following the principle of population policy in order to slow population growth through regulated fertility and planned births. Village cadres allow unplanned births, but will collect fines and attempt to persuade couples to have the IUD insertions, abortions and sterilizations that cadres need to 'complete' their tasks, especially since they find it difficult to stop couples from having children. Village cadres do not always apply administrative pressure to their fellow villagers in order to exact compliance with family planning policies made at higher administrative levels, because this may also damage the relations between cadres and the families concerned. They may at times protect their fellow villagers from harsher treatments imposed by higher authority (township and county administrations). Villagers do not always make trouble over family planning or resist village cadres; they may also collude with village cadres to falsify family planning registrations and reports to higher authorities. They also pay fines to 'save face' (*liulianmian*) with village cadres.

It should be noted that interactions between different households and cadres vary significantly in the bargaining process. The poor do not *liulianmian* to cadres, and try hard to get family planning penalties lifted. They are the ones who receive group visits during family planning campaigns, which were mainly used to press for compliance because, when visited by individual cadres, they had refused the options of paying the fine or practising contraception. They may have no better option than simply running away from cadres to escape the penalties during the family planning campaigns or paying some grain if they have no cash. Some poor families may also have their household property taken away by cadres as collateral if payment negotiations fail. This happens mostly with extremely poor families who find it difficult even to borrow money from friends or neighbours, or with families who insist they will not pay any economic fine. Rich villagers who have no close relation with cadres pay their fines without creating much trouble for village cadres. The most privileged are those who are both rich and closely related to cadres; the average villager does not know whether these families pay their fines, nor how much they pay (although they can easily afford the economic penalty). The means and effectiveness of defying family planning policies differ greatly among households.

The family member chosen as negotiator also varies among families and depends on the positions of different family members. It seems that, with the increasing decision power of the young and of women in the family, cadres are increasingly negotiating with young reproductive couples rather than with their elders. Women may also be moving to the forefront in negotiations with local cadres over their reproduction as a result of the long-term migration of husbands working outside the village. In an increasingly conflict-ridden situation, young women and young couples are increasingly playing more important roles in their reproductive decision-makings, and the influence of family elders and local cadres is declining.

New characteristics of family planning programme at the local level are not only shaped by changes within families; they are also shaped by interactions between rural households and local cadres. For example, no village cadre wants to show more enthusiasm than others in pushing fellow villagers to comply with unpopular state policies. These new characteristics are also reshaped by interactions among cadres of the same and different administrative levels. Village cadres have both direct and disguised ways to resist policies imposed by higher authorities. For example, village cadres can falsify the relevant statistics in order to get easier-to-meet family planning quotas; and can protect their fellow villagers from the harsher penalties defined by higher authorities; they can also use collective money to pay fines or to buy false certificates.

In short, state policies are increasingly mediated by both local government administrations and individual families and households, through interactions between rural households and local government administrations, and through interaction among local cadres and among cadres of various administrative levels.

Notes

[1] Mosher (1983, 1995) and Aird (1990), however, present an image of family planning cadres as coercive, merciless figures that are manipulated by the state and all behave in the same way. Articles that have appeared in Western periodicals on Chinese family planning issues in a simplistic and distorted fashion have been criticized (see Wasserstrom 1984).

[2] In my interviews, several leaders of the residential groups confirmed that they quit because 'the work was too difficult and the payment too little'.

[3] Condoms are available in the village shops; however, it seems that they are sold as toys for children rather than as contraceptives for adults.

[4] Some residents who live in the village but hold non-agricultural household registrations usually get their contraceptives from their work units. For those couples where husbands work outside and have urban household registrations and wives stay in the village and have the village's rural household registrations, it is assumed that responsibility for the couple's family planning lies with the husbands' work units, and not with the village family planning commission. However, work units find it difficult to monitor family planning; village cadres simply do not interfere.

[5] This was a county-wide activity. In other townships, Party secretary, governor of the county, and other county-level cadres together with township cadres, held the same type of village meeting.

[6] Village cadres told me (and this was confirmed later by township cadres) that a neighbouring village collected 400 *yuan* in fines for illegal or early marriage, 100 *yuan* more than the village. Although the neighbouring village was smaller, and is thus considered easier in terms of family planning work, village cadres need not match their performance, but can make their own policy according to their own situations; concrete measures in the implementation of state policy can vary from village to village.

[7] This specifically refers to the promises the village cadres made that couples accepting sterilization would not be fined for extra births.

[8] Through the loudspeaker system, the village cadres informed households with family planning problems that they should remain in the village during the family visits, and that otherwise the cadres would break in and take away household property as collateral.

[9]   Which was 300 *yuan*, but was not specified in the decision made by village and township cadres.

[10] According to township regulations, the village had to pay its expenses by requesting the township family planning implementation team to assist the family planning campaigns.

CHAPTER 9

Fertility, Contraception and Adoption

To understand the dynamics of fertility, the individual fertility motivation and interactions in fertility decision-making discussed in the preceding chapters need to be linked to quantitative fertility and contraception data. That is, we need to know not only what people say about their fertility perception, but also how they behave in practice. We need to know not only the processes through which local cadres and families mediate state policies, but also the outcomes of such mediation. It will show that in the village the age of childbirth has shifted downward, that the interval between marriage and first birth and between first and second birth are shorter; yet it will also show that the fertility level has been declining in the village since reforms. The pattern of contraception, abortion and sterilization, which affect the number and timing of births, also reflect changes in fertility motivation, in power relations within the family and in relations between families and the local authorities.

Empirical data on adoption also extends the analysis of fertility changes. Firstly, it is important to know how infertile couples adapt to the changing context brought about by economic reforms. Secondly, it appears that fertile couples use adoption to achieve the number of children or sex composition desired, when the cost of giving birth is too high. This use of adoption is becoming more common as families cope with the influences of economic reform and stringent family planning policies; rural couples are trying to avoid having many sons and to avoid liability for increasing family planning penalties.

Fertility indicators will be explored dynamically from the individual life-cycle perspective. This chapter will firstly show that fertility has declined in the village, although women are beginning child-bearing at a younger age and birth intervals are becoming shorter, women are also younger when they stop having children. It then discusses how this drop in fertility has been achieved, i.e. through the changing pattern of contraception, abortion and sterilization of rural reproductive couples. Finally the chapter discusses adoption, and shows that the adoption pattern has also changed under the new context.

CHANGING FERTILITY PATTERNS

Using the childbearing histories of women aged 20–59 from the sampling survey of the ever-married women, the number of live births and children alive at the time of the survey reported in the sampling survey of the old, and using 1982 and 1990 official population census data, the decline of women's fertility level in the village can be depicted in some detail.[1] The data reveal changes in fertility level over time, from the 1960s and the 1970s of the pre-reform collective era, to the 1980s and the early 1990s of the reform era.

Table 9.1 presents the (1993) mean and median number of children born and alive for ever-married women aged 20 and over for each five-year age group. The data show that except in the 75–79 age group, for women in age groups over 50 (all of whom have finished their repro-ductive career), the mean and median numbers of children born decline consistently as the age of the group declines. This is even more marked when age groups 45–49 and 40–44 are included, since most women over 40 years cease childbearing (see Figure 9.8 later in this chapter). Women in the 70–74 age group had, on average, given birth to 5.5 children; women in the 40–44 age group, have on average two children fewer (3.4). The median has dropped even more sharply: for women aged 70–74 years the median is 7, for women aged 40–44 years, 3. Although the number of children born has been declining successively from old to young age groups for those aged 60 and over, the number of children alive has increased. This reflects the fact that the reproductive period of the older age groups was mainly in the 1940s, 1950s and early 1960s; infant mortality was high and only started to decline dramatically after the 1959–61 famine (see Chapter 4).[2]

It is difficult to say at this moment whether the fertility level has declined dramatically since reforms, given that reform began less than 15 years before the time of the survey. However, it is clear from Table 9.1 that more than half of ever-married women aged 30–34 (who started their childbearing after reforms) have three or more living children. Also, more than half of women aged 25–29 already had two or more children. For both groups, this is far beyond the limits set by formal family planning regulations.

Change in fertility over time can also be checked by comparing childbirth patterns of women of different generations while they were at the same age, and the necessary data can be compiled from 1982 and 1990 official population census data and from my own survey of ever-married women conducted in 1993. Increases or decreases over time should be visible in a comparison of the percentage of women in

Table 9.1 Number of children born and number of children alive for ever-married women by age group, 1993

Age	Number of children alive		Number of children born		No. of cases
	Mean	Median	Mean	Median	
20–24	0.8	1	0.8	1	57
25–29	1.7	2	1.6	2	71
30–34	2.4	3	2.5	3	65
35–39	2.9	3	3.0	3	53
40–44	3.1	3	3.4	3	95
45–49	3.4	3	3.7	4	54
50–54	3.7	4	4.3	4	26
55–59	4.5	5	5.1	5	29
60–64	4.7	5	5.2	5	23
65–69	4.1	5	5.2	6	15
70–74	3.9	4	5.5	7	17
75–79	3.5	2.5	4.5	5	8

Sources: Research survey: ever-married women 1993; Research sampling survey: the elderly 1993.

each age group (focusing on the four age groups of 30–34, 35–39, 40–44, 45–49, which have experienced some or all of their reproductive years) who had four or more children at the time (1982, 1990 and 1993) the data was collected (Tables 9.2, 9.3, and 9.4).

Women who were aged 30–34 and over in 1982 had most of their children during the collective period in the 1970s. Women in the older age groups had most or all of their children in the late 1950s and the 1960s. Women who were aged 30–34 in 1993 had most of their children during the reform period in the 1980s and early 1990s. Women of other age groups in 1993 spent their reproductive period partly in the collective period and partly in the reform period.

As Figure 9.1 shows, the percentage of women in a given age group who had given birth to four or more children declined sharply between 1982 and 1993 (though the 1990 data disturbs the pattern somewhat for the age groups 30–34 and 35–39).

The declining fertility level during the reform period can be seen in the changing parity structure of births between 1983 and 1992, as shown in Table 9.5.[3] Over all, the percentage of higher parity births (third and fourth child, etc.) declined in the intervening decade, while the percentage of births of lower parity (first and second child) increased. It should be noted that the percentage of first parity births peaked in 1986, declined in the late 1980s, and again peaked in 1992. The percentage of third parity births declined until 1986, then leveled off before a further decline in the early 1990s. Two factors could contribute to the pattern: firstly, changes in marriage patterns since the reforms and secondly, the intensity of family planning programmes. The age at marriage has declined since the early 1980s

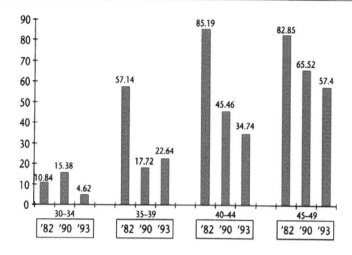

Figure 9.1   Share of ever-married women with four children and over born (per cent) by age groups in 1982, 1990 and 1993
Source: Government population census of the village 1982; Government population census of the village 1990; Research population census of the village 1993; Research survey: ever-married women 1993.

and this, together with the tendency to began to produce families soon after marriage, has contributed to the increase of births of first parities. This pattern may also be related to the implementation of family planning programmes in the county which (as mentioned in Chapter 3) was reportedly good in the early 1980s, slipped backward in the second half of the 1980s, and became much intensified again during the 1990s.

Despite declining fertility in the reform period, many couples managed to have their desired number of children, rather than to follow the state's rules for regulating family size. For example, more than half of women in the 30–34 age group in 1993, who started their reproductive lives during the reform period, managed to have three children, and a few managed to have four. Even some women in the 25–29 age group managed to have four children.

FERTILITY DECISION OUTPUTS: START CHILDBEARING, BIRTH INTERVALS AND STOP CHILDBEARING

When to start having children and with what interval?

Trying to have children of one's own is universal in the village, which can be shown by the small percentages of childless women in the various age groups (Tables 9.2, 9.3 and 9.4), and the small percentage of childless women by years of marriage (Table 9.6). Further, since centage distribution of ever-married women by number of children born and by age groups (1982)

0	1	2	3	4	5	6	7	8	9	10	Total	N
55.0	25.0	20.0									100	
8.5	46.3	39.0	3.7	2.4							100	
1.2	9.6	34.9	43.4	7.2	1.2	2.4					100	
	3.6	7.1	32.1	42.9	10.7	3.6					100	
		7.4	7.4	25.9	33.3	18.5	7.4				100	
	2.9	2.9	11.4	25.7	20.0	17.1	17.1	2.9			100	
2.9		8.6	5.7	17.1	8.6	17.1	22.9	17.1			100	
2.5	12.5	10.0	10.0	10.0	17.5	10.0	10.0	10.0	5.0		100	
	4.2	12.5	4.2	20.8	12.5	12.5	20.8	12.5	2.5	2.5	100	

ent population census of the village 1982.

centage distribution of ever-married women by number of children born and by age groups (1990)

0	1	2	3	4	5	6	7	8	9	Total	N
45.2	39.7	9.6	2.7	2.7						100	
13.0	27.5	42.0	13.0	4.4						100	
	13.5	32.7	38.5	13.5	1.9					100	
	5.1	16.5	60.8	15.2	2.5					100	
		13.6	40.9	34.9	6.1	4.6				100	
3.5	3.5	3.5	24.1	37.9	20.7	3.5	3.5			100	
		11.8	26.5	20.6	23.5	17.7				100	
	9.1	15.2	9.1	30.3	12.1	18.2	3.0	3.0		100	
	5.9	17.7		17.7	23.5	20.6	11.8	3.0	2.9	100	

ent population census of the village 1990.

0	1	2	3	4	5	6	7	8	9	Total	No
28.1	61.4	10.5								100	
5.6	33.8	43.7	14.1	2.8						100	
4.6	3.1	33.9	53.9	4.6						100	
5.7	1.9	13.2	56.6	15.1	5.7	1.9				100	
1.1	1.1	8.4	53.7	27.4	4.2	2.1	1.1			100	
1.9	3.7	3.7	33.3	38.9	13.0	1.9	3.7		1.1	100	
3.9		7.7	19.2	23.1	26.9	11.5	3.9	3.9		100	
3.5		3.5	10.3	13.8	24.1	24.1	13.8	3.5	3.5	100	
8.3		8.3	8.3	12.5	20.8	4.2	8.3	29.2		100	

opulation census of the village 1993.

ity distribution of births by year, 1983-92 (per cent)

1st parity	2nd parity	3rd parity	4th parity	5th parity	6th parity	7th parity
18.4	18.4	40.8	16.3	4.1	2.0	
27.9	21.3	37.7	8.2	1.6	3.3	
33.9	16.9	23.1	24.6			
40.0	26.0	20.0	12.0	2.0		1.5
24.6	32.3	23.1	9.2	9.2		
25.0	30.0	25.0	11.7	6.7	1.7	
32.0	36.0	24.0	6.0		2.0	
33.3	25.0	30.0	5.0	6.7		
43.3	31.7	21.7	1.7	1.7		
52.2	23.9	15.2	6.5	2.2		

urvey: ever-married women 1993.

Table 9.6 Cases of ever-married women without biological children, by year of marriage

Year of % Marriage	Childless women	Ever-married women	Childless women as % of ever-married
1950–54	0	10	0.0
1955–59	1	23	4.4
1960–64	0	16	0.0
1965–69	1	42	2.4
1970–74	0	66	0.0
1975–79	2	62	3.2
1980–84	3	76	4.0
1985–89	4	87	4.6
1990+	18	59	30.5

Source: Research survey: ever-married women 1993.

infertile couples without biological children adopt one or two children (discussed later), having no children or having only one child was an exception in the village. Villagers used to believe having no children to be a curse by heaven. Some men, believing it was their wives' fault that they had no children, divorce and remarry in order to have their own children.[4]

The age of having the first child is declining from 25 or 26 years for women who were in their 40s in 1993, to around 23 for those in their late 20s (Table 9.7). The exceptions are the 55–59 age group, most of whose marriages began in the late 1950s, when age at marriage started to increase, and the 50–54 age group, whose marriage and first births were seriously influenced by the 1959–61 famine. Women in the younger age groups may, of course, have children after the survey date. However, the problem this creates with the data can be ignored for all age cohorts except those aged 20–24 years and those who married in the 1990s (1990+), because most women in the other groups had already had their first child (see Tables 9.4 and 9.6).[5]

The age at which a woman has her first child depends on her age at marriage. Birth outside marriage is still socially unacceptable, though there have been occasional rumours spread in the village in recent years that a woman may rush to marry after discovering she is pregnant;[6] no woman had a child before marriage in the known history in the village. The age at which a woman has her first child also depends on the interval between marriage and first birth. In the village, the declining age of women having their first child is due to both the decline in the age of brides since the mid-1970s, and the shorter interval between marriage and the birth of the first child since the 1950s.

The correlation between women's age at marriage and the age at which they had their first and second child is shown in Figures 9.2,

Table 9.7 Mean and median age of the ever-married women for having child of different parity, by age groups

	Age							
	20–24	25–29	30–34	35–39	40–44	45–49	50–54	55–59
First child								
Mean	21.5	23.1	23.9	25.1	25.6	25.6	26.2	24.4
Median	22.0	23.0	24.0	25.0	26.0	25.0	24.5	24.0
No. of cases	41	68	64	50	94	53	26	28
Second child								
Mean	22.5	24.0	26.2	27.7	28.8	27.9	29.0	27.8
Median	22.6	24.0	26.0	27.0	28.0	27.0	28.0	27.0
No. of cases	6	44	61	49	93	51	26	27
Third child								
Mean		25.5	28.0	30.5	32.0	31.1	30.9	30.5
Median		26	28	30	32	31	30	30
No. of cases		12	39	42	83	49	23	27
Fourth child								
Mean	—	—	32.1	33.9	33.9	33.7	33.1	
Median	—	—	32	35	34	33	32	
No. of cases	—	—	12	33	29	18	23	
Fifth child								
Mean		—	—	36.8	34.5	36.4	34.8	
Median		—	—	37.0	33.5	36.5	34.0	
No. of cases		—	—	8	12	12	19	

Note: — Fewer than 5 cases.

Source: Research survey: ever-married women 1993.

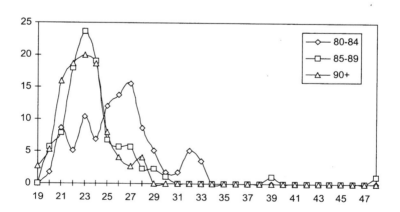

Figure 9.2 Percentage distribution of women's ages at the birth of their first child, 1980–84, 1985–89, 1990+
Source: Research survey: ever-married women 1993.

9.3 and 9.4. The age distribution at first childbirth for women who married in the early period of reforms (1980–84), is dispersed along a broader range, mainly between 19–34 years with a peak at 27 (Figure 9.2). For those women who married later, in 1985–89, the distribution has narrowed to about 19–30 years, and the peak has shifted from 27 years to 23 years. The distribution for 1990+ is moving even younger; it resembles that of 1985–89 group, but with a lower peak. The age distribution for women having their second child has similar tendencies. Although the distribution differs, the age of women having their second child is also becoming younger and concentrated in a smaller age ranges (see Figure 9.3).

These patterns follow changes in the post-reform age distribution

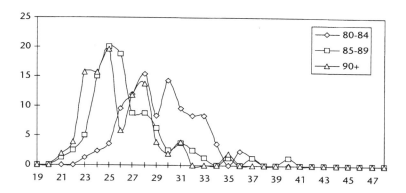

Figure 9.3 Percentage distribution of women's ages at the birth of their second child, 1980–84, 1985–89, 1990+
Source: Research survey: ever-married women 1993.

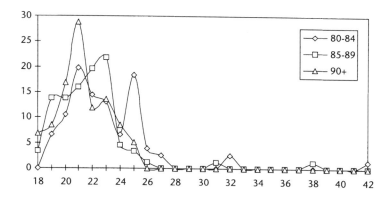

Figure 9.4 Percentage distribution of women's ages at their first marriage by date of marriage, 1980–84, 1985–89, 1990+
Source: Research survey: ever-married women 1993.

for women at first marriage, which has become younger and more concentrated in a smaller age range (see Figure 9.4).

Thus younger marriage, combined with the narrowing interval between marriage and first birth, means that the age of women having their first child is declining. As Figure 9.5 shows, the tendency for couples to have their children sooner has been especially pronounced since the 1970s.[7] The same tendency is shown in Table 9.8: an increasing percentage of women married recently are having their first child within a year of marriage, and fewer women are beginning their families two or more years after marriage, compared to those who married in the early 1970s.[8] Only about 10 per cent of women who married during the 1950s and the first half of the 1960s had their first child within one year of marriage. In 1985–89, the percentage exceeded 40 per cent. The low incidence of births within one year of marriage in the 1950s and early 1960s, and the high percentage of births after 5 or 6 years for women in this group may be due to difficulties in conception, to frequent miscarriage or to still-births, which would be consistent with the poor health and low level of health and maternal care and the famine during the period.

Like the interval between marriage and the birth of the first child, the interval between the first and the second birth has also narrowed, especially for those married in the 1970s and the 1980s (see Figure 9.6 and Table 9.9).[9] Clearly childbearing accelerated, though the Great Leap Forward and the early years of Cultural Revolution may distort the trend of the birth interval over time. This distortion can be seen especially in the 1960–64 period, when famine first widened the interval between the first and second birth, then birth compensation narrowed it. This can explain why the birth interval in this period has a larger spread than in most other periods (especially compared to later periods).

Notably, a majority of couples had their second child within four years of the first, both during the 'later, sparser, fewer' policy period and during the 'one-child' policy period. The birth interval between the first and the second parity became even shorter for women married after 1970 (see Figure 9.6), when the family planning programme was becoming increasingly intensive in the village. This trend confirms that the provincial policy to delay the birth of the second child by a four-year interval was not implemented in the village.

The impact of migration on the interval between marriage and the first birth and on birth intervals between different parities should be noted.[10] As discussed in Chapter 4, migration has become much more common since reform, and it is mainly men who migrate out, leaving their wives behind in the village. Many young men work in cities for most of the year, and in recent years many have done so within one or two months of marriage. Some scholars have argued that such disruption may have a significant effect on the timing of childbearing (and thus on birth intervals) since temporary migration involves the separation of spouses (Tan 1990, Yang 1991, Goldstein et al. 1996). If this is so, then the interval between marriage and first birth and the interval between the first and second birth should be increasing for young generations.

However, this has been shown not to be the case in this village (see Figures 9.5 and 9.6). When asked about this, some women laughed and said it was not the man who gave birth to children. They pointed out that young women easily become pregnant. For example, among the 20 or so new couples who married in early 1993, only a few husbands remain in the village (working in the collective kiln); all the

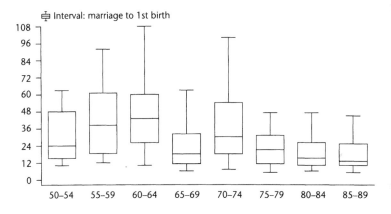

Figure 9.5 Box plots of interval between marriage and first birth (in months) for different marriage cohorts
Source: Research survey: ever-married women 1993.

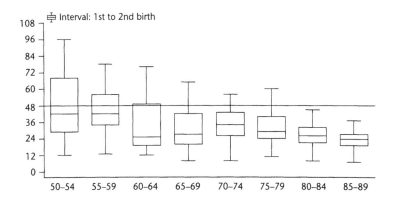

Figure 9.6 Box plots of birth interval between first and second birth (in months) for different marriage cohorts
Source: Research survey: ever-married women 1993.

others migrated out as construction workers, and some of them stayed away as long as nine or ten months in the year without coming back in between. However, all but one of the newly married women became pregnant within the first year of marriage. Villagers believed that the young at present mature both physically and psychologically at a younger age. Improved living standards, and the better health and maternal care that have developed since the reforms will also, inevitably, increase women's and as well as men's fertility and reduce the incidence of miscarriage and stillbirth.

The lower percentage of couples in the older generations who had children soon after marriage may also be explained by differences in the marriage institution. Such couples began their marriages with a lack of intimacy; there was little contact between engaged couples before marriage. It is thus possible that the declining birth interval, and the increase in births within the first year of marriage may be due to increase coital frequency early in marriage because of the intimacy that has developed among couples of the younger generations (see also the study of Korea, Malaysia and Taiwan by Rindfuss & Morgan 1983) as a result of frequent contact between the couples before marriage. This may be cancelling out the effects of male migration (including among the newly-married). Readily available information on sexuality and reproduction both as a result of the 'open-door' policy and via the continuous government family planning programme, has also greatly reshaped the sexual and reproductive behaviour of the younger generations (Wang and Yang 1996).[11]

The post-reform interest in having children earlier rather than later, combined with improved living standards and better health care, increasing intimacy between young couples, and increasing bargaining power of villagers with local cadres in fertility decision-making, are direct reasons for the declining interval between marriage and the first child and other birth intervals. In addition, since young mothers have become much busier than before, breast-feeding may be shortened. Although postnatal sexual abstinence may influence the birth interval, data on this is unavailable, and in any case it seems that the factors that are shortening the birth intervals may well offset contravening factors. Since this pattern of shortening interval between marriage and first birth and the decrease in other birth inter-vals contradicts state policy objectives, the state policies of 'later marriage and later child birth' (*wanhun wanyu*) are ineffective in this locality.

How many children and when to stop?

The parity progression ratio (PPR) indicates the likelihood that women with a certain parity will achieve parity of a higher order.[12] The PPR can be used to show the change in fertility level over time. It can also be used to show the effectiveness of family planning programmes. PPRs from first to second birth and from second to third

...rval between marriage and the first birth (women with no births excluded)

Within 1 year	>1 year, ≤2 years	>2 years, ≤3 years	>3 years, ≤4 years	>4 years ≤5 years	>5 years ≤6 years	>6 years	Total (%)	No
12.5	37.5	12.5	12.5		12.5	12.5	100	
8.7	21.7	13.0	8.7	13.0	13.0	21.7	100	
6.7	13.3	26.7	20.0	13.3	13.3	6.7	100	
33.3	23.1	20.5	2.6	7.7	7.7	5.1	100	
17.7	27.4	16.1	6.5	11.3	9.7	11.3	100	
31.6	35.1	19.3	12.3		1.8		100	
35.6	38.4	19.2	5.5	1.4			100	
41.9	31.1	17.6	4.1	4.1	1.4		100	

survey: ever-married women 1993.

...rval between the first and the second birth (women with no births excluded)

>1 year, ≤2 years	>2 years ≤3 years	>3 years ≤4 years	>4 years ≤5 years	>5 years ≤6 years	>6 years ≤7 years	>7 years	Total	No
		25.0	12.5			62.5	100	
		4.8	9.5	4.8	28.6	52.4	100	
7.1		7.1	14.3	7.1	14.3	50.0	100	
2.5	22.5	25.0	10.0	12.5	2.5	25.0	100	
1.6	4.8	19.4	16.1	8.1	21.0	29.0	100	
1.7	20.3	20.3	20.3	25.4	8.5	3.4	100	
1.4	23.9	46.5	11.3	11.3	4.2	1.4	100	
18.6	37.3	23.7	13.6	5.1	1.7		100	

survey: ever-married women 1993.

birth are of particular interest, since they are likely to indicate the demographic impact of the present family planning policy.

The period parity progression ratio may be calculated in numerous ways (see Feeney & Wang 1993, Feeney & Lutz 1991, Luther et al. 1990, Feeney et al. 1989, Tu 1993). To compare fertility between different birth cohorts, I applied the simple method of calculating cohort PPRs for each five-year age group from 15–59, using data on children ever born (see Newell 1988) as reported in the official population census of 1982 and in my population census of 1993. PPRs for older women are more accurate, because they are at or close to their final PPRs; the PPRs for younger women are smaller and do not reflect their final fertility. The timing of childbearing may also have an impact on the PPRs of younger age groups. For example, the fact that the PPRs of first-to-second birth and second-to-third birth for women aged 25–29 were higher in 1993 than that in 1982 (see Figure 9.7) may not show an increasing level of fertility of the new generation, but does show that childbearing has shifted to earlier ages (as discussed earlier).

Firstly, the PPRs in Figure 9.7 confirm that the one-child policy did not succeed in the village and even the two-child policy did not work well. PPRs for younger age groups, especially the age groups 30–34, 35–39 and 40–44, for whom childbirth is in the present or in the past one or two decades, shows that nearly all women have had one or two children, and nearly 90 per cent of women aged 35–39 who had two children then had a third. Most importantly, the PPRs of lower-order births (from 0→1, 1→2, 2→3) for groups aged between 25 and 44 have remained essentially unchanged, showing that younger generations in 1993 have a pattern similar to that of older generations, at least in terms of the first three children. Only births of higher orders (fourth parity or higher) differ between the generation that was young in 1993 and the generation that was young in 1982. It seems that the state's 'later, sparser and fewer' policy of the 1970s and 'one-child family' policy of the 1980s, both of which strongly prohibit third-parity births, failed in this village in their stated objective, although births of higher parity are becoming less common.

Secondly, the village has experienced tremendous fertility decline in recent years, despite the failure to carry out rigidly formal family planning policies. PPRs for fourth or higher parity births have been declining significantly, though the degree varies among different age groups. Cohorts who were in the 55–59 age group in 1982 (and who finished their reproductive lives in the early 1970s) had significantly higher PPRs for higher parity births (including sixth, seventh, and eighth parities) than did the group of cohorts who were in the 55–59 age group in 1993 (who finished their reproductive period in the early 1980s).[13] A drop in fertility from six children per woman in the early 1970s to around three children per woman in the early 1990s is evident in the data on the 50–54 age groups, and also in the 45–49 and 40–44 cohort groups. Differences in childbearing patterns

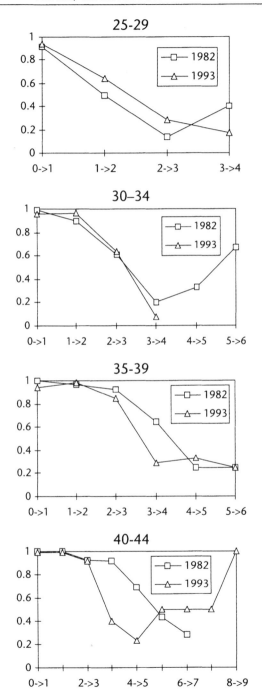

Figure 9.7 Parity progression ratios for married women in 1982 and 1993

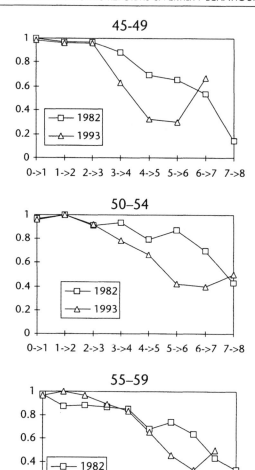

Figure 9.7 (Continued)
Note: Number of women for age group 25–29, 30–34, 35–39, 40–44, 45–49, 50–54, 55–59 are 83, 83, 28, 27, 35, 36, 41 respectively in 1982 and 71, 65, 53, 95, 54, 26, 29 respectively in 1993.
Sources: Government population census of the village 1982, and my field research survey: ever-married women 1993.

between the 1982 and 1993 survey data are more pronounced for higher parities (e.g. the higher parity women in the 50–59 age group), but these differences are beginning to appear even with the fourth or fifth birth. The gap between PPRs of the two cohort groups grows further in slightly lower parities for women of 45–49, and is also growing for women aged 40–44. Fertility has clearly declined tremendously in the village between the 1970s and the early 1990s, though this transition was less significant than that in the Chinese countryside as a whole (see period PPRs from 1967–87 presented in Feeney & Wang 1993).

A couple's decision to cease having children depends on the number and sex composition of children born and alive in the family. Few couples will stop having children before they have at least one son (see Table 9.10; also Ahn 1994). This shows either that parents intend to balance the sex composition of families, or the persistence of China's traditionally strong son preference. Childbearing in relation to son preference can be expressed in either of two ways when fertility supply is higher than fertility demand. One is to control the sex of children in the family, through selective abortion of female

Table 9.10 Sex composition of children for those couples having a fifth or higher parity birth after 1985

7th	Year birth of last child	Age of wife (1993)	Sex 1st parity	Sex 2nd parity	Sex 3rd parity	Sex 4th parity	Sex 5th parity	Sex 6th parity	Sex 7th parity
I	1985	50	F	F (D)	F	F	F	M	F
II	1986	50	M(D)	M(D)	F	M	M		
III	1987	45	F	F	M	M	M(D)		
IV	1987	45	F	M	M	F	F		
V	1987	42	F	F	F	F	F		
VI	1987	38	F	F	M	F	M		
VII	1987	45	F	F	F(D)	F	F	M	M
VIII	1988	50	M(D)	F	M	M	F		
IX	1988	42	F	F	F	M	M		
X	1988	37	M(D)	F	F	F	M		
XI	1988	42	M	M(D)	F	M(D)	M		
XII	1989	37	M(D)	F	F	F	M	F	
XIII	1990	30	M	M	M	M	F		
XIV	1990	38	F	F	F	F	F		
XV	1990	37	F	F(D)	F	F	F		
XVI	1990	38	F	M	F	F	F		
XVII	1991	40	M	M(D)	F	F	F		
XVIII	1992	40	F	F	F	F	M		
XIX	1993	42	F	F	F	F	F		

Source: Research survey: ever-married women 1993.

Notes: M = male child; F = female child; D = deceased.

fetuses, female infanticide, or the adopting out of baby girls. The other is to continue having children, to increase the chances of having one or more sons. In the village, the second option has been adopted. Though some villagers are aware of ultrasound technology that can ascertain the sex of the fetus, I uncovered no cases of selective abortion during my fieldwork; there was not even a rumour that such an event had occurred. It is also possible that there were no infanticides in the village in recent history, if neglect of infants is not counted as infanticide.[14]

The decision to have (or not to have) an additional child also depends on the intensity of the family planning programme. In 1990–93 when family planning was intensified, seven couples in the village managed to have their fifth child. Four of them had had all girls prior to the fifth child, and of these, one couple succeeded in having a son. Two already had one living son, hoped to have another, and did not succeed. One couple with four sons succeeded in having a girl. In the late 1980s, most couples who were either without a son or had only one son tried to have an additional child, although in two cases, couples with two sons still had a fifth child. There were even cases in which couples had births of seventh or higher parities (see Table 9.11). However, between 1972 and 1981, when a less intensified version of family planning was being promoted, very high parity births seem mainly to have been due to contraception failure or to a couple's failure to use contraception even when no more children were desired.

Since reform, couples with two sons are most likely to stop having more children once they have a girl. One couple with three sons adopted a girl in the early 1990s; they were afraid of having another son if they tried to have a daughter through a fourth pregnancy.[15]

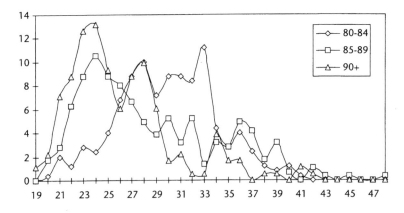

Figure 9.8 Percentage distribution of ages of women who gave birth to children 1980–84, 1985–89 and 1990+
Source: Research survey: ever-married women 1993.

Table 9.11 Sex composition of children for those couples having a 7th or
higher parity birth between 1970 and 1981

Birth of last child	Age of wife	Sex 1st parity	Sex 2nd parity	Sex 3rd parity	Sex 4th parity
I	1972	59	M	M	F	M(D)
II	1972	59	M	F	M	M
III	1973	59	M(D)	M(D)	F	M
IV	1973	53	F	M	M(D)	F(D)
V	1973	56	M	M	F	F
VI	1976	56	M	M(D)	F	M(D)
VII	1977	57	M(D)	M(D)	F	M
VIII	1979	57	M(D)	M	F(D)	M
IX	1980	53	F	M	M(D)	F(D)
X	1981	47	F	F	M	M

Birth of last child	Age of wife	Sex 5th parity	Sex 6th parity	Sex 7th parity	Sex 8th parity	Sex 9th parity
I	1972	59	M(D)	M	F	M	M
II	1972	59	F(D)	F	M		
III	1973	59	M	F	M		
IV	1973	53	M	M	M		
V	1973	56	M	F	M(D)		
VI	1976	56	M	M	M		
VII	1977	57	F	F	M		
VIII	1979	57	F	F	M	F	
IX	1980	53	M	M	M	M	
X	1981	47	M	M	F		

Source: Research survey: ever-married women 1993.
Notes: M = male child; F = female child; D = deceased.

Most couples stop having children once they turn 40 years old, a
choice that became possible only in recent decades when modern
family planning methods became available. As Figure 9.8 shows, the
number of women who gave birth to children after age 40 is small.
There is some sense in the society that couples should not continue
to have children when their older children have grown, married, and
started having children themselves. Couples may also prefer not to
have more children as they reach middle age, because having a child
after age 40 means they will be busy arranging that child's marriage
and so on, when they themselves are in their 60s. Mothers in the early
1990s are on average younger than mothers in the first half of the
1980s, and these early 1990s mothers are also likely to stop having
children sooner than did older generations.

CONTRACEPTION, ABORTION AND STERILIZATION

Traditional Chinese herbs, postnatal sexual abstinence, and prolonged breast-feeding have all been used to prevent unwanted births in Chinese societies in the past (see Wang et al. 1995, Rigdon 1996). However, some traditional contraceptives were ineffective or dangerous. One woman said that her grandmother had died after using a medicine prescribed by a local 'doctor' for contraception. Before contraceptives became available, pregnant women would also attempt to induce spontaneous abortion by doing heavy physical work or pressing the stomach with a heavy object. Infanticide was never mentioned in the village as a means for controlling family size. However, as mentioned earlier, it was not rare in the past to adopt out children the family could not afford feed. It therefore should be understood that villagers were not against all elements of family planning, when contraceptives became available through state programmes. Villagers may resist the methods when they dislike, but they do make use of available contraceptives when they need them. Many older women said they would have had fewer children, if effective contraceptives had been known and available to them in the past.

Family planning without penalties was introduced and promoted in the first half of the 1970s, but was not immediately effective. For example, in 1975 one Huang family had its ninth child. This family, like others, would not necessarily have chosen to have so many children. However, effective contraception and abortion were either not easily accessible, or villagers were unaccustomed to them. In the early years of family planning, people felt shy talking about contraception, and only after years of continuous family planning in the village were rural couples used to modern contraceptive methods, safe abortions, and sterilization.

At the same time, even in 1993 many couples used no contraceptives. Table 9.12 shows that over half of all couples in age groups over 25 used no contraceptives, and 94 per cent of those in the 20–24 age group also used no contraceptives, though over 10 per cent of the latter group had already had two children. Those who used contraceptives mostly chose either contraception or sterilization after they had three children, though younger age groups (e.g. 25–29) started to use contraception after two children (Table 9.14).

As mentioned in Chapter 8, local cadres heavily rely on IUDs, abortion, and sterilization in the implementation of family planning. In 1993, couples using contraceptives mostly used IUDs, female sterilization was nearly as important as IUDs, a few took contraceptive pills, and no couples used condoms (Table 9.12).

Individual couples also prefer the IUD to condoms or pills. Couples not intending to have children any more almost invariably opt for an IUD (if they can manage to avoid sterilization). However, many still do not use any effective contraceptive method, and instead pay for an abortion if the wife becomes pregnant. Some women have had three

Table 9.12 Percentages distribution of couples with and without contraception

Age	Female sterilization	Male sterilization	IUD	Pill	No contraception	Total	No. of cases
20–24			5.3		94.8	100	57
25–29	14.1	5.6	15.5		64.8	100	71
30–34	18.5	13.9	10.8	1.5	55.4	100	65
35–39	13.2	5.7	24.5		56.6	100	53
40–44	23.2	1.1	21.1		54.7	100	95
45–49	22.2	3.7	24.1	1.9	48.2	100	54
Total	16.0	4.8	17.0	0.5	61.8	100	395

Source: Research survey: ever-married women 1993.

Table 9.13 Basic information of the cases of women who reported their number of abortions as three times and more

	Age	No. and sex order of children	No. of abortions	Contraception	Reported time of contraception for the first time
I	44	MFM	7	IUD	After 2nd child born
II	44	MMF	6	NO	N.A.
III	49	MMMF	4	NO	After 3rd child born
IV	41	MMFM	4	NO	After 2nd child born
V	38	MFFM	4	Female sterilization	After 4th child born
VI	48	MMMM	3	IUD	After 4th child born
VII	45	MMF	3	Male sterilization	After 2nd child born
VIII	43	FFM	3	Female sterilization	After 1st child born
IX	40	FFFFM	3	NO	N.A.

Source: Research survey: ever-married women 1993.
Notes: M = male child; F = female child.

or four abortions, and a few women in their late 40s have had as many as seven abortions. Note that the data in Table 9.13, which lists couples who reported four or more abortions as of 1993, would be underreported since women are generally reluctant to expose this information.

In general couples use no contraception immediately after marriage, since the couples generally wish to have children quickly. As mentioned, among the 20 or so newly married couples in 1993, only one newly married-in wife was not been pregnant in the first year of her marriage. There might be special cases where women would use contraception without their husbands' knowledge. For example, a woman in her 30s took contraceptive pills after marriage because she wanted a divorce.

Ironically, even with stringent family planning programmes, it is

Table 9.14 Contraception use rates (including male and female sterilization) among ever-married couples by parity and sex of children born and by age groups in 1993[16]

No. and sex by order of parities	20–24	25–29	30–34	35–39	40–44	45–49
No children born	0	0	0	0	0	0
One parity	9	15	0	0	0	0
M	16	7	0	0	0	0
F	0	30				0
Two parities	0	39	29	50	47	100
MF	0	50		33	40	
FM	0	29	25	0	0	
Three parities		88	61	35	47	48
MMM			67	50	57	50
MMF		100	100	25	17	50
MFM			33	50	33	67
MFF		50	33	0	63	50
FMM		100	67	100	50	50
FMF		100	50	50	50	33
FFM		50	80	0	75	0
FFF		100	50	0		
Four parities		100	100	83	48	55
Five parities				75	33	100
Six parities					50	100
Seven parities						0

Source: Research survey: ever-married women 1993.

not easy for young couples (except teachers, contract workers, and government employees) to gain access to contraception, even when they would like to. The norm that one should have children soon after marriage is prevalent. Delaying childbirth intentionally is considered strange, especially because family planning is becoming more and more intensive, and having extra births is much more difficult. Parents will scold the young if they discover that the young want to delay parenthood. One young couple, who married in 1993 and wanted to postpone having the first child so that they could do business together in Beijing, did not use contraceptives. They were too shy to ask for contraceptives from family planning cadres, and did not buy contraceptives in the city. Within a month, the wife was pregnant. His mother warned them not to have an abortion, saying that the wife might have difficulties getting pregnant afterwards. They did go to Beijing together for half a year, and then the wife came back to the village for the birth of their child.

Most couples used no contraceptives even after the first child was born. They used IUDs, abortion or sterilization only after their second or third. Sterilization has been mostly female rather than male sterilization. According to my survey, from the late 1970s, when the first group of women were sterilized, until 1993, for more than 80 per cent of the 83 couples that had opted for sterilization, the partner who was sterilized was the wife (Table 9.15). The 1993 survey data also shows that among all reproductive couples aged 20–49, one-fifth had one sterilized partner; and 77 per cent of these sterilizations were of the wife. Some villagers told me that many reported male sterilizations (and probably female sterilization also) were false (several couples gave birth to children after they had reported either male or female sterilization). In the early 1990s when male sterilization could be performed in the township hospitals, many men managed to get false male sterilization certificates (this was relatively easier at the township level than in county-level hospitals). The county family planning commission discovered the problem, and decided that sterilization had to be performed only in designated hospitals in the county, to guard against fraud.[17]

The five cases of female sterilization in 1978 were the first group of women sterilized in the village (Table 9.15). Three are wives of the then-village cadres; villagers said that they believed that cadres in the collective era did take the lead in responding to the call of the state and the Party for family planning, and that local cadres implemented family planning programmes seriously. As Table 9.15 shows, there were more cases of sterilization in 1983, and again in 1991 and 1992. This is consistent with the intensification of the family planning programme in these years; the early 1980s (after the call for one child for each couple) was a 'high tide' for family planning, as was the early 1990s, when family planning in the countryside was intensified.

Though sterilization has gradually become accepted through two decades of family planning programmes, many men still resist the idea of male sterilization. They believe that male sterilization will cause them to lose their physical power, and that it will also influence their sexual ability. They choose female sterilization, saying that they see this as 'easier', and that women can recover 'easily' from opera- tions. However, this male resistance may be weakening; it is possible that the ratio of male to female sterilization is higher in younger age

Table 9.15 Number of female and male sterilizations in the village

Year	Female sterilization	Male sterilization	Year	Female sterilization	Male sterilization
1978	5		1987	2	
1980	4		1988	4	
1981	1		1989	2	1
1982	2		1990	3	2
1983	8	1	1991	22	12
1984	1		1992	9	
1985	1		1993	2	
1986	1		Total	67	16

Source: Research survey: ever-married women 1993.

groups than in older age groups (see Table 9.12). This probably shows that younger men are increasingly taking responsibility for contraception, and if contraception patterns are gradually changing, this may be related to the increasing bargaining power of young women.

Most sterilizations involve couples with at least three children, or, in more recent years, couples with two children. According to the sampling survey of the married couples, nearly three-fifths (58.5 per cent) of the 84 couples that report a sterilization had the operation performed after the third child, just over one-fifth (20.7 per cent) did so after the second child, and just under one-fifth (18.3 per cent) after the fourth child.

ADOPTION OF CHILDREN

Although reproductive couples make up the majority of the rural population and are the focus of this research, the strategies infertile couples are using to adapt to the changing environment of the reform era must also be included to compose a complete picture of the influence of economic reforms on fertility. Fertility behaviour encompasses not only by giving birth to children, but also adopting children. What is new in the reform era in this village is both infertile couples and fertile couples are adopting children. The adoption of children has many functions. It is a way for infertile couples to have children, who can then meet their needs for security and mobility in present Chinese society.

The practice of adopting infant girls who were to be reared as future daughters-in-law, which previously existed in rural China, has essentially died out; there were no reported instances in the village in either the collective or the reform period.[18] What is new in recent years is that, as family planning has intensified, parents with children have started to adopt an additional child in order to have a child of the desired sex, even when they can biologically have children.

In the past, only infertile couples, or those who could not have additional children after giving birth to girls, adopted children, and invariably they adopted boys. Adoption of a boy was not really for continuation of family line, since only biological sons were believed to continue bloods and family lines. Children were adopted on the basis of practical consideration of labour demand, risk aversion and old age security. Couples usually adopted infants. They did not adopt older children, for fear that the child might run away or fail to provide good care when they knew that the couples were not their biological parents. For the same reason, parents did not divulge information about the adoption to their children, but told them that they were their biological parents. Rural couples who adopted usually limited this to one or two children; adopted infants were costly to raise, and couples would need to have enough money to purchase milk powder and other necessities. Health care was insufficient, and infant mortality was high. No couples adopted more than two children (see Table 9.16 for a list of adoptions in the village in the past three decades).

Table 9.16 List of cases for adoption of children and general information on each adoption

No. of cases for adoptions	Sex of adopted child	Year of adoption	General descriptions about the adoption
I	M	1966	The couple did not give birth to another child for some time after having a girl. Three years after adopting a boy, another boy was born.
II	M	1970	The couple was unable to give birth to children, after giving birth to one girl.
III	F M	1972 1972	The infertile couple first adopted a girl, then a boy. The two adopted children married when they grew up, and had a baby in 1993.
IV	M	1972	The couple was unable to give birth to children, after giving birth to one girl.
V	M	1974	The couple was unable to give birth to children, after giving birth to three girls.
VI	F M	1977 1990	The infertile couple first adopted a girl; many years later, having lost hope of having children biologically, they adopted a son.
VII	M	1977	The couple adopted a son. About ten years later, they gave birth to two girls.
VIII	F	1982	The couple adopted a girl. A few years later they give birth to three more girls
IX	F	1985	After having a boy, the wife suffered heart and liver problems. They adopted a girl.
X	F	1985	The infertile couple adopted a girl, and would like to have a son-in-law join the family when the girl grows up.
XI	F F	1986 1991	The infertile couple adopted two girls, and at the time of the study (1993) had no plans to adopt a boy.
XII	F	1986	The infertile couple adopted a girl; felt it was too expensive to adopt a boy.
XIII	F	1987	The couple adopted a girl from the husband's sister, who had four girls and intended to have a boy. The girl lived with them until 1993, and it was not known whether she would return to her parents.

Table 9.16 (Continued)

No. of cases for adoptions	Sex of adopted child	Year of adoption	General descriptions about the adoption
XIV	F	1990	The possible infertile couple adopted a girl, and still hope to have biological children later on.
XV	F	1991	After having a boy, the husband became ill; the wife was over 40; they adopted a girl.
XVI	M	1992	The infertile couple adopted a son from the husband's sister.
XVII	F	1993	The couple had three boys first, and later aborted a boy (without the knowledge of the sex of the fetus before abortion). They did not want another son, and would have been requested to undergo sterilization if the wife gave birth a fourth time. They adopted a girl instead.
XVIII	F	1993	The husband was over 40 in 1993. His marriage had been delayed until the 1990s since his 'class label' was rich peasant. The wife, from Sichuan province, was also over 40 and could no longer have children. They adopted a girl in 1993.
XIX	F	1993	The couple had no biological children after seven years of marriage.
XX	F	1993	The couple produced two sons, did not want another boy but they did want a daughter. Rather than try for a girl by themselves, they spent 700 *yuan* and adopted a girl from Shanxi province, where many villagers work as migrant construction workers. The decision to adopt was due to to the strict family planning policy.
XXI	F	1993	The couple produced three sons, did not want another boy but did want a daughter. They adopted, the decision to adopt was due to the strict family planning policy.

Note: Most adopted children were infants when adopted. Thus the year of adoption was mostly within a year of birth.

Child adoption only occurs in a limited number of families. However, cases of child adoption increased significantly since the 1980s.[19] Both infertile and fertile couples adopt. Because living standards and health care have both improved, infant mortality is lower, and the probability that an adopted child might die has become small. People have enough food and money to feed and clothe the adopted child. Most importantly, the intensified family planning programme has made the cost of giving birth to an extra child more costly than adopting a child of the desired sex, so adoption is both a cheaper and more controllable alternative to having further biological children.

In the village, only biological children are counted when the family planning cadres levy fines, or require abortion or sterilization. Couples who convincingly claim that they have adopted a child rather than giving birth to her or him can avoid sanctions. Many couples use this as a loophole, claiming their own births to have been adoptions, or adopting out their unplanned children during family planning campaigns. As a result, in April 1992 the county, following the state promulgation of adoption law, created new regulations for adoption. Persons who want to adopt children needed to satisfy the following three conditions: (1) no children; (2) the ability to rear and educate the adopted child; and (3) adoptive parents must be at least 35 years of age. In addition, the county regulations specified that each adoption that failed to meet these conditions would be liable for a fine of 500–1,000 *yuan*. This policy was not, however, implemented in the village.

Another feature of adoption at present is that couples mostly adopt girls rather than boys. Those with several sons who would like to have a daughter would rather adopt a girl than risk giving birth to another son. Infertile couples also tend to adopt a girl instead of a boy, especially when they are poor (since adopting a girl is much cheaper).[20] This may indicate that more girls than boys are available for adoption. However, some households prefer girls not because adopting boys is too expensive, but because they feel that the adopted daughters will care to them better than would adopted sons. This also reflects the recent changes in the relationship between parents and married daughters: daughters have much more ability and flexibility to support their parents than in the past. Many couples who adopted girls rather than boys believe that in raising a girl they will eventually also gain a son-in-law for their old age support. The settling of a husband in his wife's family is increasingly accepted in the society, and the free arrangements of labour and work after the reforms provide much more flexibility to arrange such situations.

The fertility level in the village declined during the collective period (starting in the 1970s) and continued to decline in the post-reform period (from the 1980s into the early 1990s). However, this does not mean that rural couples follow the state's formal rules for regulating family sizes and timing of childbearing. The fertility outcomes are increasingly mediated by a couple's own wishes. Since economic reforms, rural couples have tended to marry younger and give birth younger with shorter intervals. However, rural couples also tend to stop having children at a younger age, and have fewer children overall. The one-child-per-couple policy never worked in the village being studied, and even when complemented with 'one girl plus another child' the policy did not work well in the village. In contrast to the (1970s) family planning policy of 'later, sparser and fewer', the current fertility pattern in this village is 'fewer', but neither 'later' nor 'sparser'.

Contraception is used by rural couples mainly to regulate ending childbearing, rather than to regulate timing of births. IUDs are mostly used by rural couples when they wish to cease childbearing entirely; both the couples and local cadres prefer IUDs, which are more effective and reliable than other contraceptives such as condoms and pills. Women, rather than men, bear the main burden for contraception, abortion and sterilization.

A new phenomenon concerning post-reform fertility is that some couples now adopt (usually one child) to achieve the desired number and sex composition of their family, even when they are biologically able to give birth. This is a break from the past, when only infertile couples adopted. Such adoption allows couples to have larger families and still avoid harsh family planning penalties. It also shows a notable preference for the adoption of girls. As shown in the previous chapters, the changing social and economic relations of wives with their husbands and of daughters with their parents and parents-in-law affect the adoption motivation of infertile couples, and of reproductive couples as well.

Notes

1   Using the number of children born and alive by age groups of surviving mothers to show the change of fertility may be biased by the differential mortality of mothers of different age groups, especially for higher age groups (60s and 70s). Migration can also have an impact.

2   The famine did occur in the village; villagers said there was little to eat during the period, and that some women found it difficult to become pregnant or to give birth. Fertility intervals during the period were longer since most women delayed their childbearing.

3   This starts in 1983 mainly because the data was collected on the birth histories of women aged 15–59 in 1993, and a share of births to women who were aged below 49 before 1983 was thus not captured in the survey.

4   A girl from the village married out to a man in a neighboring village but divorced after four years. Some villagers believed that the marriage ended mainly because the woman did not give birth to any children.

5   Similarly, for other indicators concerning the first parity, the right censusing problem for marriage cohorts except 1990+ and age cohorts of 20–24 could be ignored. For birth interval or other indicators concerning second parity, the right censusing problem (i.e. those having not yet had first child born at the time of the survey) for marriage cohort except 1985–89, and 1990+ could be ignored.

6   I heard of only one such case during my fieldwork. Almost all marriage ceremonies are held in winter during the Spring Festival. Villagers suspect

that couples who marry at other times of the year may have 'problems', implying the wife may be pregnant and the family trying to cover it up.

[7] The right censusing problem can be ignored for marriage cohorts except those married in the 1990s, since more than 95 per cent of the women in each marriage cohort had already had at least one child (see Table 9.6).

[8] This is quite different from a study conducted in a village in central Hebei province in post-1978 reform period. 'A . . . significant departure from earlier norms of both the republican era and the collective years is that by the late 1980s many young couples were not producing offspring in the first several years of marriage. By contrast, prior to the 1980s, virtually every couple produced a child within the first year or two of marriage.' (Selden in Davis & Harrell 1993: 149). However, Wang Feng & Yang Quanhe (1996: 299) claim that '[a] long interval between marriage and the couple's first birth (the first birth interval) was one of the most prominent features of the Chinese demographic regime before the 1970s'. Using the *Two-Per-Thousand Fertility and Birth Control Survey* conducted by China's State's Family Planning Commission in 1988, they showed the continuous decline of the first birth interval at the national level over the 1970s and the first half of the 1980s. For birth intervals from the 1940s to the 1970s, see Coale, Li & Han (1988).

[9] There were 87 women in marriage cohort 1985–89, among whom 27 had not had a second child, and there were 59 women in marriage cohort 1990+ among whom only four had a second child. In the other cohort groups, nearly all women had a second child. Birth intervals for women of marriage cohorts 1985–89 and 1990+ could be ignored since right censusing problems of the data.

[10] Some studies on migration and fertility in the reform period suspect that increasing migration may be linked to higher fertility, because some couples migrate intentionally to have larger families and it is extremely difficult for government family planning officials to intervene and address family planning work towards temporary migrants (Xu & Ye 1990, Tian 1991). However, the respective shares of rural-urban migration specifically to have 'unplanned' births and migration for market and work opportunities are unknown. Of the hundreds of people who migrated out of the village, only three couples migrated together in 1993, one couple to Beijing and the other two to Shanxi. It is said that one wife who had an unplanned birth within the village stayed with her husband (who was working in construction in Shanxi), to avoid economic penalties. A survey of 231 temporary migrants in Dalian circa 1990 shows that they desire fewer children than would normally be expected (Anonymous 1992). Another survey of 4,641 households in Anhui in 1989 shows that the fertility of temporary migrants was lower than that of non-migrants at rural areas (Liu 1993, Xu 1992, Yang 1991).

[11] Information on sexuality and reproduction is now widely available through television, films, videos, magazines and various forms of literature in China. The young, who have more education and more migration opportunities, are much more exposed to this information than were former generations; some young people have even managed to see pornographic videos, which are strictly prohibited in China.

[12] PPR is defined for parity i ($i =0$, 1, 2, . . .) as the proportion of women who proceed to the next birth, $i+1$, among those who have had an ith birth. In

this chapter, cohort PPRs for women of different age groups from 25–59 are calculated separately. Thanks are given to Griffith Feeney for his kind comments on this section of the chapter; I bear complete responsibility for any remaining shortcomings.

[13] Higher progression ratios of higher order progressions are relatively unimportant compared with the PPRs of lower order births.

[14] See, however, Scrimshaw (1983, cited in Hariss & Ross 1987:6) who includes seven common forms of infanticidal behaviour, including deliberate killing, abandonment, and low biological and emotional support. In the village in the early 1980s, one handicapped boy died when he was fourteen mainly due to his long-term illness. However, villagers said that the father used to say it was better for the boy to die. Infanticide (using the most inclusive definition) has not been common in this village. Readers may refer to Croll (1995) for a general discussion of infanticide in China.

[15] In the county, a facility for checking the sex of the fetus was available, and some couples in the village had the knowledge of the sex of the fetus through a prenatal check. However, the county had strict regulations prohibiting access to this information, and I heard of no cases of abortion based on prenatal check of the sex of a fetus in the village (nor in the county).

[16] Contraceptive use rates are the numbers of ever-married couples of a certain group (e.g., by parity of children and age of couples) practising any kind of contraception (including male or female sterilization) per 100 ever-married couples of the same group in a given period of time.

[17] Though the data were cross-checked with informants from the village who knew more about the true incidence of sterilization, it is not possible to be entirely certain that the data is reliable, since some false sterilization were undoubtedly not known even to neighbors. Nevertheless, the data presented here does represent the cases of sterilization known to the villagers, and can be used to indicate changes in the number of sterilizations over time, and the relative proportions of male and female sterilization.

[18] There was one case in which an infertile couple adopted both a boy and a girl in the early 1970s, and then arranged that the two marry each other when they had grown up.

[19] Adoption only happens in a limited number of families, though there are increasing cases of adoption of children recently. Unfortunately, I do not have much information on the biological parents of the adopted children nor on regions from which they were adopted. I also do not have systematic information on families adopting out children in the village. I heard that six girls had been adopted out of the village in recent years. However, such out-adoption of girls could also be a strategy for peasant households to avoid family planning penalties and the adopted girls might have been taken back later (see Chapter 8).

[20] Adoption of children is not cost free, unless one can adopt a child from a relative (the cost would then be in other non-monetary forms). Most villagers who adopt use informal channels, and pay money to the parents, or 'buy a child' from child traffickers

Conclusion

The principle concern of this study has been to analyse changing individual fertility behaviours within the changing context brought about by economic reforms that began in rural China in the late 1970s. Based on in-depth empirical field research in a northern Chinese village, this study is intended to shed light on the processes and mechanisms through which macro-economic reforms influence individual fertility behaviour by affecting intermediate institutions and intermediate variables.

The study employed an institutional approach to relation between economic change and individual fertility behaviour, considering that the main fertility theories that locate fertility at different levels of macro- and micro-analysis – fertility transition theory and microeconomic theories of fertility – do not incorporate the institutional context in their analyses. That is, classical demographic transition theory assumes invariant institutions: the functions of institutions and the principles governing demographic change are seen as uniform, even for different societies. Similarly, microeconomic fertility theory assumes inevitable institutions: all non-neoclassical explanations of human behaviour are thus shunned. From a social demographic perspective, socio-economic factors must work to affect fertility through intermediate fertility variables. Many correlation analysis of socio-economic development, family planning and fertility variables, linked by intermediate variables, provide some explanations of fertility determinants, reveal certain patterns and pose many questions. However, they fail to recognize that the nature of the effect of macro–socio-economic factors on fertility is filtered as well as reshaped by existing social institutions. Observed quantitative correlations do matter, but they are contingent and context-specific, and can only be understood in the light of the historically specific character of the socio-economic developments in which they arise (Wuyts 1997). As this study shows, the study of the social institutions that regulate socio-economic activities and mediate state policies holds considerable promise in the analysis of human fertility. Taking institutions into account in fertility studies can provide a better understanding of changes in individual fertility behaviours as well as of dramatic aggregate fertility change in rapidly shifting contexts (e.g. in modern China). Understanding the social institutions within which individual fertility decisions are made can help one explain more fully not only fertility outcomes, but the mechanisms and processes through which government policies and socio-economic factors influence fertility within a particular historical and cultural context. This closes the gap in understanding the relations between socio-economic development and demographic change. As Potter (1983) noted, bringing social institutions into the picture enables us to overcome one of the stumbling blocks we face – the much-discussed schism between macro and micro levels of analysis.

At the macro level, tremendous variations exist in socio-economic development, family planning programmes and fertility among China's provinces. No doubt variations among the hundreds of thousands of villages in rural China also exist. The institutions through which macro-economic policies influence individual fertility behaviours in different localities could vary, as could their mechanisms and processes. The study shows that existing institutions matter a great deal in shaping and filtering the mechanisms and processes through which macro forces influence micro behaviours. The study does not intend to generalize about rural China as a whole. It was designed to capture elements that might be shared with other villages, while avoiding idiosyncratic elements clearly limited to the specific village studied. In this sense, the study provides a starting point for a comparative study of many other villages in China; it should serve as a model and as background for further, detailed micro studies.

This research analyses the ways in which individual fertility motivations, perceptions, and interactions in fertility decision-making have been influenced by two decades of state-instigated economic reforms and by the consequent changes in the context within which people work and live. It focuses on intermediate-level institutions through which the macro-economic reforms influence micro fertility behaviours. It considers the intermediate level institutions regarding marriage and family, and local authority and power, and demonstrates the following three points:

(1) Institutional context is important in shaping individual fertility perceptions, in influencing interactions in fertility decision-makings and thus in determining individual fertility behaviour.

(2) Individuals are not merely subject to and constrained by social institutions. Their responses to the context within which they live and work in turn also reshape the character of social institutions.

(3) State policies influence and are at the same time mediated and filtered by existing societal institutions. Mediation of

state policies by intermediate institutions is complex and can lead to unintended outcomes.

OVERVIEW OF FINDINGS

In this county and village, as elsewhere in rural China, the most dramatic reform-era changes have been the introduction of the responsibility system, the dismantling of the commune system, the introduction of a contracting system for rural collective enterprises, the coexistence of the state, collective and private economy, and the gradual opening up of the market. Economic reforms initiated in the late 1970s have influenced almost every aspect of rural Chinese life, and touched almost every corner of rural Chinese society. The village studied has similarly experienced tremendous changes, especially in its economic organization and structure and in education, health, and social welfare systems. Increase in family income and a higher living standard have led to better health in general population and better health among children in particular. Education has, in general, not been adversely affected in the village. Social differentiation has, however, been widening since reforms began; increasing social differentiation and the weakening roles of the collective have engendered varying degrees of vulnerability for various subgroups within the village. This escalating social differentiation has been buffered significantly by more or less even contracting of land to rural households; access to land provides a certain level of security for the rural Chinese.

The labour structure has become complex and diversified in the village. With the opening up opportunities, many people have left agriculture in favour of sidelines or non-agricultural activities. They may now run household enterprises with self-employed labour, or they may engage in private enterprises and recruit other, non-household labour. At the same time, the related risks and uncertainties have become more significant for rural peasants, who since the retreat of the state must now rely more on themselves. Also, the differentiated roles between men and women and between generations, in agriculture, sidelines, rural industry and non-agricultural paid jobs linked to migration, are markedly asymmetrical. Agriculture has been increasingly feminized; this is consistent with what is happening elsewhere in rural China, where women have become the primary labour force in agriculture.

These changes have brought about corresponding changes in many other intermediate institutions. Marriage as a social institution, the age at marriage and the proportion who marry, the key intermediate variables through which socio-economic factors influence fertility, have experienced tremendous changes. For example, in sharp contrast to the pre-reform trend in the village, age at first marriage has been declining both for men and women, with age at marriage of men declining faster than that of women. The 'exchange marriage' (in which parents in two or more households arrange marriages for their sons by exchanging their daughters as daughters-in-law) and the 'mercenary marriage' (in which men purchase women as their wives from traffickers in women) have both re-emerged. An increasing proportion of marriages involves men and women in nearby villages, though there is no significant change in village endogamy. Both bride price and dowry have increased significantly. Importantly, the ratio of dowry to brideprice has nearly become an equal exchange. The younger generation has much more say in decision-making for their own marriages, in contrast to the fact that the majority of those in former generations were arranged by their parents or during the commune system heavily influenced by local cadres. The changing marriage pattern (e.g. declining age at marriage and increasing proportion married) has not only had an impact on the timing of childbearing and on the fertility level of the whole population, it is also linked to a restructuring of familial relations and thus in turn has implications for interactions among family members concerning fertility decision-making.

Changing marriage patterns such as the declining age at marriage might partially reflect changing fertility motivations, e.g. a desire for earlier childbirth, as many scholars postulate. However, changes in the marriage institution mainly reflect the responses of individuals to broader changes. For example, the declining age at marriage is one strategy peasant families use to set up alliances and compete or cooperate with other peasant families, to make use of available opportunities and to cover increasing risks and uncertainties. This pattern of responses differs by social group. The rich, who are situated in advantageous positions in the marriage market, can have their children married earlier. The sons of the poor marry later, because their parents occupy a disadvantaged position in society and experience more difficulty in arranging marriages for their sons.

With respect to families and households in village society, social differentiation has increased. The inter-generational and intra-generational relationships within households are also changing, mainly because the available opportunities and increasing vulnerabilities, risks and uncertainties after reforms are asymmetrical for different households, generations and genders. Household size is decreasing, and household structure is becoming nuclearized, following the trend in the collective period. Increasingly the period of co-residence of the young married couples with their parents or parents-in-law is becoming shorter. Young couples are separating from their parents sooner after marriage. Within the household, the division of labour has also been reshaped, with far more men than women engaging in non-agricultural activities, whether in the village, in nearby villages, or through migration; women are taking care of agriculture, agricultural sidelines, and household chores. Within the household, the power is being shifted from the old generation to the young generation and the old generation is losing its leading position. The traditional primary relation between father and son is gradually being replaced by the relation between husband and wife. Older parents, once their children marry and form procreative units, cannot stop the occurrence of em'otional nuclearization; for some parents, this creates dissatisfaction, complaint, or even desperation. Meanwhile, these changes mean that many young women in their 20s and 30s have increased their bargaining power, both with their husbands and with their parents-in-law. This increased power is also related to changes in kinship relations, which during the collective period heavily favoured paternal kin, but which is now more balanced. Women have frequent contact with their native kin, and kinship has become more important as an organizing principle in social relations. The many aspects of the changing roles of women also indicate that women's positions within the household has become socially more differentiated and in general more complex. Some women from poor families may face less favourable situations; for example, some of them are traded by their families in exchange marriages. Some women in rich families may have an increased living standard, but do not necessarily have increased decision-making power, especially with regard to income-related decisions.

The dismantling of collective institutions has destroyed the base on which the fertility perception and motivation of the older generations were formed, and the new institutional environment has reshaped the fertility perceptions of present reproductive couples. In the absence of the collective, the roles of children have changed: children are contributors to household economy, insurance against increasing risks and various contingencies to the household members as a whole, and especially providers of old-age support for their parents. In these respects, the roles of sons and daughters have both changed. Children contribute more to the household before their marriage than they did in the collective period. However, the earlier age at marriage and the earlier division of the household after marriage imply that the total labour children perform under their parents' control has decreased. Having a large number of children, which during the collective period could be useful for claiming a greater share of collective resources (e.g., private plots, grain rations, etc.) and work opportunities, is no longer so desirable. Furthermore, there is increasingly a sense that sons are unreliable and that sons are less willing to provide care to elderly parents than are daughters. At the same time, daughters are more able to provide such care to their natal parents, given their improved situation in their newly formed nuclear households. The new labour and mobility arrangements also make daughters valuable to their natal parents.

Meanwhile, childbearing and childrearing have become increasingly costly, whether measured in terms of the child's marriage, education and similar direct expenses, or as indirect opportunity cost. The increasing opportunity cost for having children in the reform period easily makes some households lag behind others. During the collective period, a substantial share of such costs was borne by the society as part of the more egalitarian production, distribution and social policies in education, health and welfare. The transformation of collective institutions into market and household-based ones and the increasing commercialization of services and goods have meant that individual parents now bear costs which were once shared, and also that the costs have increased in monetary terms. Increasingly, are peasants tending to have fewer children; their motivation for having girls is becoming stronger; they tend to have children earlier with shorter intervals; and they stop having children at earlier ages. Giving birth to children has become increasingly a conscious choice.

Shifts of collective institutions to market- and household-based ones reshape the character of fertility control. It reshapes the ways and mechanisms of local cadres in implementation of state policies. The decollectivization, in which collective resources like land and other major means of production and work opportunities have been reallocated, changed the position of local cadres in relation to peasantry. It reinforces the roles of the individual households and their bargaining power and weakens the roles of grassroots cadres. Local cadres have now less effective means in the reform period than they otherwise would have as in the collective period in implementation of rigid family planning policies. For example, mass meeting and study groups, which were effectively organized in the collective period, are no longer valid in the reform era. Cadres can no longer deduct work points from peasant households as penalties: they must now go door-to-door to collect family planning fines. Also, pregnancy and childbirth are no longer easily monitored, because household labour is organized freely by the individual households themselves rather than by the collectives.

However, the village and township cadres have gained some autonomy in relation to the higher authorities. Thus the rigid state family planning policies are seldom exactly followed at the local level, but are translated into modified local policies. These local policies, implemented at the village level, reflect the bargaining processes between peasants and local cadres. This bargaining process, in turn, exhibits conflicts and cooperation among cadres and peasants that leads to a compromise between private childbearing of individuals and the social control over fertility and family planning imposed by local authorities. It shows that individual fertility behaviour since the reforms is increasingly mediated by individual design, by individual families, and by grassroots government administrations.

The roles of local cadres as mediators of state policies are complex. There have been problems between township cadres (who are official government employees) and village cadres (who are members of the village society). The transfer of state policies creates problems between village and township cadres, because although village cadres are duty-bound to carry out state policies, they are attached to family clans, neighbours and rural enterprises. Village cadres and peasants do cooperate to resist unpopular policies. Village cadres can show directly their reluctance to complete tasks assigned to them from above. They also need villagers' cooperation in order to implement family planning policy. They must persuade (or force) fellow villagers to comply with state policies (or modified versions of these policies). It should be noted that interactions between different households and cadres in family planning programmes vary significantly in the bargaining process. Some households are much more effective than others in their defiance of family planning policies. Furthermore, the chief negotiator in the family also varies among families; who negotiates depends on the position of different family members within the family. Since reform, local cadres are increasingly negotiating directly with young reproductive couples or with the women themselves, an indication that the young generation has gained more control over its reproduction in the family and also a reflection of the fact that many men are migrating outside the village for non-agricultural activities. Meanwhile, township cadres, with no effective means to press village cadres to be loyal to higher-level administrations, can only bargain by assigning higher quotas for the specific family planning tasks.

These findings are consistent with the research findings of Parish & Whyte (1978) on social change before the reforms, i.e. that the extent of change does not correspond in any clear and simple way with government priorities and pressure. Individual couples have increasingly gained autonomy in decision-making over their own fertility, an area which formerly was more controlled either by elder family members or by local authorities. This finding has not been reported by most other researcher, who tend to link the success of Chinese family planning programmes to the extensive structure of government control and which emphasize the determining role of government control in the fertility decline.

Although many scholars have suspected that economic reforms would strengthen the motivation of rural couples to have more children (especially sons), this is not the case in the village. This study has shown that the mechanisms and processes through which state instigated economic reforms influence individual fertility perception and fertility decision making are complex, and there are economic mechanisms at work which constrain fertility. *Since the reforms, rural Chinese are more likely to marry at earlier ages and to have children earlier with shorter birth intervals; nevertheless, they also stop their reproduction earlier and thus have fewer children.* In contrast to the arguments of many scholars, early marriage and early childbirths do not necessarily mean more births. This study has shown that the *timing* of marriage and of childbearing have been shifted to earlier ages, but they are not the mechanisms at family level for increasing fertility.

The changing fertility pattern is an outcome of changing individual fertility perceptions and fertility motivations, and of interactions within families between generations and between husbands and wives, and in the larger community between families and local cadres. The changing perceptions and interactions are in turn reshaped by the changing institutional context. The changing, interrelated and intertwined social, economic and political institutions of the reform period are consequences of both contextual changes brought about by deliberate rural reforms and strategic or tactical responses of the rural Chinese to this rapidly changing context in which they live and work. Earlier marriage, earlier childbearing and shorter birth intervals are the outcomes of a mediation process between existing institutions regarding marriage, family relations (including gender relations and inter-generational relations within the family institution) and relations of local power and authority. This negotiated outcome cannot be characterized in terms of either the 'one-child-per-family' policy, nor even the 'later, sparser and fewer' policy.

It should be noted that the major findings of the present study, concerning patterns of marriage, timing of childbirth and birth intervals, are consistent with macro patterns. In rural China age at marriage rose continuously before 1980 and then started to decline (Wang & Yang 1996), the age of primapara women has decreased since reforms began (Chen 1991); and birth intervals continue to shorten in rural China as a whole (Feeney & Wang 1993, Wang & Yang 1996). It is clear that the Chinese check on population growth has been operating rather more effectively in stopping reproduction than in delaying its start or broadening the spacing pattern.

However, processes and mechanisms of the reforms that are influencing individual fertility behaviour may vary in different villages. Comparing this research with other studies, one can easily recognize that differences exist in marriage and family and in the implementation of family planning programmes. For example, the sex ratio at birth does not show abnormalities in this village, but these are observed at the macro level and indicate that certain variations exist among villages in the vast area of rural China. Variations among villages may reflect different local economic, ecological, political and social circumstances to which individuals must respond. Variations also exist among households within the village, given that social differentiation has widened greatly since reforms began. Variations among households in the same village reflect the different responses of individuals to their social context according to their own characteristics (e.g., gender, age, etc.). The important thing is that this village study shows the importance of social context in delimiting individual behaviours.

RETHINKING ECONOMY, INSTITUTIONS AND FERTILITY IN
RURAL CHINA

The findings of the present study are contrary to the suspicion that reforms are reinforcing peasant motivations for having more children (especially sons), but consistent with the views that peasants tend to marry and have children at earlier ages. Nevertheless, many previous studies have no intensive empirical evidence to bear this out. Some who have argued that there is stronger motivation to have many children and to have children earlier rather than later see this as the result of traditional restoration in the reform period. They argue that traditional ideas of having children, especially sons, have been strengthened because collective institutions have been dismantled and the traditional household mode of production has been reinstated. They also argue that the motivation to have many children has been strengthened because children help to meet increasing needs for labour and for old-age security while the cost of having children in rural areas has been small; for these researchers, this process is possible because the erosion of the power of local cadres makes it increasingly difficult for them to implement family planning programmes.

Such arguments are also based on the assumption that relations between collectivization and fertility were such that the economics of collective life gradually lowered peasant fertility aspirations. They assume that under the collective economic regime, many traditional family functions were taken over by the team, eroding the advantages children had historically conferred on rural parents.

This study shows both continuity and change in the village throughout the collective and post-reform period. It is the society's new institutional fabric – reshaped by macroeconomic reforms and micro individual responses which are historically inherited – which in turn influences individual fertility behaviours. Tremendous socioeconomic development has been achieved since reforms began. Peasants' fertility perceptions, and fertility decision-making, would be totally different in other economic situations. The idea of a restoration of tradition concerns only partially on changes in certain aspects, and neglects change and continuity in other aspects. The idea that rural China is reverting to tradition focuses primarily on the restoration of the household as the unit of production, but ignores the new nature of 'the household', as well as changing ways in which production is organized and changes in the division of labour within the family as economic opportunities are released by the reforms. Furthermore, such 'restoration' does not include land. Prior to collectivization, land was privately owned and sons were the major means of wealth accumulation. This is not presently the case, since land is still owned by the collective.

Institutions are path dependent; they are not independent of time and space, and thus history matters. Twenty years of the commune system and collectivization have had a profound impact on the life of rural Chinese people; their effects can be assumed to continue into the reform period. As this study has shown, the characteristics of social institutions such as marriage and family, gender, and local authority, all of which mediate and are influenced by social policies, are much different than they were before collectivization. For example, collectivization brought rural women out of the domestic sphere to participate in social production in the collectives. Once women's role in production outside the household was initiated during the collective period, the market-oriented economic reforms could not push them back into the 'pre-collectivization' household. They instead have become the main labour force in agriculture. Their important roles in agriculture, agricultural sidelines and in non-agricultural production since reforms had never existed before. Furthermore, within the family the young generation had already gained some autonomy concerning their marriages, and there had been an erosion of power of the older generation in the collective period. Since reform, the trend of increasing autonomy for the young has not reversed; it has not only continued, but in many respects it is taking new forms as families adjust to the new context.

Institutions transfer information, provide guidance to human behaviour and reshape human perceptions. Individual perception is also reshaped within the rapidly changing context. The comparison of present with past provides peasants with guidance for future action. Post-reform perceptions of childbearing are closely related to those that prevailed during the commune system. The interaction between peasants and cadres since reform, as cadres are losing their power and authority, would be much different if that power and authority had never existed.

The costs and benefits of childbearing have changed: the increased demand for security and social mobility may not be met through the contribution of children's labour, and children may not provide the satisfactory old age support that could be assumed during the collective period. However, it is clear that perceptions of childbearing go beyond the economic notion of individual maximization based on the calculation of the costs and benefits of having children. It is not simply cost-benefit analysis that causes post-reform reproductive couples to differ in their fertility behaviours from similar couples in the collective period. Changing power relations affect individual fertility behaviour even when there has been no change in the costs or benefits of children. The important factor that determines the reproductive processes of individuals in post reform era may be such shifting power relations: within couples, between generations within the family, and between families and local authorities.

The role of local cadres has weakened in the reform era, but this does not indicate that cadres had absolute power and authority over peasants in the collective period. During the commune system and the 'later, sparser and fewer' family planning policy in the 1970s, peasants still arranged for their children to marry young, and had more children with little consideration for the birth interval set as the state norm. Increasing age at marriage during the collective period was in line with the demand of a girl's family to retain her labour and with her reluctance to leave her natal family while very young. As

Parish and Whyte concluded, in their study of Guangdong villages, 'changes have occurred primarily through indirect responses of peasants to the structural transformations of rural life rather than through direct change efforts by the government' (Parish & Whyte 1978: 154).

While the roles of individuals in shaping the character of institutions, in modifying formal rules and in creating informal rules might be hidden and obscured during the collective period, such roles have become obvious since reform. For example, during the collective period, unpopular policies could be met by silence: peasants would withdraw cooperation as much as they possibly could, hoping that local cadres would change or modify the rules. Peasants now can openly resist and protest unpopular policies (though most often in an unorganized manner). The processes of rural reform and the difference between national family planning policy and local-level policies reflect this change in the bargaining process between cadres and peasants.

This is not to deny that state policies have an impact. State policies do influence the economic and social lives of peasants. Years of government anti-natalist policies have ensured that peasants' fertility behaviour is a matter of conscious choice. Expansion of the education and health care systems and government efforts to raise the status of women may also have greatly facilitated the rapid fertility decline seen during the collective period. The government's influence on individual behaviour seems to have been more effective during the collective period than during the reform period, however in both periods the state's effect on local society and the individual could not have been achieved without the mediation of intermediate institutions. Such mediation can alter government intentions: some may work their way to the local level basically unaltered, others may be altered to varying degrees, and still others may engender completely transformed, in unintended ways.

This study has shown that intermediate institutions play important roles in mediation between macro socio-economic forces and micro fertility behaviours. Relations and linkages between macro forces and micro behaviour in the reform era are different from those in the collective period. The mechanisms and processes which are filtered and reshaped by social institutions (and through which macro state policies and socio-economic development influence individual fertility in these two particular historical periods) are different. It should not be assumed that 'development' will automatically lead to fertility decline, with institutions taking care of themselves, as posed by conventional demographic transition theory. It should be understood (though microeconomic theories of fertility do not) that individuals do not live in an institution-free world and that power relations and their impact on the complex reproductive processes must be taken into account in the study of individual fertility behaviour. This empirical study of economic reforms and fertility behaviour in rural China has shown that changes in intermediate institutions matter a great deal; they affect the process and mechanisms through which macro socio-economic factors influence micro fertility behaviours. These intermediate institutions shape and filter the nature of the effects of macro socio-economic policies on fertility. Thus, considering the changes within social institutions in a society can provide a better understanding of individual fertility behaviour, and of the levels and dynamics of fertility in society.

Appendices

A Note on Fieldwork

Investigation in the field followed a two-step procedure: first in the county-town and second in the village. Selection of the county cannot escape some degree of arbitrariness, mainly because of the consideration of convenience for the study. However, before the county was selected, the available quantitative data was processed and a selection of officials and local residents were interviewed, mainly on policy processes, economic development and population growth of the 16 counties of Handan prefecture, to ensure that the chosen county and village are not exceptional, and that the findings would be valid and useful in understanding other parts of rural China as well. The data and interviews confirmed that the county, like many other counties in China, follows the national policies in economic reforms and family planning. Reform processes, evolution of the family planning policies, economic development and population growth at the county level are, as chapter three has shown, not exceptional compared with many other Chinese counties. Investigation of the background information of the county preceded the selection of one village for intensive study.

Applying an institutional approach to studying Chinese economic reforms and fertility behaviour requires a context-specific study. I will firstly explain why an intensive micro-level village study was needed, and I will then introduce my investigation of the county and selection of the village. Finally I will discuss the detailed information about investigation in the village.

1. METHODOLOGY: WHY A VILLAGE STUDY?

Studies of the relation between Chinese fertility change and socio-economic development and family planning policies are mainly of a macro nature. Methodologically, such studies tend to analyse fertility and fertility change at the aggregate level. Though fertility indicators may be analysed at the individual level, they are mainly used as dependent variables whose variations are explained by individual or family socio-economic characteristics through correlation and regression analysis. Data used is mainly quantitative, and collected through short-term demographic surveys with structured questionnaires. This tendency to rely on quantitative analysis, may, as Martin King Whyte (1992: 322) points out, be due to the fact that '[m]any professional colleagues in China consider in-depth ethnographic research to be "old fashioned" and unscientific, and feel that only work with "modern" quantitative methods, surveys and computers will advance them in their own careers'; though at the same time, as Whyte also pointed out, Chinese scholars have certain limitations in conducting fieldwork, and they may avoid dealing with sensitive issues.

Macro quantitative studies provide information on patterns of fertility and fertility change; however, they fail to provide insights into or explanations of the processes and mechanisms through which various social, economic and political factors influence fertility change. Applying an institutional approach to relations between reforms and fertility mediated and shaped by intermediate institutions in rural China needs context-specific research at the micro level. Further, a micro study can help obtain accurate data which is vital to understanding social reality. Interviewees who intend to mislead researchers and try to influence policy-makings to their advantage are not rare. Intensive study through long term residence is necessary to gain sufficiently accurate data; this is impossible using short-term, large-scale, structured questionnaire surveys, because rapport with interviewees is a prerequisite for the kinds of discussions which would expose true information, and is also needed when researchers intend to understand and verify the accuracy of the data (Srinivas 1988).

Intensive village-level study is also needed to understand the complex intermediate institutions, and their roles in mediating and linking macro policies and micro behaviours. The vertically dynamic processes cannot be simply studied by macro investigation of socio-economic aggregates. The essence of the process is how certain institutional changes bring forth other adjustments and adaptations in the social institutional fabric of society, since changes in any one institution or institution set produce changes in other institutions. Understanding this requires detailed analysis of the complexities of institutions and institutional change.

Studying institutions in society, not only to know how individuals perceive how they work, but to see how they actually work in practice, needs intensive study through interaction with people and participation in their work and daily life (e.g. Cain 1985). Such an intensive village study guards against making unwarranted generalizations based on the analysis of observed associations between macro aggregates.

The micro study is the first step toward having a complete, clear picture emerged through ongoing study and debate. Generalization is giving way to intensity. I am not looking for an 'average' village which could represent all or even part of rural China; this would be impossible before knowledge about various villages has been obtained. The study in a single village is used as one example to show that policy-induced institutional changes mediate state policies which may bring about unexpected outcomes. This study shows that institutions matter in the mediation of economic reforms and fertility in rural China. However, I am not intending to claim from this particular village study that institutions matter in rural China in the same manner as in this village. The processes and mechanisms through which intermediate institutions mediate state policies and individual fertility behaviour in other villages may differ, and thus many similar village studies will be needed for a complete picture of reforms and fertility in rural China.

2. COUNTY INVESTIGATION AND SELECTION OF THE VILLAGE

I started my fieldwork in July 1992. I formally entered the county at the end of the month and stayed in the county town for two months. I had two main purposes in mind at this initial stage of the fieldwork: I wanted to get sufficient background information about the county, and I planned to use this information to choose one village for further detailed study. County data, with its general patterns, could be compared with data on other counties and higher-level regions to indicate similarities and differences with other counties, and to provide a reference point and context for the village study, linking it with the province and the nation. Both qualitative and quantitative data were collected, including quantitative data such as statistics from regular registrations, censuses and sampling surveys, and qualitative data such as reports and documents and data collected by interviewing officials, workers, teachers, students, hairdressers, businessmen and many others. This helped me to become familiar with the reform processes, the evolution of family planning, the population structure and its trends, and the economic structure and development in the county. It also helped me to have a firm base for choosing a village for my intensive study. The county investigation also served as a trial period for further village investigation. Before selecting and going into the village for further study, I already had some detailed information about what was going on in the county and some of its villages, such as what have been changed in marriage, family structure, implementation of family planning programmes, etc. This helped me reformulate research questions and hypotheses, better understand the difficulties I might encounter in the later village study, and equipped me with some solutions.

I was aware that the research would not be easy, not only because I was a young male scholar intending to understand one intimate aspect of human life (individual fertility behaviour) but mainly because this study is related closely to the Chinese family planning programme, which in recent years has been one of the most controversial area of China's programmes, both domestically and abroad. The most apparent problems concern implementation of the family planning programme at the local level. Thus local cooperation with my research was the main determinant on my research outcome. Without this cooperation of both people and cadres, the research would not have been possible.

In the county investigation I was particularly interested in how family planning campaigns were organized at county level. I visited many county family planning officials, attended mobilization meetings for family planning campaigns, observed and visited rural couples coming to the county hospitals for family planning operations, and visited family planning technicians and doctors. Family planning cadres were surprisingly open-minded. Most of them felt free to talk with me about their perception of population problems and population policies, and about problems and difficulties in the implementation of provincial family planning policies.

The process of collecting and processing secondary data and interviewing local people in the county town also informed my choice of village. Many people working, studying or living in the county town came from the various county villages. They had frequent contact with their natal families and villages, and some even lived in their villages while working in the towns. From the detailed and in-depth talks, I came to know the situation on reforms, family planning and various changes occurring in some of the villages. Complementing this information with the quantitative data from the county statistics bureau on village information such as number of households and population, per capita arable land and per capita income, I shortlisted 30 or so villages from among the 421 villages of the county using certain, though not strict, criteria. Villages with fewer than 300 households were dropped, based on the consideration of statistical significance. Villages with overly high or low per capita income were removed from the list. Villages in the county were categorized into three groups based on village cadres' performance in carrying out state policies, with the best and the worst in the first and third categories and those in between in the second category. Villages in the first and third categories were dropped so that the selected village would be one in which the performance of cadres in carrying out the state policies was in the middle group. Villages in border area with other counties were dropped, since the implementation of state policies in those villages could be influenced by the implementation of state policies in the nearby villages of other counties. Three villages within the 30 shortlisted villages had also been among the nine selected for 1987 national population sampling survey. They received particular attention given the availability of historical data, based on which I could know better the process of change. However, I dropped the idea of choosing one of these three villages for my village study after I attended and observed the process of a similar population sampling survey organized by the county statistics bureau, because the data collected for the survey was seriously distorted (see Appendix II). For example, population was underreported to make the assigned family planning tasks easier; the number of births was underreported to show the 'good' performance of cadres in fertility control, as has been shown in Chapter 8.

I did not visit each of the villages one by one, but simply approached people familiar with villages on my list. I asked them about economic reforms, implementation of family planning, and socio-economic changes that occurred in the village before and after the reforms, especially changes in labour structure, social differentiation, and the development of non-agricultural enterprises. I then visited two villages and three townships which I thought appropriate for the village study, through county administrative channels. I explained the purpose of my research and made it as specific as possible. I mentioned that one aspect of the study would concern family planning. After further discussions with the cadres about their villages, I tried to assess the possible cooperation of township cadres and village cadres especially, and finally decided on one village for the study. Though the above process was all conducted through the channel of government administrations, the choice of the village was made by myself.

3. THE VILLAGE INVESTIGATION

With the county background and context in mind, I started my village investigation soon after the village was selected. I lived with a family in the village, as arranged by village cadres. In addition to qualitative data collected through participant observation and interviews, quantitative data was collected through population censuses and surveys conducted at various stages of the fieldwork. The total period of fieldwork in the village was exactly one year, beginning in November 1992 and finishing at the end of November 1993.

Qualitative data collection: Participant observations and interviews

The village was chosen, and my entry arranged through administrative channels. However, settling down in the village was not straightforward. I faced some resistance, not so much from the township cadres, but mainly from the village cadres. Their major worry was that I might have come to investigate their implementation of family planning programmes. The form this resistance took was not directly rejecting my study, but delaying my settling in the village, in the hope that I would withdraw and shift to another village. I explained the village cadres as well as township cadres about my purpose of the study, first to convince the township cadres and later convince the village cadres with the help from the township as well as the county cadres. I did not give up to shift to another village. I knew I would face the same situation if I did so.

The difficulties encountered in settling down in the village also derived from the fact that villagers were not familiar with the idea that scholars would stay in the village for a long period simply for academic research. Their experiences with outsiders residing in the village for some period were with government officials in work teams (gongzuedui) for various campaigns, and with young urban intellectuals sent to be educated by peasants during Cultural Revolution. They wondered why an urban young 'university student' studying abroad wanted to reside for a full year in a rural village, when essentially all intellectual youth had returned to the cities 20 years ago. There was only one of these young intellectuals from Tianjin who married a man in the village and stayed there afterwards. However, this is believed to be extremely rare. For some time I explained many times that I was a student studying abroad, born in the county, who wanted to do academic work in the village.

The family with whom I lived included three generations: the host and hostess, their four children, the wife of the eldest son and one granddaughter. The family was well respected in the village. The host and two sons worked in the county town in government departments and state enterprise. One son had joined the army. The hostess took care of the contracted land and household chores. The little daughter was in the secondary school. During the whole period, I lived in a room with the second son, who graduated from a special secondary school (zhongzhuan). He helped me in many ways related to my study, and became one of my local assistants for the population census. I was treated as one of their family members. I ate with them, gave help when I could, e.g. planting corn, reaping wheat, watering the field, helping with cooking and household chores. The hostess was extremely helpful, in ways too numerous to be listed fully here. She answered patiently my endless questions, whether personal or general, introduced me to other villagers at the initial stage of the fieldwork, and even asked me to attend their family meetings, besides cooking for one more person in the family during my one-year fieldwork. I learned a great deal about their lives in particular and village life in general from discussions and observations while working and living with the family.

After settling down in the village, I tried to present myself to my host family, the neighbours, and many other villagers. I kept introducing myself to people I met along the streets or in shops. The fact that I was born in the county helped me increase the degree of my local identification and I was easily accepted by the villagers. I developed a rapport with many families during my long-term residence. I could easily approach them and ask questions, and I could note down what they told me in my small notebook without problems. With many people the interview was quite informal, except for the structured questionnaire surveys. I simply had the questions in mind, asked them and listened to the replies, sometimes guiding the direction of the talk, and made notes afterwards. With these forms of interview, people felt at ease; they appeared to like to chat with me. Many people even approached me to tell their own stories.

Besides participating the household work and giving help in agricultural work in the fields in my host family, I also visited the village collective brick kiln, the private plastic factory, and the household-run small charcoal-making enterprise. I often gave a hand there while we were talking, since they were busy and simply had no time to leave their work. From this participation, I could understand better the detailed process of agricultural work and non-agricultural activities, and the roles of men as well as women, the old and the young, in their agricultural and non-agricultural work. I also visited people running small shops in the county town. At a very late stage of the fieldwork, I went to Changzhi, a city in Shanxi province, to visit the migrant workers from the village who worked in construction.

Though I intended to interview as many villagers as possible, of different occupations, sexes, ages and social groups, I faced difficulties in interviewing certain groups, and in covering certain topics. Talks with young unmarried women and with new brides could be problematic, especially on marriage, childbirth and family planning. The village society is still conservative, and talking alone with them was not seen as appropriate. Most information concerning marriage, childbirth and family planning was from men or women with some children. Talking with men and some married women with children was not so difficult, even on many intimate aspects of their lives.

Unlike foreign scholars doing fieldwork in China, who were usually accompanied by government officials during the interviews (e.g. Croll 1994, Judd 1994), I was free to go everywhere and interview anyone without official restrictions. This ensured high data quality and detailed information with wide scope. In particular, I could observe how the family planning campaign was implemented in the village. I feel fortunate that I could observe all four family planning campaigns during 1993, since the focus and methods of each family planning campaign differed.

The timing of my entry into the village was serendipitous. The initial months were just after the autumn harvest, when people had some leisure time, and many migrant labourers started coming home. It was the period when families arranged their children's marriages. I was introduced by my host family, cadres, and neighbours and welcomed to attend marriage ceremonies; people liked to tell me about their marriage customs. Later when I became familiar with people and families in the village, I was allowed and even asked to participate in marriage rituals such as transporting dowries, receiving brides and receiving guests from brides' families, as a member of the groom's family.

My population census was conducted after three months' stay in the village, during the Chinese spring festival when almost all family members return home; by then I had come to know a part of the village population well. As explained below, the object of the census was the *de jure* population. Because almost all migrant labour came back to celebrate the spring festival, they could be captured by the census, and the information could be ensured to be of high quality. Soon after the completion of the population census, the first of the year's four family planning campaigns started. Each family planning campaign lasted for about a month and was followed by a one or two month interval. Each campaign differed in its focus: fines, contraception, abortion, or sterilization. Knowledge of all of the campaigns was essential for understanding the different aspects of family planning work at the local level.

As this description of data collection shows, the whole process was an exploration. I kept my ears and eyes open and tried to penetrate every aspect of the village's social and economic life. During the fieldwork I found that not all villagers would know how a particular institution works, or how it should work. Some people knew certain institutions much better than others. Even the villagers would consult 'institution experts' (e.g., in marriage, burial arrangements, etc.) to guide their behaviour. I also approached and interviewed these experts, for a detailed understanding of such institutions.

Quantitative data collection: Censuses and surveys

One census and four surveys were conducted to collect quantitative data. These were a population census, a survey of the birth histories of all ever-married women aged 15–59, a survey of married couples in the same age category, a survey of unmarried young aged 5–24, and a survey of those aged 60 and over. As mentioned, the population census was conducted after three months' stay in the village. The surveys of married women, married couples, the young and the old, were conducted after nine months' stay in the village. The questionnaires were prepared before the fieldwork and modified during the fieldwork. In the survey of married couples, I simplified many questions concerning fertility and family planning, to guarantee the quality of data. Some questions were deleted, because it was difficult to get reliable information, or the information was irrelevant, or it was inapplicable in practice. For example, the original questionnaire asked whether they had a baby after they received the birth permission certificate according to the formal state requirement, but this question was dropped, since the cadres never put this state requirement into practice in this village. Questions suggested by the fieldwork were added; these concerned marriage, family and the relevant issues. The wording of questions was also modified to make them easily understood in local terms.

Population census
The main purposes of the census were fourfold: (1) getting to know the general background information of the village concerning individual and household characteristics, socio-economic structure and migration patterns; (2) preparing for the survey of ever-married women by identifying those women; (3) creating a base for selecting samples for questionnaire surveys at later stage; and (4) collecting data for analysis in combination with that from the other surveys. The questions concerned individual and household characteristics, such as the number of household members, their age, sex, marital status, occupation, migration, education level and household property. Since villagers always combined their economic activities with many other activities, the primary and secondary activity and their time period during the year was included in the census. Yearly income was included in the census, however data quality was poor and this indicator was not used in the analysis. Family property, like ownership of housing, main means of production, livestock and durable consumer goods was used to represent the economic situation of the family.

The object of the population census was the *de jure* population, not the *de facto* population. The unit for the census was the family, which included all institutional family members whether or not they resided in the village. Husbands working in urban areas either in state enterprises or in private enterprises, unmarried sons in the army or being educated outside the village were included as family members. Holders of non-agricultural registrations, such as former state employees who came back to reside in the village were included in the census. A few families who held the village's agricultural household registration were not included in my census, since all family members had migrated out of the village several year earlier; although their fellow villagers still regarded them as village members, they are in fact out-migrants. The standard time set for the census was 23 January 1993, the day of Chinese lunar new year.

Village cadres were initially reluctant to allow me to conduct the population census. They had two worries. They worried that villagers would respond to my census in ways that relate to family planning policies. For example, one local family planning regulation was that a woman with extra children was not required to undergo sterilization if she was above 40 years of age. Village cadres worried that reproductive women would report their ages as over 40 in my census, and then expect the answer to be accepted by village cadres, thus exempting them from sterilization. Cadres also worried that the results of my population census would be exposed to higher authorities, who would see that the population number was higher than the reported number, and that the higher authorities would then assign heavier family planning tasks and increase their work burdens, since family planning tasks were in part based on the size of a village's population.

I assured them that I would not share my data with anyone else for any other purpose except academic research, and assured them that I would clarify this for families before asking questions and filling in the questionnaire. The cadres also made a public announcement about my census to the villagers through a loudspeaker, specifying that my population census would not be used as a basis for policy implementation. Further, the cadres were not involved in the census to insure villagers that my census was only for my own study. I was happy with this arrangement, and in fact I tried to avoid involving cadres in my research throughout the fieldwork.

I asked two local assistants to help me conduct the census. One was my roommate, and the other was our neighbour. Both had graduated from the same special normal school, and they also worked together as state employees in the county town. Because they were familiar with the village they were already known to and accepted by the villagers and could assess data quality. Most importantly, they knew my purposes of the village study and had confidence in my research. We divided the village into three parts, and each of us covered a different part and conducted the survey separately. Every day we met and discussed the census; members of my host families and also my neighbours enjoyed helping me to cross-check the questionnaire so that wrong reports could be corrected.

The most problematic areas, as expected, concerned the ages of married women and the number of children. The families with whom I had become familiar, and families without problems in family planning, usually cooperated. However, some families met for the first time over-reported their ages and under-reported their number of children. I could sometimes determine their ages and the number of children by their appearance, their attitude as they answered questions, and the number of children playing around them. Wrong reports were also corrected through cross-checks; some people also approached me later to correct their wrong reports after they gained confidence in my study. During the census, one family did not answer my questions at the beginning but had the questionnaire filled in with the help of my neighbours. One family used pseudonyms. Reports for other questions had minor problems; for example I discovered later that one single, elderly man reported his marital status as widowed, and one young, divorced woman reported her marital status as single.

Survey of ever-married women, of married couples, of the old and of the unmarried young

After nine months' stay in the village, and six months after the population census, I conducted the survey of ever-married women aged between 15–59, the survey of married couples between 15–59, the survey of the unmarried young, and the survey of those over 60, roughly at the same time.

The survey of ever-married women concerned only basic questions on women's history: marriage, childbirth, contraception, and present contraception methods. Its purpose was to know individual fertility behaviours and fertility patterns aggregated at group level and the village level as a whole. All married women aged 15–59 captured by the population census were objects of this survey. Inclusion of women over 49 was based on the consideration of comparison of births within wider age groups, since women aged over 40 were within their reproductive age in part of the 1980s and in the 1970s. The final survey size, 450 women, accounted for 97.2 per cent of the ever-married women aged 15–59.

The survey of the married couples was more comprehensive. Questions were divided into four parts: marriage, family, economic activities, and fertility motivations. The survey of the unmarried young asked only about their schooling and their economic activities. The survey of the old concerned their family life and socio-economic activities, and their attitudes toward childbirth and old age. The survey size, 254, accounted for 54.9 per cent of all married couples aged 15–59. The survey of the young covered 244 persons, or 33.2 per cent of those in this category. The sample size of those aged 60 and over was 95 persons, and accounted for 66.0 per cent of the older population.

Conducting these surveys was much easier than was the population census. The cadres approved the survey without problems. Most families cooperated well. I could ask women about childbirth and even their contraception history and present contraceptive methods. After years of family planning programmes most people were able to openly discuss contraception, abortion, and sterilization, although some young women would be shy in answering my questions. Data on number of children, timing of births and timing of miscarriages and abortions were, however, better than data on contraception methods. For contraception methods like IUD and sterilization, some responses were false; women kept their secrets not only from me but also from village cadres and even their neighbours. In addition, 'extra' babies who were sent outside the village into hiding for some period of time were exposed neither to the public nor to my survey, although children not reported by their parents in the survey but known to the public were added during cross-checking.

I had two female assistants helping me to conduct the surveys. One was a mother of three children in her 30s from the village, and the other was a graduate student majoring in anthropology at a university in Beijing. The survey was not conducted strictly on a random basis. We simply went to the households one by one, and skipped those households where people were not at home. However, I ensured that the sample covered a wide range by cross-checking the households surveyed with household information collected by the census, and thus that the sample could be statistically meaningful by subgroups according to variations in household properties.

There were some problems with attitudinal questions. Though I tried to interview husband and wife separately, without the presence of others, sometimes they had to be interviewed together, and sometimes even in the presence of neighbours and friends, when private interviews were not practical. Interviews were mostly conducted when the villagers were off job, sometimes chatting with neighbours and friends, doing household chores, watching television or having dinner. Furthermore, the questions in my questionnaires were quickly known in the whole village, and within one or two days after I started my interviews people were chatting about the questions and discussing their own attitudes with each other. It would have been very difficult to control the situation so that it perfectly fit the research requirements. From participating in the whole process of interview and through direct observation, however, I knew myself what data for which items were of good quality and could be used with confidence, which data had problems and demanded careful interpretation, and which data had problems so serious that they could not be used to support arguments.

Data processing and interpretation

Immediately after the census and the surveys, I had the data input to computer, had a preliminary check and then processed the data in the field. It was much easier to check logical errors which could then be corrected in the field. For example, cases in which birth intervals were shorter than ten months were rechecked. Preliminary processing of the data in the field made it possible to revisit the family where data presented problems, and also to cross-check with other informants. I also rechecked cases in which I had doubts about data which, though theoretically possible, was not always plausible, or simply where it was worthwhile to visit the relevant families again. For example, I listed all cases in which couples used contraception before the first or second child was born, the age of marriage was below 18, the number of children was over four, and those who had the first child before 1988 but no children afterwards, etc.; I revisited the family or cross-checked to see if there were data problems or special circumstances. For example, among eight cases who had only one child before 1988 but no children afterwards (four cases had their only child in the 1960s or 1970s), I found that three couples could not give birth to another child after the first one because of physical problems, two couples were infertile and the reported child was actually adopted, and two couples underreported the number of children; I suspected another couple had more than one child but I could not verify this.

After processing of the preliminary data, dynamic patterns with respect to births, birth intervals, marriage, family structure, etc. became clear to me, and these guided my further fieldwork. I did not find much inconsistency between patterns of various variables in my own tables and figures and what I heard from the villagers themselves. However, some questions arose. I showed various figures and tables to villagers, explained the message and asked the villagers to interpret. They could easily give me explanations which I had not noticed during previous open-ended interviews and participant observations. This also helped them to clarify some of their own doubts and impressions based on their own experiences but perhaps not always consistent with the actual pattern for the village as a whole. In this sense my research was not only mainly exploratory but also was participated in by both the villagers and myself, as we tried to delineate the relations between reforms and fertility.

Some Problems in Official Statistics

1. NORMAL VITAL REGISTRATION

Cadre's purposeful misreporting in statistics, as a strategy for local governments to mediate state policies according to local or individual interests, is
discussed in the previous chapters. I will only provide a few of the empirical
examples found during my fieldwork.

The degree of misreporting in reports and statistics is related to the degree
of sensitivity of the issues concerned. It is more serious in more sensitive
issues, and less so in less ones. Regarding population and family planning in
rural China, areas in which cadres may misreport range from number of population to number of births, abortions, sterilization, and family planning fines.
Unplanned births may not be registered. Family planning cadres are reluctant
to report unplanned births because they will be assigned higher family planning quotas in the following family planning campaigns, or will be evaluated
as having performed badly in their family planning work. Moreover, individual couples will not report unplanned births in order to avoid certain
punishments according to the county and provincial family planning regulations. The tendency to underreport births is supported not only by the fact
that family planning tasks are assigned on the basis of total population in the
village, but also because agricultural tax, levies, and other assignments are
collected based on the population numbers. More population means more
agricultural tax and levies to be collected.

This can be seen if we consider the data on population, births, deaths
reported by the CSB from 1949 to 1990, and number of migration calculated
from the number of population at the end of the year and number of births
and deaths of the year. As shown in Table A.1, in the 40–year period from 1949
to 1989, net immigration ranged from 227 to 4372 persons annually, while net
emigration ranged from 203 to 6544 persons. In 1990, the net immigration
based on the calculation of reports of population, births, and deaths increased
to 52,224 persons, 11 times higher than the historical peak of net immigration
in 1982. The official population census was conducted in 1990. The report of
end year population by CSB could not be smaller by mid-year population from
the census. However, reports of number of births were intentionally kept low,
and tremendous number of births of the year and of previous years were
counted as immigrants in 1990.

Cadre misreporting in statistics is not exceptional only in the researched county. It occurs in many other counties as well. According to an investigation conducted by the provincial statistics bureau at the end of 1993, one county in Handan prefecture underreported 49.3 per cent of its births (HRZ 1994). In another survey conducted in 1993 to examine the problem of underreporting in 32 villages in Hebei and Hubei provinces (42,514 individuals), it was estimated that 37.3 per cent of rural births were not reported, and it was suggested that local officials may well have encouraged and even organized individuals to underreport (Zeng 1996).[1] Fifty of the 52 towns and townships of Jinhua County in Zhejiang Province had under-reports of births in 1988, 52 in 1989, 48 in 1990, and 49 in 1991, and among the under-reports, 47.1 per cent were underreported intentionally by family planning cadres (see Bao 1993).

The problem of underreporting also exists in the fourth official population census conducted in 1990.[2] Yearly reports of deaths were more consistent with census results, with no tendency of underreporting.

2. SAMPLING SURVEY CONDUCTED BY THE PROVINCIAL STATISTICS BUREAU: ILLUSTRATION OF A CASE

At the end of September 1992, the County Statistics Bureau (CSB) conducted a population sampling survey. It was an annual sampling survey organized by the Provincial Statistics Bureau (PSB). The purpose was twofold: to evaluate the yearly family planning work and to understand the situation of population growth, thus to provide data base for policy recommendations.

Three villages in the county were selected for the sampling survey. Villages were selected rather randomly, according to CSB officials. However, local cooperation was considered when making the selection. On 26 September, the CSB called the nine relevant village and township cadres together for a meeting in the county town. The director and three staff of the CSB gave an introduction of the sampling survey, including the purpose of the survey, how the three villages were selected, and how to conduct the survey. The structured questionnaire for the survey was designed by the PSB. It included the items like household size, name of the household head, age of the reproductive woman, and births distinguished by planned births and unplanned births. The filled-in questionnaire were to be submitted to the PSB for aggregation, and not kept by the CSB.

The director stressed the importance of data quality. He mentioned that purpose of the survey was not for evaluation of family planning work of the individual villages selected for the survey. Further, the county government would not refer the survey results to punish for bad performance in family planning or award otherwise. He specified that the questionnaire should be filled in by household visits, and that planned and unplanned births, distinguished by having birth permission certificate or not, should be filled in the form separately. Births without permission certificates were treated as unplanned births, even if it was the first child.

After the meeting, a banquet was held. Discussion of the survey was still going on, and in this informal setting, other staff from CSB talked with village and township cadres about filling in the questionnaires. 'Do not make many corrections in the questionnaire', 'In general, women at their reproductive ages would account for 20 per cent of the total population. If you did not report the truth and there was a big gap, the problem would be easily recognized', they told the lower level cadres.

On 27 September, I witnessed the sampling survey conducted in one of the

Table A.1 Number of population, births, deaths reported by CSB and calculated number of net migrations in the researched county, 1949–90

Year	EoY population	No. births	No. deaths	Net immigration	Net emigration
1949	258,297	3,943	3,310		
1950	260,906	4,413	3,245	1,441	
1951	263,636	4,406	3,514	1,838	
1952	266,262	4,619	4,407	2,414	
1953	267,008	5,525	3,390	1,389	
1954	275,815	6,655	2,825	4,977	
1955	287,128	11,036	1,589	1,866	
1956	290,485	11,045	3,845	3,843	
1957	303,635	12,220	2,795	3,725	
1958	309,014	8,380	3,690	689	
1959	313,130	8,129	3,810		203
1960	303,843	3,588	6,331		6,544
1961	302,213	2,484	2,922		1,192
1962	305,869	7,094	2,067		1,371
1963	312,300	12,362	3,137		2,794
1964	313,232	8,838	2,711		5,195
1965	319,142	8,367	1,927		530
1966	327,744	9,315	2,122	1,409	
1967	335,502	8,886	1,952	824	
1968	344,814	9,598	2,088	1,802	
1969	352,148	8,689	2,009	654	
1970	359,509	9,033	2,004	332	
1971	363,582	8,594	1,999		2,522
1972	371,771	10,154	2,192	227	
1973	379,245	9,209	2,320	585	
1974	385,567	7,717	2,385	990	
1975	390,126	5,909	2,794	1,444	
1976	393,720	5,292	2,967	1,269	
1977	397,302	4,802	3,001	1,781	
1978	401,011	5,322	2,449	836	
1979	406,943	5,540	2,649	3,041	
1980	414,376	6,522	2,291	3,202	
1981	422,646	7,853	2,530	2,947	
1982	431,272	6,594	2,340	4,372	
1983	436,099	6,528	2,374	673	
1984	441,113	6,326	2,796	1,484	
1985	445,447	5,883	2,381	832	
1986	450,265	5,750	2,495	1,563	
1987	454,601	5,443	2,353	1,246	
1988	458,623	5,526	2,692	1,188	
1989	463,078	6,437	2,719	737	
1990	521,696	8,971	2,577	52,224	

Notes: EoY population = total number of population at the end of the year. Net immigration is calculated based on total number of population at the end of the year and number of births and deaths in the year.
Source: County Statistics Bureau 1992.

three villages. One staff from CSB, three family planning cadres of the township led by vice-township governor came to the village, and conducted the survey together with the village Party secretary and village governor. They did not visit households to complete the questionnaire as requested by CSB, but simply stayed in the village government site to fill in the questionnaire by themselves, referring to household registration books and family planning registrations held by the village and township governments.

The village, and most likely the township, did not have single birth permission certificate distributed to their reproductive couples according to requirements of the county and provincial family planning regulations. The township family planning cadres brought the certificates with them, and asked the village cadres to collect some photos of reproductive couples to be stuck on the certificate, and to distribute them after they were completed.

Reporting of number of births was a bit headache for the cadres, who did not want to report a high number, nor a too-low number. A high number meant that village cadres would have higher family planning quotas during the following family planning campaigns, increasing the difficulty of completing the task. The county family planning cadres mentioned that since they had already reported the 'number' of births to County Family Planning Commission, the data reported in this survey should not surpass that number, for the sake of report consistency. Some suggested the number of births as four, however, the fertility rate would then have been four per thousand (the village was around 1000 population with over 200 households). Higher-level officials would not believe such a low rate, and might request that cadres redo the survey, which would mean more trouble for both the village and the township cadres. Finally, it was decided that the number of births in the village in 1992 was reported as nine to the PSB.

Problems also arise as to how many unplanned births should be reported. The township family planning cadres suggested a number. However, the vice-governor of the township did not agree to put any number for unplanned births, though the village cadres did not put forward their opinions. The final decision was that there were no unplanned births in the village this year.

The whole survey in the village took about five hours. The township cadres left the village in the afternoon, leaving village cadres to collect photos for birth permission certificates. This would take a bit more time, because village cadres needed at least to explain why some couples were requested to hand in photos but not others.

A popular Chinese saying: 'Statistics, statistics, seven statistics, three estimates' (*tongji tongji, qifen tongji, sanfen guji*), implies that 30 per cent or so of statistics involve estimates and guesses. Still, such estimates may have to be mostly (if not always) approved by certain key officials before they are reported to higher level administrations.

Notes

[1] For discussion of data problems concerning population and fertility existed in contemporary China, see also Hermalin & Liu 1990, Bao 1993, and Sun & Qin 1993, Smith 1994.

[2] Tu Ping & Liang Zhiwu (1992) estimate that for China as a whole, around 4 per cent of births were not registered in the census.

Bibliography

Ahmad, Ehtisham & Athar Hussain (1991) 'Social Security in China: A Historical Perspective', pp. 247–304 in Ehtisham Ahmad, Jean Drèze, John Hills & Amartya Sen (eds) *Social Security in Developing Countries*. Oxford: Clarendon Press.

Aird, John S. (1978) 'Fertility Decline and Birth Control in the People's Republic of China', *Population and Development Review* 4(2): 225–54.

Aird, John S. (1990) *Slaughter of the Innocents: Coercive Birth Control in China*. Washington, DC: American Enterprise Institute.

Anker, Richard (1975) 'An Analysis of Fertility Differentials in Developing Countries', Population and Employment Working Paper 16. Geneva: ILO.

Arnold, Fred & Liu Zhaoxiang (1986) 'Sex Preference, Fertility, and Family Planning in China', *Population and Development Review* 12(2): 221–46.

Ash, Robert F. (1988) 'The Evolution of Agricultural Policy', *The China Quarterly* 116: 529–55.

Ashton, S., K. Hill, A. Piazza & R. Zeitz (1984) 'Famine in China', *Population and Development Review* 10(4): 613–45.

Aslanbeigui, Nahid & Gale Summerfield (1989) 'Impact of the Responsibility System on Women in Rural China: An Application of Sen's Theory of Entitlements', *World Development* 17(3): 343–50.

Banister, Judith (1984) 'Population Policy and Trends in China, 1978–83', *The China Quarterly* 100: 717–41.

Banister, Judith (1987) *China's Changing Population*, Stanford University Press.

Bao Wenyue (1993) 'Zhejiang Jinhuaxian 1598 ge Yinger Chusheng Loubao Yuanyin Fenxi Jiqi Duice Tantao' (Under-reporting of 1598 births in Jinhua County, Zhejiang Province: Analysis of Causes and Discussion on Solutions). *Renkou Yanjiu* 1: 53–56.

Becker, Gary (1965) 'A Theory of the Allocation of Time', *The Economic Journal* 75: 493–517.

Becker, Gary (1976) 'An Economic Analysis of Fertility', pp. 171–94 in Gary Becker (ed.) *The Economic Approach to Human Behaviour*. Chicago: University of Chicago Press.

Beijing Review (1985) Beijing (22 July).

Birdsall, N. & Dean T. Jamison (1983) 'Income and Other Factors Influencing Fertility in China', *Population and Development Review* 9(4): 651–75.

Boerma, Jan Ties (1996) *Child Survival in Developing Countries: Can Demographic and Health Surveys Help to Understand the Determinants?* Amsterdam: Royal Tropical Institute.

Bongaarts, John (1978) 'A Framework for Analyzing the Proximate Determinants of Fertility', *Population and Development Review* 4(1): 105–32.

Bongaarts, John (1982) 'The Fertility-inhibiting Effects of the Intermediate Fertility Variables', *Studies in Family Planning* 13(6–7): 179–89

Bramall, Chris, & Marion E. Jones (1993) 'Rural Income Inequality in China since 1978', *Journal of Peasant Studies,* 21(1): 41–70.

Buck, John Lossing (1937) *Land Utilization in China.* Nanking: University of Nanking.

Cain, Mead (1981) 'Risk and Insurance: Perspectives on Fertility and Agrarian Change in India and Bangladesh', *Population and Development Review* 7(3): 435–74.

Cain, Mead (1983) 'Fertility as an Adjustment to Risk', *Population and Development Review* 9(4): 688–702.

Cain, Mead (1985) 'Intensive Community Studies', pp. 213–23 in John B. Casterline (ed.) *The Collection and Analysis of Community Data.* Voorburg, the Netherlands: International Statistical Institute.

Cain, Mead (1991) 'The Activities of the Elderly in Rural Bangladesh', *Population Studies* 45(2): 189–202.

Caldwell, John (1980) 'Mass Education as a Determinant of the Timing of Fertility Decline', *Population and Development Review* 6: 225–55.

Caldwell, John (1985) 'Strengths and Limitations of the Survey Approach for Measuring and Understanding Fertility Change: Alternative Possibilities', pp. 45–63 in John Cleland & John Hobcraft (eds) in collaboration with Betzy Dinesen. *Reproductive Change in Developing Countries.* Oxford: Oxford University Press.

Caldwell, John C. & Pat Caldwell (1987) 'The Cultural Context of High Fertility in Sub-Saharan Africa', *Population and Development Review* 13(3): 409–37.

Caldwell, John C., Allan G. Hill & Valerie J. Hull (1988) *Micro-Approaches to Demographic Research.* London: Kegan Paul.

Caldwell, John C., P.H. Reddy & Pat Caldwell (1988) *The Causes of Demographic Change: Experimental Research in South India.* Wisconsin: University of Wisconsin Press.

Caldwell, John C., Pat Caldwell & Bruce Caldwell (1987) 'Anthropology and Demography', *Current Anthropology* 28(1): 25–43.

Cao Jingchun (1985) 'A Discussion of the Effect of Development of Commodity Economy on Rural Fertility Trend in the Countryside', *Population Research* 4: 16–9.

Cao Jingchun (1989) 'Shangpin Jingji de Fazhan yu Nongcun Jihua Shengyu' (Development of Commodity Economy and Rural Family Planning). *Renkou yu Jingji* (1).

Cao Jingchun (1990) 'Shixi Nongmin Shengyuguan Zhuanbian de Jingji Tiaojian he Linjieduan' (A Tentative Analysis of Economic Condition and Critical Points in the Transformation of Peasant Fertility Concept). *Renkou yu Jingji* (3): 19–24.

CASS, Zhongguo Shehui Kexueyuan Renkou Yangjiusue (1988) *Zhongguo Renkou Nianjian 1987 (Almanac of China's Population 1987).* Beijing: Jingji Guanli Chubanshe.

CASS, Zhongguo Shehui Kexueyuan Renkou Yangjiusue (1994) *Zhongguo Renkou Nianjian 1987 (Almanac of China's Population 1994).* Beijing: Jingji Guanli Chubanshe.

Chai, Cecilia Lai-wan (1995) 'Gender Issues in Market Socialism', pp. 188–215 in Linda Wong & Stewart Macpherson (eds) *Social Change and Social Policy in Contemporary China*. Avebury: Aldershot.

Chan, Anita, Richard Madsen, & Jonathan Unger (1984) *Chen Village: The Recent History of a Peasant Community in Mao's China*. Berkeley: University of California Press.

Chang, Kyung-Sup (1996) 'Birth and Wealth in Peasant China: Surplus Population, Limited Supplies of Family Labour, and Economic Reform', pp. 21–45 in Alice Goldstein & Wang Feng (eds) *China: The Many Facets of Demographic Change*. Boulder CO: Westview Press.

Chen Ping (1993) 'Xingbie Pianhao de Lianghua Hengliang Jiqi yu Shengyulu Guanxi de Tantao' (Probe into the Relation of Sex Preference to Fertility and Its Measurement). *Zhongguo Renkou Kexue* (2): 42–47.

Chen Youhua (1991) 'Zhongguo Nuxing Chuhun Chuyu Nianling Biandong de Jiben Qingkuang Jiqi Fenxi' (Basic Condition and an Analysis on Change of Age at First Marriage and First Birth for Chinese Women). *Zhongguo Renkou Kexue* (5): 39–45.

Cheng Du (1992) 'Nongcun Funu Zeou Wenti Diaocha' (An Investigation on Rural Women's Choice of Spouse). *Renkou yu Jingji* (1): 44–49.

Cheng, Chaoze & Fernando Rajulton (1992) 'Determinants of Fertility Decline in China, 1981: Analysis of Intermediate Variables', *Social Biology* 39(1–2): 15–26.

China Population Today (1992) 'Survey and Analysis of Childbearing Intentions of the Floating Population', *China Population Today* 9(5): 4–5.

Choe, Minja Kim, Tsuya & O. Noriko (1991) 'Why Do Chinese Women Practice Contraception? The Case of Rural Jilin Province,' *Studies in Family Planning* 22(1): 39–51.

Coale, Ansley J. (1984) *Rapid Population Change in China, 1952–82*, Washington D.C.: National Academy Press.

Coale, Ansley J. & Cheng, Sheng Li (1987) Basic Data on Fertility in the Province of China, 1940–82. A Paper of East-West Population Institute, No. 104.

Coale, Ansley J. & Judith Banister (1994) 'Five Decades of Missing Females in China', *Demography* 31(3): 459–79.

Coale, Ansley J., Shaomin Li & Jing-Qing Han (1988) The Distribution of Interbirth Intervals in Rural China, 1940s to 1970s. Papers of the East-West Population Institute, No. 109.

Cohen, Myron L. (1976) *House United, House Divided: The Chinese Family in Taiwan*. New York: Columbia University Press.

Cohen, Myron L. (1992) 'Family Management and Family Division in Contemporary China', *The China Quarterly* (130): 357–77.

Cook, Karen S. & Margaret Levi (1990) *The Limits of Rationality*. Chicago: University of Chicago Press.

CPIRC (China Population Information and Research Centre). *China Population Data Sheet 1993*. Beijing: CPIRC.

CPIRC) (1983) *Zhongguo Renkou Ziliao Shouce 1983* (Handbook of Chinese Population Information, 1983). Beijing: China Population Information and Research Center.

Croll, Elisabeth J. (1981a) *The Politics of Marriage in Contemporary China*. Cambridge: Cambridge University Press.

Croll, Elisabeth J. (1981b) 'A Conflict for Control of Marriage Patterns: Primary Groups versus Political Organizations', pp. 231–55 in Sidney L. Greenblatt, Richard W. Wilson & Amy Auerbacher Wilson (eds) *Organizational Behaviour in Chinese Society*. New York: Praeger.

Croll, Elisabeth J. (1987a) 'Some implications of the rural economic reforms for the Chinese peasant household', pp. 105–36 in Ashwani Saith (ed.) *The Re-emergence of the Chinese Peasantry: Aspects of Decollectivisation*. London: Croom Helm.

Croll, Elisabeth J. (1987b) 'New Peasant Family Forms in Rural China', *The Journal of Peasant Studies* 14(4): 469–99.

Croll, Elisabeth J. (1994) *From Heaven to Earth: Images and Experiences of Development in China*. London: Routledge.

Croll, Elisabeth J. (1995) *Changing Identities of Chinese Women: Rhetoric, Experience and Self-Perception in Twentieth-Century China*. Hong Kong: Hong Kong University Press.

Croll, Elisabeth J. (1988) 'The New Peasant Economy in China', pp. 77–100 in Stephen Feuchtwang, Athar Hussain & Thierry Pairault (eds) *Transforming China's Economy in the Eighties, Volume I: The Rural Sector, Welfare and Employment*. Boulder CO: Westview Press & London: Zed Books.

CSB (various years) *Guomin Jingji Tongji Ziliao* (Statistics on National Economy of the County), County Statistics Bureau.

CSBPCO (1982) *Nian Renkou Pucha Jiqi Huizong Ziliao* (Data Compilation of Population Census 1982) County Statistics Bureau, Population Census Office.

CSBPCO (1990) *Nian Disici Renkou Pucha Jiqi Huizong Ziliao* (Data Compilation of the Forth Population Census 1990) County Statistics Bureau, Population Census Office.

CSC (China. State Council) Information Office (1991) *Human Rights in China*. [online] http: //www.cityu.edu.hk/HumanRights/index.htm [downloaded 12 February 1997].

CSC (China. State Council) Information Office (1996) 'Chinese Government White Paper on Family Planning', *Population and Development Review* 22(2): 385–90.

Dai Kejing (1991) 'The Life Experience and Status of Chinese Rural Women from Observation of Three Age Groups', *International Sociology* 6(1): 5–23.

Dankert, Gabriele, Li Lan & Li Zhongyi (1990) 'Changing First Birth Intervals, Marriage Patterns and Fertility Control in Three Provinces of China', pp. 87–102 in M.J. Titus & H.A.W. van Vianen (eds) *Perspectives on Population and Development in Third World Countries*. The Hague: Netherlands Demographic Society.

Davin, Delia (1988) 'The Implications of Contract Agriculture for the Employment and Status of Chinese Peasant Women', pp. 137–46 in Stephen Feuchtwang, Athar Hussain & Thierry Pairault, (eds) *Transforming China's Economy in the Eighties, Volume I: The Rural Sector, Welfare and Employment*. Boulder CO: Westview Press & London: Zed Books.

Davin, Delia (1990) 'Never Mind If It's a Girl, You Can Have Another Try', in *Remaking Peasant China: Problems of Rural Development and institutions at the Start of the 1990s*, (eds) Jorgen Delman, Clemens Stubbe Ostergaard & Flemming Chiristiansen. Aarhus, Denmark: Aarhus University Press.

Davis, Deborah & Stevan Harrell (eds) (1993) *Chinese Families in the Post-Mao Era*. Berkeley: University of California Press.

Davis, Kingsley (1945) 'The World Demographic Transition', *Annals of the American Academy of Political and Social Science* 237: 1–11.

Davis, Kingsley & Judith Blake (1956) 'Social Structure and Fertility: An Analytical Framework. *Economic Development and Social Change* 4(4): 211–35.

Davis-Friedman, Deborah (1985) 'Intergenerational Inequalities and Chinese Revolution', *Modern China* 11(2): 177–201.

De Bruijn, Bart (1991) 'The Concept of Rationality in Social Sciences', Groningen University, Population Research Centre, Working Paper.

De Bruijn, Bart (1992) 'Interdisciplinary Backgrounds of Fertility Theories', Groningen University, Population Research Centre, Working Paper.

De Bruijn, Mirjam (1996) 'The Position of Fulbe Pastoral Women: Milk and Social Relations', Research Seminar of Rural Development Studies at the Institute of Social Studies, The Hague, The Netherlands.

Dixon, Ruth B. (1979) 'On Drawing Policy Conclusions from Multiple Regressions: Some Queries and Dilemmas', *Studies in Family Planning* 9(10–11): 286–88.

Easterlin, Richard A. & Eileen M. Crimmins (1985) *The Fertility Revolution: A Supply-Demand Analysis.* Chicago: University of Chicago Press

Eberstadt, Nick (1981) 'Recent Declines in Fertility in Less Developed Countries, and What Population Planners May Learn From Them', in Nick Eberstadt (ed.) *Fertility Decline in Less Developed Countries.* New York: Praeger Publishers.

Ebrey, Patricia (1984) 'Introduction: Family Life in Late Traditional China', *Modern China* 10(4): 379–85.

Ebrey, Patricia B. (1991) 'Introduction', pp. 1–24 in Rubie S. Watson & Patricia B. Ebrey (eds) *Marriage and Inequality in Chinese Society.* Berkeley: University of California Press

Eisenstadt, Shmuel N. (1968) 'Social Institutions', in *International Encyclopaedia of the Social Sciences* 14, ed. David L. Sills. New York: Macmillan & Free Press.

Feeney, Griffith & Wang Feng (1993) 'Parity Progression and Birth Intervals in China: The Influence of Policy in Hastening Fertility Decline', *Population and Development Review* 19(1): 61–101.

Feeney, Griffith & Wolfgang Lutz (1991) 'Distributional Analysis of Period Fertility', pp. 169–95 in Wolfgang Lutz (ed.) *Future Demographic Trends in Europe and North America: What Can We Assume Today?* New York: Academic Press.

Feeney, Griffith & Yuan Jianhua (1994) 'Below Replacement Fertility in China? A Close Look at Recent Evidence', *Population Studies* 48: 381–94.

Feeney, Griffith, Feng Wang, Mingkun Zhou & Baoyu Xiao (1989) 'Recent Fertility Dynamics in China: Results from the 1987 One Percent Population Survey', *Population and Development Review* 15(2): 297–322, 394–95.

Fei Hsiao-tung (1939) *Peasant Life in China: A Field Study of Country Life in the Yangtze Valley.* London: Routledge & Kegan Paul.

Feng Guoping (1995) 'Changing Patterns in Determinants of Fertility Decline in China in the 1980s', unpublished research paper, Population and Development Programme, Institute of Social Studies, The Hague.

Feng Litian (1992) '80 Niandai Zhongguo Shengyulu de Biandong yu Shehui Jingji Yinsu de Fenxi' (Dynamic Fertility Change and Socio-economic Development in China in the 1980s). *Zhongguo Renkou Kexue* (1): 42–47, 56.

Freedman, Ronald & Bernard Berelson (1976) 'The Record of Family Planning Programmes', *Studies in Family Planning* 7(1): 1–40.

Freedman, Ronald, Xiao Zhenyu, Li Bohua & William R. Lavely (1988) 'Local Area Variations in Reproductive Behaviour in the People's Republic of China, 1973–1982', *Population Studies* 42(1): 39–57.

Fudan Study Group (1993) 'Gaishan Shequ Huanjing, Zhili Duohai Shengyu' (Improve Community Environment and Deal With Many Births) in Jiang Yiman (ed.) *Zouchu Zhaozedi: Duohai Shengyu de Genyuan yu Duice.* Beijing: Qixiang Chubanshe.

Gamble, Sidney D. (1954) *Ting Hsien: A North China Rural Community.* Stanford: Stanford University Press.

Gao Er-sheng, Chen Run-tian, Wang Shu-lin, Gu Xing-yuan, Chen Chang-zhong & Hu Ying (1991) 'Analysis of Proximate Determinants of Fertility in Shanghai City, Hebei Province and Shaanxi Province' in *Fertility in China*, Proceedings of the International Seminar on China's In-Depth Fertility Survey held in Beijing, 13–17 February 1990. Voorburg, the Netherlands: International Statistical Institute.

Goldstein, Alice, Michael White & Sidney Goldstein (1996) 'Migration and Fertility in Hubei Province, China', PSTC working papers No. 96–08 [online] http:// pstc3.pstc.brown.edu: 80 /papers/wp-1996/96–08.html [downloaded 14 February 1997].

Goody, Jack (1990) *The Oriental, the Ancient and the Primitive: Systems of Marriage and the Family in the Pre-industrial Societies of Eurasia.* Cambridge: Cambridge University Press.

Greenhalgh, Susan (1988) 'Fertility as Mobility: Sinic Transitions', *Population and Development Review* 14(4): 629–74.

Greenhalgh, Susan (1990a) 'Toward a Political Economy of Fertility: Anthropological Contributions', *Population and Development Review* 16(1): 85–106.

Greenhalgh, Susan (1990b) 'Socialism and Fertility in China', pp. 73–86 in Samuel Preston (ed.) *World Population: Approaching the Year 2000*, special issue of *The Annals the American Academy of Political and Social Sciences.*

Greenhalgh Susan (1992) 'State-Society Links: The Political Dimensions of Population Policies and Programs, with Special Reference to China', in James F. Phillips & John A. Ross (eds), *Family Planning Programmes and Fertility*. Oxford: Clarendon Press.

Greenhalgh, Susan (1993) 'The Peasantization of Population Policy in Shaanxi,' pp. 219–50 in Deborah Davis & Stevan Harrell (eds) *Chinese Families in the Post-Mao Era.* Berkeley: University of California Press.

Greenhalgh, Susan (1994a) 'Controlling Births and Bodies in Village China', *American Ethnologist* 21(1): 1–30.

Greenhalgh, Susan (1994b) 'The Peasant Household in the Transition from Socialism: State Intervention and Its Consequences in China', pp. 43–64 in Elizabeth Brumfiel (ed.), *The Economic Anthropology of the State.* Lanham: University Press of America.

Greenhalgh, Susan (1995) *Situating Fertility: Anthropology and Demographic Inquiry.* Cambridge: Cambridge University Press.

Greenhalgh, Susan & Li Jiali (1995) 'Engendering Reproductive Policy and Practice in Peasant China: for a Feminist Demography of Reproduction', *Signs: Journal of Women in Culture and Society* 20(3): 601–41.

Greenhalgh, Susan, Zhu Chuzhu & Li Nan (1994) 'Restraining Population Growth in Three Chinese Villages, 1988–93', *Population and Development Review* 20(2): 365–95.

Griffin, Keith & Ashwani Saith (1981) *Growth and Equality in Rural China.* Singapore: Maruzen.

Griffin, Keith & Kimberley Griffin (1985) 'Institutional Change and Income Distribution in the Chinese Countryside', in Chi-Keung Leung & Joseph C. H. Chai (eds) *Development and Distribution in China.* Hong Kong: University of Hong Kong.

Griffin, Keith & Zhao Renwei (eds) (1993) *The Distribution of Income in China.* New York: St. Martin's Press.

Gu Baochang (1987) 'Lun Shehui Jingji Fazhan he Jihua Shengyu zai Woguo Shengyulu Xiajiang zhong de Zuoyong' (On Roles of Socio-economic Development and Family Planning in China's Fertility Decline). *Zhongguo Renkou Kexue* (2): 2–11.

Gu Baochang (1996) 'Fertility: From the 1970s to the 1990s,' pp. 69–80 in Alice Goldstein & Wang Feng (eds) *China: The Many Facets of Demographic Change*. Boulder CO: Westview Press

Gu, Baochang & Yi Xu (1994) 'A Comprehensive Discussion of the Birth Gender Ratio in China', *Chinese Journal of Population Science* 6(4): 417–31.

Hajnal, J. (1982) 'Two Kinds of Preindustrial Household Formation System', *Population and Development Review* 8: 449–94.

Hamilton, Lawrence C. (1993) *Statistics with Stata*. California: Duxbury Press.

Hammel, E.A. (1990) 'A Theory of Culture for Demography', *Population and Development Review* 16(3): 455–85.

Hammel, E.A. & Diana Friou (1997) 'Anthropology and Demography: Marriage, Liaison or Encounter?' in D. Kertzer & T. Fricke (eds) *Anthropological Demography: Toward a New Synthesis*. Chicago: University of Chicago Press [online] http: //boserup.qal.berkeley.edu/%7Egene/brown.94.rev.2.html [downloaded on 5 December 1996].

Han Min (1993) *Lineage Continuity in Northern Anhui: A Response to Revolution and Reform*. PhD dissertation, Department of Cultural Anthropology, University of Tokyo.

Han Min & J.S. Eades (1995) 'Brides, Bachelors and Brokers: The Marriage Market in Rural Anhui in an Era of Economic Reform', *Modern Asian Studies* 29(4): 841–69.

Handwerker, W. Penn (1986) 'Culture and Reproduction: Exploring Micro/Macro Linkages', pp. 1–28 in *Culture and Reproduction: An Anthropological Critique of Demographic Transition Theory*. Boulder CO: Westview.

Hardin, Russell (1990) 'The Social Evolution of Cooperation', pp. 358–82 in Karen S. Cook & Margaret Levi (eds) *The Limits of Rationality*. Chicago: University of Chicago Press.

Harrell, Stevan (1992) 'Aspects of Marriage in Three South-western Villages', *The China Quarterly* 130:323–37.

Harrell, Stevan (1993) 'Geography, Demography, and Family Composition in Three Southwestern Villages', pp. 77–102 in Deborah Davis & Stevan Harrell (eds) *Chinese Families in the Post-Mao Era*, Berkeley: University of California Press.

Harris, Marvin & Eric B. Ross (1987) *Death, Sex, and Fertility: Population Regulation in Pre-industrial and Developing Societies*. New York: Columbia University Press.

Harris, Olivia (1981) 'Households as Natural Units', pp. 49–68 in Kate Young, Carol Wolkowitz & Roslyn McCullagh (eds) *Of Marriage and the Market: Women's Subordination in International Perspective*. London: CSE Books.

Hayes, Adrian C. (1994) 'The Role of Culture in Demographic Analysis', Australia National University Working Paper No.46.

HDBW (Hebeisheng Difangzhi Bianzhuan Weiyuanhui) (1987) *Hebei Difangzhi: Renkouzhi* (The Annals of Hebei Province: Population Volume). Shijiazhuang: Hebei Renmin Chubanshe.

HDBW (Hebeisheng Difangzhi Bianzhuan Weiyuanhui) (1989) *Hebei Shixian Gaiquang* (Profile of Cities and Counties in Hebei Province). Shijiazhuang: Hebei Renmin Chubanshe.

HDRPB (1985) *Handan Diqu Disanci Renkou Pucha Huizong Ziliao*. Handan Diqu Renkou Pucha Bangongshi, Population Census of Handan Prefecture.

HDRPB (1992) *Handan Diqu Disanci Renkou Pucha Huizong Ziliao*. Handan Diqu Renkou Pucha Bangongshi (Population Census of Handan Prefecture).

HDW (Hebeisheng Diming Weiyuanhui) (1991) *Hebeisheng Diming Cidian*

(Dictionary of Place Names in Hebei Province). Shijiazhuang: Hebei Kexue Jishu Chubanshe.

HDXGT (various years), *Handan Diqu Guomin Jingji Tongji Ziliao*. Handan Diqu Xingzheng Gongshu Tongjizhu (Statistics Bureau of Handan Prefecture).

Hermalin, Albert I. & Xian Liu. 'Gauging the Validity of Response to Questions on Family Size Preferences in China', *Population and Development Review* 16(2): 337–54.

Hernandez, Donald J. (1981) 'A Note on Measuring the Independent Impact of Family Planning Programs on Fertility Declines', *Demography* 18(4): 627–34.

Hodgson, Geoffrey M. (1988) *Economics and Institutions: A Manifesto for a Modern Institutional Economics*. Cambridge: Polity Press.

Hong, Lawrence-K. & Joan D. Mandle (1987) 'Potential Effects of the One-Child Policy on Gender Equality in the People's Republic of China', *Gender and Society* 1(3): 317–26.

Hou Wenrue (1981) 'Population Policy', pp. 55–76 in Liu Zheng et al. (eds) *China's Population Problems and Prospects*. Beijing: New World Press.

Hou Wenruo (1988) 'Zhongguo Renkou Zhengce Pinggu' (Evaluation of Chinese Population Policy). *Renkou Yanjiu* (6): 32–37.

Howell, Nancy (1986) 'Demographic Anthropology', *Annual Review of Anthropology* 15: 219–46.

HRZ (Hebeisheng Renmin Zhengfu) (1994) *Heibei Jingji Tongji Nianjian 1994* (Economic Statistical Yearbook of Hebei Province). Beijing: Zhongguo Tongji Chubanshe.

Huang, Shu-min (1989) *The Spiral Road: Change in a Chinese Village Through the Eyes of a Communist Party Leader*. Boulder CO: Westview Press.

Huang, Shu-min, Kimberley C. Falk & Chen Su-min (1996) 'Nutritional Well-being of Preschool Children in a North China Village,' *Modern China* 22(4): 355–81.

Hull, Terence H. (1990) 'Recent Trends in Sex Ratios at Birth in China', *Population and Development Review* 16(1): 63–83, 207, 209.

Hull, Terence H. & Quanhe Yang (1991) 'Fertility and Family Planning', in Wang Jiye & Terence H. Hull (eds) *Population and Development Planning in China*, Sydney: Allen & Unwin.

Ikels, Charlotte (1990) 'The Resolution of Intergenerational Conflict: Perspective of Elders and Their Family Members', *Modern China* 16(4): 379–406.

Ji Yonghua (1992) 'Fertility Change of Chinese Women in the 1980s', Paper prepared for International Seminar on China's 1990 Population Census, 19–23 October, Beijing.

Jiang Zhenghua, Zhang Erli & Chen Shengli (1994) *1992 nian Zhongguo Shengyulu Chouyang Diaocha Shujuji* (Data of 1992 Chinese Fertility Sampling Survey). Beijing: Chinese Population Publisher.

Jiang Zhenghua (1986) 'Shehui Jingji Yinsu dui Zhongguo Shengyulu de Yingxiang' (Influence of Social Economic Factors on Chinese Fertility). *Renkou Yanjiu* (3): 25–30.

Jin H. (1995) 'A Study of Rural Women's Decision-Making Power on Reproduction and Fertility', *Chinese Journal of Population Science* 7(3): 241–57.

Johansson, Sten (1995) 'Lun Xiandai Zhongguo de Shouyang' (Adoption in Contemporary China). *Renkou Yanjiu* 19(6): 20–31.

Johansson, Sten & Nygren, Ola (1991) 'The Missing Girls of China: A New Demographic Account', *Population and Development Review* 17(1): 35–51, 201, 203.

Johnson, D. Gale (1988) 'Economic Reforms in the People's Republic of

China', *Economic Development and Cultural Change* 36(3): s225–s245, supplement.

Johnson, D. Gale (1994) 'Effects of Institutions and Policies on Rural Population Growth with Application to China', *Population and Development Review* 20(3): 503–31.

Johnson, Graham E. (1993) 'Family Strategies and Economic Transformation in Rural China: Some Evidence from the Pearl River Delta', pp. 103–36 in Deborah Davis & Stevan Harrell (eds) *Chinese Families in the Post-Mao Era*. Berkeley: University of California Press.

Johnson, Kay Ann (1983) *Women, the Family, and Peasant Revolution in China*. Chicago: University of Chicago Press.

Judd, Ellen R. (1989) 'Niangjia: Chinese Women and Their Natal Families', *The Journal of Asian Studies* 48(3): 525–44 (August).

Judd, Ellen R. (1990) 'Alternative Development Strategies for Women in Rural China', *Development and Change* 21(1): 23–42 (January).

Judd, Ellen R. (1994) *Gender and Power in Rural North China*. Stanford: Stanford University Press.

Kelkar, Govind (1985) 'Impacts of Household Contract System on Women in Rural China', *Economic and Political Weekly* 20(17).

Kelkar, Govind (1990) 'Women and Rural Economic Reform in China', *Indian Journal of Social Science* 3(3): 395–430.

Kertzer, David I. & Dennis P. Hogan (1989) *Family, Political Economy, and Demographic Change: The Transformation of Life in Casalecchio, Italy, 1861–1921*. Madison WI: University of Wisconsin Press.

Krishnaji, N. (1992) 'Agrarian Structure and Family Formation: A Tentative Hypothesis', pp. 152–67 in *Pauperising Agriculture*. Oxford: Oxford University Press.

Lang, Olga (1946) *Chinese Family and Society*. New Haven: Yale University Press.

Langlois, Richard N. (1986) 'Rationality, Institutions, and Explanation', pp. 225–55 in Richard N. Langlois (ed.) *Economics as a Process*. Cambridge: Cambridge University Press.

Lardy, Nicholas R. (1978) *Economic Growth and Distribution in China*. Cambridge: Cambridge University Press.

Larsen, Kield A. (1990) 'Regional Policies in Post-Mao China', *Copenhagen Papers in East Asian Studies* 5.

Lavely, William (1991) 'Marriage and Mobility under Rural Collectivism', pp. 286–312 in Rubie S. Watson & Patricia B. Ebrey (eds) *Marriage and Inequality in Chinese Society*. Berkeley: University of California Press.

Lavely, William & Xinhua Ren (1992) 'Patrilocality and Early Marital Co-residence in Rural China, 1955–85', *The China Quarterly* 130: 378–91.

Lesthaeghe, Ron (1980) 'On the Social Control of Human Reproduction', *Population and Development Review* 6(4): 527–48.

Levi, Margaret (1990) 'A Logic of Institutional Change', in Karen Schweers Cook & Margaret Levi. (eds) *The Limits of Rationality*. Chicago: University of Chicago Press.

Levy Jr., Marion J. (1949) *The Family Revolution in Modern China*. Cambridge, MA: Harvard University Press.

Li Jingneng & Wu Guocun (1985) 'Jingji Fazhan dui Renkou Zhuanbian de Zuoyong: Tianjin de Shili' (Roles of Economic Development in Population Transition). *Renkou Lilun he Diaocha Yanjiu* (1).

Li Rongshi (1992) 'A Study on Early Marriage in China'. Paper presented at International Seminar on China's 1990 Population Census, 19–23 October, Beijing.

Li Yongping (1993) 'Yinger Xingbiebi Jiqi he Shehui Jingji Bianliang de Guanxi: Pucha de Jieguo he Suofanying de Xianshi' (Infant Sex Ratio and its Relationship with Socio-economic Variables: Result of Population Census and the Reflected Realities). *Renkou yu Jingji* (4): 3–14.

Li Jiali & Rosemary Santana Cooney (1993) 'Son Preference and the One-child Policy in China: 1979–88', *Population Research and Policy Review* 12: 277–96.

Li Li (1993) 'Chinese Women's Participation in Fertility Discussions', *International Journal of Sociology of the Family* 23(1): 33–42.

Lin Fude & Yao Yuan (eds) (1993) 'Zhongguo Nongcun Renkou yu Fazhan Xingeju' (*New Pattern of Chinese Rural Population and Development*). Beijing: Zhongguo Renkou Chubanshe.

Lindenberg, Siegwart (1990) 'Homo Socio-oeconomicus: The Emergence of a General Model of Man in the Social Sciences', *Journal of Institutional and Theoretical Economics* 146(4): 727–48

Liu Chuanjiang (1991) 'Zeou Fanwei yu Nongcun Tonghunquan' (Mate Selection and Marriage Market in Rural China) *Renkou yu Jingji* (4): 47–50.

Liu Gang (1993) 'Family planning programs in Anhui: challenges of population redistribution', Paper presented at the Annual Meeting of the Population Association of America, Cincinnati, OH (1–3 April).

Liu Suinian & Wu Qungan (1986) 'China's Socialist Economy: An Outline History (1949–1984)'. Beijing: *Beijing Review.*

Liu Zheng (1992) 'Zhongguo 80 Niandai Shengyulu de Xintedian yu Duice' (New Characteristics of Fertility in the 1980s and Fertility Control Measures) *Renkou Yanjiu* (5): 1–6.

Liu, Shuang (1986) 'A Brief Discussion on the Differences in the Sex Ratio at Birth of China's Population', *Population Research* 3(3): 46–7, 45.

Lorimer, Frank (1954. *Culture and Human Fertility: A Study of the Relation of Cultural Conditions to Fertility in Non-industrial and Transitional Societies.* Paris: UNESCO.

Luther, Norman Y., Griffith Feeney & Zhang Weimin (1990) 'One-child families or a baby boom? Evidence from China's 1987 One-per-Hundred Survey', *Population Studies* 44: 341–57.

Mackintosh, Maureen (1995) *Economics and Changing Economies.* Milton Keynes: The Open University.

Marsh, Catherine (1988) *Exploring Data: An Introduction to Data Analysis for Social Scientists.* Cambridge: Polity Press.

Mauldin, W. Parker & Bernard Berelson (1978) 'Conditions of Fertility Decline in Developing Countries, 1965–75', *Studies in Family Planning* 9(5): 90–147.

McKinley, Terry (1993) 'The Distribution of Wealth in Rural China', pp. 116–34 in Keith Griffin & Zhao Renwei (eds) *The Distribution of Income in China.* New York: St. Martin's Press.

McKinley, Terry & Keith Griffin (1993) 'The Distribution of Land in Rural China', *The Journal of Peasant Studies* 21(1): 71–84.

McNicoll, Geoffery (1975) 'Community-level Population Policy: An Exploration,' *Population and Development Review* 1(1): 1–21.

McNicoll, Geoffery (1978) 'On Fertility Policy Research', *Population and Development Review* 4(4): 681–93.

McNicoll, Geoffery (1980) 'Institutional Determinants of Fertility Change', *Population and Development Review* 6(3): 441–62.

McNicoll, Geoffery (1985) 'The Nature of Institutional and Community Effects on Demographic Behaviour: A Discussion', pp. 177–84 in John B. Casterline (ed.) *The Collection and Analysis of Community Data.* Voorburg, the Netherlands: International Statistical Institute.

McNicoll, Geoffrey (1994) 'Institutional Analysis of Fertility', in *Population, Economic Development, and the Environment*, pp. 199–230 in Kerstin Lindahl-Kiessling and Hans Landberg (eds) Oxford: Oxford University Press.

McNicoll, Geoffrey & Mead Cain (1990) 'Institutional Effects on Rural Economy and Demographic Change', pp. 3–42 in Geoffrey McNicoll & Mead Cain (eds) *Rural Development and Population: Institutions and Policy*. New York: Population Council.

Messkoub, Mahmood (1992) 'Deprivation and Structural Adjustment', pp. 175–98 in Marc Wuyts, Maureen Mackintosh & Tom Hewitt (eds) *Development Policy and Public Action*. Oxford: Oxford University Press.

Michelson, Ethan & William L. Parish (1996) 'Gender Differentials in Economic Success: Rural China in 1991', Paper presented in conference on 'Gender, Households, and the Boundaries of Work in China' at the University of North Carolina, Chapel Hill (25–27 October).

Mosher, Steven W. (1983) *Broken Earth: The Rural Chinese*. London: Robert Hale.

Mosher, Steven W. (1995) *A Mother's Ordeal: One Women's Fight Against China's One-Child Policy, The Story of Chi An*. London: Warner Books.

Nee, Victor & Su Sijin (1990) 'Institutional Change and Economic Growth in China: The View from the Villages', *The Journal of Asian Studies* 49(1): 3–25.

Newell, Colin (1988) *Methods and Models in Demography*. London: Belhaven Press.

Ng, Siu-Man & Baochang Gu (1995) 'Dimensions of Fertility Transition in the Third World: Level, Timing and Quality,' Paper prepared for the 1995 Population Association of America Annual Meeting, 6–8 April, San Francisco CA. [http://www. cpc.unc.edu/pubs/paa_papers/1995/ng.gu .html].

Nolan, Peter & J. Sender (1992) 'Death Rates, Life Expectancy and China's Economic Reforms', *World Development* 20(9): 1279–304.

North, Douglass C. (1990) *Institutions, Institutional Change and Economic Performance*. Cambridge: Cambridge University Press.

North, Douglass C. (1994) 'Economic Performance Through Time', *The American Economic Review* 84(3): 359–68.

Notestein, Frank W. (1945) 'Population – The Long View', pp. 33–62 in T. Schultz (ed.) *Food for the World*. Chicago: University of Chicago Press.

Notestein, Frank W. (1983) 'Population Growth and Economic Development,' *Population and Development Review* 9(2): 345–60.

Nugent, Jeffery B. (1985) 'The Old-Age Security Motive for Fertility', *Population and Development Review* 11(1): 75–97.

O'Driscoll, Gerald P., Jr. & Mario J. Rizzo with a contribution by Roger W. Garrison (1985) *The Economics of Time and Ignorance*. New York: Basil Blackwell.

Palmer, Michael (1995) 'The Re-emergence of Family Law in Post-Mao China: Marriage, Divorce and Reproduction', *The China Quarterly* 141: 110–34.

Parish, William L. & Martin King Whyte (1978) *Village and Family in Contemporary China*. Chicago: University of Chicago Press.

Peng Xizhe (1987) 'Demographic Consequences of the Great Leap Forward in China's Provinces', *Population and Development Review* 13(4): 639–70.

Peng Xizhe (1989) 'Major Determinants of China's Fertility', *The China Quarterly* 117: 1–37.

Peng Xizhe (1990) 'China's population control and the reform in the 1980s', *Population Research* 7(3): 1–17.

Peng Xizhe (1991) *Demographic Transition in China: Fertility Trends since the 1950s*. Oxford: Clarendon Press.

Peng Xizhe (1993) 'Regional Differentials in China's Fertility Transition', in R. Leete and I. Alam (eds) *The Revolution in Asian Fertility*. Oxford: Clarendon Press.

Peng Xizhe & Dai Xingyi (1993) 'Shixi Fengxian Zuixiaohua Yuanze zai Shengyu Jueding zhong de Zuoyong' (Roles of Minimizing Risks Principle in Fertility Decision Making). *Renkou Yanjiu* (6): 2–7.

People's Daily (Renmin Ribao): 5 July 1957.

People's Daily (Renmin Ribao): 26 September 1980.

Platteau, Jean-Phillippe (1991) 'Traditional Systems of Social Security and Hunger Insurance: Past Achievements and Modern Challenges', pp. 33–62 in Ehtisham Ahmad, Jean Drèze, John Hills & Amartya Sen (eds) *Social Security in Developing Countries*. Oxford: Clarendon Press.

Poston, Dudley & Jia Zhongke (1990) 'Zhongguo Xianji Shehui Jingji Fazhan yu Shengyulu Bianhua de Guanxi' (Relations Between Socio-economic Development and Fertility Change at County Level in China). *Renkou yu Jingji* (2): 15–22.

Poston, Dudley L. & Gu Bao Chang (1987) 'Socio-economic Development, Family Planning, and Fertility in China', *Demography* 24(4): 531–51.

Potter, Joseph E (1983) 'Effects of Societal and Community Institutions on Fertility', pp. 627–65 in Rodolfo A. Bulatao & Ronald D. Lee (eds) *Determinants of Fertility in Developing Countries, Vol. 2, Fertility Regulation and Institutional Influences*. New York: Academic Press.

Potter, Sulamith H. & Jack M. Potter (1990) *China's Peasants: The Anthropology of a Revolution*. Cambridge: Cambridge University Press.

Putterman, Louis (1993) *Continuity and Change in China's Rural Development: Collective and Reform Eras in Perspective*. Oxford: Oxford University Press.

Rigdon, Susan M (1996) 'Abortion Law and Practice in China: An Overview with Comparisons to the United States,' *Social Science and Medicine* 42(4): 543–60.

Rindfuss, Ronald R. & S. Philip Morgan (1983) 'Marriage, Sex and the First Birth Interval: The Quiet Revolution in Asia', *Population and Development Review* 9(2): 259–78.

RIVM (National Institute of Public Health and Environmental Protection) (1994) 'Fertility Change: A Global Perspective.' Groningen, Netherlands: RIVM and Population Research Centre of the University of Groningen. RIVM Report No. 461502008.

Robinson, Jean C. (1985) 'Of Women and Washing Machines: Employment, Housework, and the Reproduction of Motherhood in Socialist China', *The China Quarterly* 101: 32–57 (March).

Robinson, Warren C. & Sarah F. Harbison (1980) 'Toward a Unified Theory of Fertility', pp. 201–35 in Thomas K. Burch (ed.) *Demographic Behavior: Interdisciplinary Perspectives on Decision-Making*. Boulder CO: Westview Press.

Saith, Ashwani (1987) 'China's New Population Policies: Rationale and Some Implications', pp. 211–49 in Ashwani Saith (ed.) *The Re-emergence of the Chinese Peasantry: Aspects of Decollectivisation*. London: Croom Helm.

Saith, Ashwani (1994) 'Rural Bases of Successful Transition: Some Chinese Lessons for Reforming and Developing Economies', Seminar paper presented at the Institute of Social Studies, The Hague.

Schultz, Theodore W. (1973) 'The Value of Children: An Economic Perspective', *Journal of Political Economy* 81(2): s2–s13.

Selden, Mark (1993) 'Family Strategies and Structures in Rural North China', pp. 139–64 in Deborah Davis and Stevan Harrell (eds) *Chinese Families in the Post-Mao Era*. Berkeley: University of California Press.

Sen, Amartya (1990) 'Cooperation, Inequality, and the Family,' pp. 61–76 in Geoffrey McNicoll & Mead Cain (eds) *Rural Development and Population: Institutions and Policy*. New York: Population Council.

Simmons, Ruth, Gayl D. Ness & George B. Simmons (1983) 'On the Institutional Analysis of Population Programs,' *Population and Development Review* 9(3): 457–74.

Simon, Herbert A. (1978) 'Rationality as Process and as Product of Thought', *The American Economic Review* 68(2): 1–16.

Simon, Herbert A. (1982) *Models of Bounded Rationality*. Cambridge MA & London: MIT Press

Siu, Helen, S. (1993) 'Reconstituting Dowry and Brideprice in South China', pp. 165–88 in Deborah Davis & Stevan Harrell (eds) *Chinese Families in the Post-Mao Era*. Berkeley: University of California Press.

Smith, Herbert L. (1989) 'Integrating Theory and Research on the Institutional Determinants of Fertility', *Demography* 26(2): 171–84.

Smith, Herbert L. (1994) 'Nonreporting of Births or Nonreporting of Pregnancies? Some Evidence From Four Rural Counties in North China,' *Demography* 31(3): 481–86.

Smith, Richard M. (1981) 'Fertility, Economy, and Household Formation in England over Three Centuries', *Population and Development Review* 7(4): 595–622.

Song Ruilai (1990) 'Fengxian Yuqi yu Nonghu de Shengyu Xingwei' (Risk Expectancy and Fertility Behaviour in Rural Household). *Zhongguo Renkou Kexue* 5: 19–24.

Srinivas, M.N. (1988) 'The Use of the Method of Participant Observation in the Study of Demographic Phenomena', in John C. Caldwell, Allan G. Hill & Valerie J. Hull (eds) *Micro-Approaches to Demographic Research*. New York: Kegan Paul.

SSB (State Statistics Bureau) (1985) *China Statistical Yearbook 1985*. Beijing: China Statistical Publishing House.

SSB (1989) *China Statistical Yearbook 1989*. Beijing: China Statistical Publishing House.

SSB (1992) *China Statistical Yearbook 1992*. Beijing: China Statistical Publishing House.

SSB (1993) *China Statistical Yearbook 1993*. Beijing: China Statistical Publishing House.

SSB (1995) *China Statistical Yearbook 1995*. Beijing: China Statistical Publishing House.

Stacey, Judith (1983) *Patriarchy and Socialist Revolution in China*. Berkeley: University of California Press.

Stokes, C. Shannon (1995) 'Explaining the Demographic Transition: Institutional Factors in Fertility Decline', *Rural Sociology* 60(1): 1–22.

Summerfield, Gale (1994) 'Chinese Women and the Post-Mao Economic Reforms', in Nahid Aslanbeigui, Steven Pressman & Gale Summerfield (eds) *Women in the Age of Economic Transformation: Gender Impact of Reforms in Post-Socialist and Developing Countries*. London & New York: Routledge.

Summerfield, Gale & Nahid Aslanbeigui (1992) 'Feminization of Poverty in China', *Development* (4): 57–61.

Sun Xueli & Qin Kaishi (1993) 'Chusheng Loubao de Zhengjie ji Jianyi Caicu de Cueshi' (The Crux of Under-reporting and Suggested Measures). *Renkou yu Jingji* (1): 49–51.

Sun Yuesheng & Wei Zhangling (1987) 'The One-Child Policy in China Today', *Journal of Comparative Family Studies* 18(2): 309–25.

Szreter, Simon (1993) 'The Idea of Demographic Transition and the Study of Fertility Change: A Critical Intellectual History', *Population and Development Review* 19(4): 659–701.

Tan Xiaoqing (1990) 'Zhongguo Nongcun Qianyi Funu de Shengyulu Bianhua' (Fertility Changes of Migrant Women in China's Countryside). *Renkou yu Jingji* (4): 6, 13–15.

Thompson, Warren (1929) 'Population,' *American Journal of Sociology* 34(6): 959–75.

Tien, H. Yuan (1983) 'Age at Marriage in the People's Republic of China', *The China Quarterly* 130: 90–107.

Tian, H. Yuan (1991) 'Population Movement, Marriage, and Fertility Change', *Chinese Journal of Population Science* 3(1): 27–44.

Tien, H. Yuan (1985) 'Provincial Fertility Trends and Patterns', in Elisabeth J. Croll et al. (eds) *China's One-Child Family Policy*. London & Basingstoke: Macmillan.

Tien, H. Yuan (1991) 'Zaohun Furan Yinyin Kuitan' (Potential Causes for the Revival of Early Marriage). *Zhongguo Renkou Kexue* (5): 32–38.

Tien, H. Yuan (1984) 'Induced Fertility Transition: Impact of Population Planning and Socio-economic Change in the People's Republic of China', *Population Studies* 38(3): 385–400.

Tu Ping (1993) 'Zhongguo Funu de Shengyu Moshi: Haici Dijin Fenxi de Jieguo' (Fertility Model of Chinese Women: Results from Parity Progression Analysis). *Zhongguo Renkou Kexue* (4): 1–5.

Tu Ping & Liang Zhiwu (1992) 'An Evaluation of the Quality of Enumeration of Infant Deaths and Births in China's 1990 Census', Paper presented at International Seminar on China's 1990 Population Census on 19–23 October, Beijing.

United Nations, (1990) *Socio-Economic Development and Fertility Decline: A Review of Some Theoretical Approaches*. New York: United Nations.

Van De Kaa, D.J. (1996) 'Anchored Narratives: The Story and Findings of Half a Century of Research into the Determinants of Fertility', *Population Studies* 50(3): 389–432.

Vlassoff, M. & Carol Vlassoff (1980) 'Old Age Security and the Utility of Children in Rural India', *Population Studies* 34(3): 487–99.

Waltner, Ann (1984) 'The Loyalty of Adopted Sons in Ming and Early Qing China,' *Modern China* 10(4): 441–59.

Wang Hongsheng (1995) *From Revolutionary Vanguards to Pioneer Entrepreneurs: A Study of Rural Elite in a Chinese Village*. PhD dissertation. University of Amsterdam, Amsterdam.

Wang Wei (1985) 'Guanyu Jihua Shengyu Gongzuo Wenti' (On Family Planning Work), speech given at the Party School of the CCP on 15 November 1985, pp. 4–11 in *Zhongguo Renkou Ziliao Shouce*, (Handbook of Chinese Population Information).

Wang Y. (1996) 'The Impact of Boy Preference on Fertility in China', *Chinese Journal of Population Science* 8(1): 69–75.

Wang Feng (1988) 'The Roles of Individuals' Socio-economic Characteristics and the Government Family Planning Program in China's Fertility Decline', *Population Research and Population Review* 7: 255–76.

Wang Feng (1996) 'A Decade of the One-Child Policy: Achievements and Implications', in Alice Goldstein & Feng Wang (eds) *China: The Many Facets of Demographic Change*. Boulder CO: Westview Press.

Wang Feng & Yang Quanhe (1996) 'Age at Marriage and the First Birth Interval: The Emerging Change in Sexual Behavior among Young

Couples in China', *Population and Development Review*, 22(2): 299–320, 410, 412.

Wang Feng, James Lee & Cameron Campbell (1995) 'Marital Fertility Control among the Qing Nobility: Implications for Two Types of Preventive Check', *Population Studies* 49(3): 383–400.

Wang Jichuan (1990) 'Women's Preferences for Children in Shifang County, Sichuan, China', *Asian and Pacific Population Forum* 4(3): 1–12.

Wasserstrom, Jeffrey (1984) 'Resistance to the One-Child Family', *Modern China* 10(3): 345–74.

Watson, Andrew (1983) 'Agriculture Looks for 'Shoes that Fit': The Production Responsibility System and Its Implications', *World Development* 11(8): 705–30.

Watson, Rubie S. (1985) *Inequality among Brothers: Class and Kinship in South China*. Cambridge: Cambridge University Press.

Watson, Rubie S. (1991) 'Marriage and Gender Inequality', in Rubie S. Watson & Patricia B. Ebrey (eds) *Marriage and Inequality in Chinese Society*. Berkeley: University of California Press.

Watson, Rubie S. & Patricia B. Ebrey (eds) 1991. *Marriage and Inequality in Chinese Society*. Berkeley: University of California Press.

Wei Jinsheng (1988) 'Evaluation of Population Growth Control in China in Recent Ten Years', Paper submitted for seminar of Ten Years Anniversary of the Third Plenary Session of the Eleventh Central Committee of the Chinese Communist Party, Beijing (December).

Wei Jinsheng (1989) 'Evaluation of Chinese Population Control in the Past Decade and the Countermeasures in the Future', *Chinese Journal of Population Science* 1(4): 385–401.

Wen Xingyan (1993a) 'Effect of Son Preference and Population Policy on Sex Ratios at Birth in Two Provinces of China', *Journal of Biosocial Science* 25(4): 509–21.

Wen Xingyan (1993b) *Current and Desired Fertility: Reflections on Fertility Decline in China*. PhD dissertation, Division of Demography and Sociology, Australian National University.

White, Ben (1976) 'The Economic Importance of Children in a Javanese Village', pp. 127–46 in Moni Nag (ed.) *Population and Social Organization*. The Hague: Mouton.

White, Ben (1980) 'Rural Household Studies in Anthropological Perspective', in Hans P. Binswanger, Robert E. Evenson, Cecilia A. Florencio & Ben White (eds) *Rural Household Studies in Asia*. Singapore: Singapore University Press.

White, Ben (1982) 'Child Labour and Population Growth in Rural Asia', *Development and Change* 13: 587–610.

White, Gordon (1992) 'Changing Patterns of Public Action in Socialist Development: The Chinese Decollectivization', in Marc Wuyts, Maureen Mackintosh & Tom Hewitt (eds) *Development Policy and Public Action*. Oxford: Oxford University Press.

White, Tyrene (1987) 'Implementing the '"One-Child-per-Couple" Population Program in Rural China: National Goals and Local Politics', in David M. Lampton (ed.) *Policy Implementation in Post-Mao China*. Berkeley: University of California Press.

White, Tyrene (1990) 'Postrevolutionary Mobilization in China: The One-Child Policy Reconsidered', *World Politics* 43: 53–76.

White, Tyrene (1994) 'The Origins of China Birth Planning Policy', in Cristina K. Gilmatin, Gail Hershatter, Lisa Rofel & Tyrene White (eds) *Engendering*

China: Women, Culture and the State. Cambridge MA & London: Harvard University Press.

Whyte, Martin King (1992) 'Introduction: Rural Economic Reforms and Chinese Family Patterns', *The China Quarterly* 130: 317–22.

Whyte, Martin King & Gu Shengzu (1987) 'Popular Responses to China's Fertility Transition', *Population and Development Review* 13(3): 471–93.

Willekens, Frans J. (1991) 'Models of Man in Demography', Paper presented at the symposium 'Dynamics of Cohort and Generations Research', Utrecht 12–14 December; NIDI, The Hague.

Williams, Linda B. (1990) *Development, Demography, and Family Decision-Making: The Status of Women in Rural Java*. Boulder CO: Westview Press.

Wolf, Arthur P. (1986) 'The Preeminent Role of Government Intervention in China's Family Revolution', *Population and Development Review* 12(1): 101–16.

Wolf, Arthur P. & Chieh-Shan Huang (1980) *Marriage and Adoption in China. 1845–1945*. Standford: Standford University Press.

Wolf, Margery (1985) 'Marriage, Family, and the State in Contemporary China,' in Kinsley Davis (ed.) *Contemporary Marriage: Comparative Perspectives on a Changing Institution*. New York: The Russell Sage Foundation.

World Bank (1993) *China: Social Economic Development*. Washington DC: The World Bank.

Wu Cangpin & Zhong Sheng (1992) 'Nongcun Shenhua Gaige yu Shengyulu Xiajiang Jizhi Tansuo' (On Reforms and Fertility Decline Mechanisms in Rural China), in *Nongcun Shenhua Gaige yu Renkou Fazhan* (Deepening Rural Reforms and Population Development). Beijing: Zhongguo Renmin Daxue Chubanshe.

Wu Cangping (1986) 'Zhongguo Shengyulu Xiajiang de Lilun Jieshi' (Theoretical Explanation of Chinese Fertility Decline). *Renkou Yanjiu* (1).

Wu Naitao (1994) 'How China Handles Population and Family Planning,' *Beijing Review* (1–8 August): 12.

Wuyts, Marc (1992) 'Deprivation and Public Need', in Marc Wuyts, Maureen Mackintosh & Tom Hewitt (eds) *Development Policy and Public Action*. Oxford: Oxford University Press.

Wuyts, Marc (1997) 'Migrant Labour, the Marriage Valve and Fertility in Southern Africa: Some Conceptual Issues,' The Hague: Institute of Social Studies, Economic Research Seminar Paper 97/03.

Xie, Y. (1989) 'Measuring Regional Variation in Sex Preference in China: A Cautionary Note', *Social Science Research* 18: 291–305.

Xu Bing (1993) 'Male Sterilization in China', *British Journal of Family Planning* 19: 243–45.

Xu Dixin et al. (1982) *China's Search for Economic Growth: The Chinese Economy since 1949*. Beijing: New World Press.

Xu Tianqi & Ye Zhendong (1990) 'Shilun Nongcun Renkou Liudong de Shengyu Xiaoying' (Preliminary Studies on the Birth Effect of Rural Floating Population). *Zhongguo Renkou Kexue* (6): 39–53.

Yanagisako, Sylvia Junco (1979) 'Family and Household: The Analysis of Domestic Groups', *Annual Review of Anthropology* 8: 161–205.

Yang Zihui & Sha Jicai (1990) 'Zaolian, Zaohun, Zaoyu Huisheng Yuanyin jiqi Duice Yanjiu' (Analysis on Early Love, Early Marriage and Early Childbearing and Its Counter-measures). *Renkou Yanjiu* (5): 1–7.

Yang, C.K. (1959) *Chinese Communist Society: the Family and the Village*. Cambridge, MA: MIT Press.

Yang Haiou & David Chandler (1992) 'Intergenerational Relations: Grievances of the Elderly in Rural China', *Journal of Comparative Family Studies* 23(3): 431–53.

Yang Zihui (1991) 'Lun Liudong Renkou de Shengyu Xingwei' (Fertility Behaviour of Temporary Migrants). *Renkou yu Jingji* (3): 3–13.

Ye Mingde (1991) 'Luetan Woguo Chuantong Wenhua dui Shengyu de Yingxiang' (Impacts of Tradition and Culture on Fertility in China). *Renkou yu Jingji* (1): 37–41.

You Jingshan (1993) 'Does the Gender of the Child Affect Acceptance of the One-Child Certificate? The Case of Shaanxi Province, China', *Asia-Pacific Population Journal* 8(3): 47–59.

Zeng Yi (1986) 'Changes in Family Structure in China: A Simulation Study', *Population and Development Review* 12(4): 675–703.

Zeng Yi (1991) *Family Dynamics in China: A Life Table Analysis.* Wisconsin: University of Wisconsin Press.

Zeng Yi (1996) 'Is fertility in China in 1991–92 Far Below Replacement Level?' *Population Studies* 50(1): 27–34.

Zeng Yi & Li Xiaoli (1990) 'Cong Hunan Shanxi Diaocha Kan Nongcun Funu Jiating Shengming Licheng yu Jiating Jiegou Bianhua' (Rural Women's Family History and Changes in Family Structure: A Report on Investigation in Hunan and Shanxi). *Renkou yu Jingji* (2): 33–37.

Zeng Yi, Li Xiaoli & Ma Zhongdong (1991) 'The Trend and the Model Schedule of Leaving the Parental Home after Marriage in China', in *Fertility in China*, Proceedings of the International Seminar on China's In-Depth Fertility Survey held in Beijing, 13–17 February. Voorburg, the Netherlands: International Statistical Institute.

Zeng Yi, Tu Ping, Guo Liu & Xie Ying (1991) 'A Demographic Decomposition of the Recent Increase in Crude Birth Rates in China', *Population and Development Review* 17(3): 435–58.

Zeng Yi, Zhang Chunyuan & Peng Songjian (eds) (1990) *Changing Family Structure and Population Aging in China: A Comparative Approach.* Beijing: Peking University Press.

Zeng Yi, Ping Tu, Baochang Gu, Yi Xu, Bohua Li and Yongping Li (1993) 'Causes and Implications of the Recent Increase in the Reported Sex Ratio at Birth in China', *Population and Development Review* 19(2): 283–302, 425, 427.

ZGFLNJ (Zhongguo Falu Nianjian Bianjibu) (1992) Zhonghua Renmin Gongheguo Shouyang Fa (Adoption Law of PRC) 1991, pp. 169–71 in *Zhongguo falu nianjian 1992* (Law Yearbook of China 1992). Beijing: Falu Chubanshe.

ZGNYNJ (Zhongguo Nongye Nianjian Bianjibu) (1980) *Zhongguo Nongye Nianjian 1980.* Beijing: Agricultural Press.

ZGNYNJ (Zhongguo Nongye Nianjian Bianjibu) (1981) *Zhongguo Nongye Nianjian 1981.* Beijing: Agricultural Press.

ZGNYNJ (Zhongguo Nongye Nianjian Bianjibu) (1984) *Zhongguo Nongye Nianjian 1984.* Beijing: Agricultural Press.

ZGNYNJ (Zhongguo Nongye Nianjian Bianjibu) (1985) *Zhongguo Nongye Nianjian 1985.* Beijing: Agricultural Press.

Zhai Zhenwu (1991) A Historical Review of China's Rural Economic Development and Population Growth. *Population Research* 8(3): 1–10.

Zhang Tianlu (1989) *Minzu Renkouxue* (Ethnic Population Studies). Beijing: Zhongguo Renkou Chubanshe.

Zhang Weiguo (1998) 'Rural Women and Reform in a North Chinese Village', in Flemming Christiansen & Junzuo Zhang (eds) *Village Inc. – Chinese Rural Society in the 1990s*. Richmond and London: Curzon Press.

Zhang Xuguang (1990) 'Qiantan Nongcun Jingji Tizhi Gaige yu Nongcun Renkou Kongzhi Wenti' (A Brief Discussion on Structural Reform of Rural Economy and Population Control). *Renkou yu Jingji*, (5): 25–28.

Zhang Junsen (1994) 'Socio-economic Determinants of Fertility in Hebei Province, China: An Application of the Sequential Logit Model', *Economic Development and Social Change* 43(1): 67–90.

Zhao Dexing (1989) *Zhonghua Renmin Gongheguo Jingji Zhuanti Dashiji 1967–1984* (Chronicle of Economic Events in the People's Republic of China 1967–1984). Henan: Henan Renmin Chubanshe.

Zhao Renwei (1990) 'Income Distribution', in Peter Nolan & F.R. Dong (eds) *The Chinese Economy and Its Future*. Cambridge: Polity Press.

Zhao, Simon Xiaobin (1996) 'Spatial Disparities and Economic Development in China', *Development and Change* 27(1): 131–63.

Zhou Yun (1995) 'Renleixue dui Renkou Yanjiu de Qishi' (Enlightenment of Anthropology to Population Studies). *Renkou Yanjiu* (3): 19–26.

Zhou Yun (1996) 'Shengyulu de Xiajiang yu Qinshu Guanxi' (Fertility Decline and Kin Relations). *Zhongguo Renkou Kexue* (1): 37–41.

Zhu Guohong (1989) 'Renkou Zhuanbian Lun: Zhongguo Muoshi de Miaoshu he Bijiao' (On Population Transition: Description and Comparison of Chinese Model). *Renkou yu Jingji* (2).

Zonabend, Francoise (1996) 'An Anthropological Perspective on Kinship and the Family', in Andre Burguiere, Christiane Klapisch-Zuber, Martine Segalen, Francoise Zonabend (eds) *A History of the Family*. Cambridge: Polity Press.

Zweig, Davia (1989) *Agrarian Radicalism in China 1968–1991*. Cambridge MA: Harvard University Press.

Index

For Product Safety Concerns and Information please contact our EU
representative GPSR@taylorandfrancis.com Taylor & Francis Verlag GmbH,
Kaufingerstraße 24, 80331 München, Germany

Printed and bound by CPI Group (UK) Ltd, Croydon, CR0 4YY
11/04/2025
01844008-0012